TBC
C (Hul)

Sociology and

ment

STUDIES IN SOCIOLOGY

Series Editor, Professor W M Williams, University of Swansea

The aim of this series is to provide essential surveys of key concepts in sociology. Each book will review the present state of the art, identify major issues and problems, and examine possible solutions and future avenues of research.

Other titles in the series include:

Friendship: Developing a Sociological Perspective
Graham Allan, University of Southampton

Imagine No Possessions: Towards a Sociology of Poverty
Brian Taylor, Roehampton Institute, London

Towards a Spatial Sociology
Peter Dickens, University of Sussex

Sociology and Development

THEORIES, POLICIES
AND PRACTICES

DAVID HULME
Institute for Development Policy and Management
University of Manchester

MARK M. TURNER
Department of Political and Social Change
Australian National University

HARVESTER WHEATSHEAF
NEW YORK   LONDON   TORONTO   SYDNEY   TOKYO

First published 1990 by
Harvester Wheatsheaf
66 Wood Lane End, Hemel Hempstead
Hertfordshire HP2 4RG
A division of
Simon & Schuster International Group

Typeset in 10/12pt Sabon
by Inforum Typesetting, Portsmouth

Printed and bound in Great Britain by
Billing and Sons Limited, Worcester

British Library Cataloguing in Publication Data

Hulme, David, *1952–*
  Sociology and development: theories, policies and
  practices. – (Harvester Wheatsheaf Studies in Sociology).
  1. Economic development. Social aspects
  I. Title   II. Turner, Mark M.
  306′.3

  ISBN 0–7450–0468–7
  ISBN 0–7450–0681–7 pbk

---

1 2 3 4 5   94 93 92 91 90

CONTENTS

PREFACE

The origins of this book stretch back a decade to when two Liverpudlians, who had never previously met, found that chance had allocated them adjoining offices on the shores of the Coral Sea. Over the years a close friendship and working relationship has developed and this book is one of the outcomes of that relationship. It is fortunate that our time in Papua New Guinea gave us opportunities to discuss many of the topics examined in this volume, as otherwise the task of jointly writing a book while living at opposite ends of the globe might have proved more daunting.

Writing a book on sociology and development has presented us with a number of problems. Some of these are inherent in the subject: a sociological specialisation that seeks to understand what is happening to three-quarters of the world's population and reflect on how this is influenced by the remaining quarter of mankind! Other problems stem from the present state-of-the-art of sociological knowledge and development. The 1980s have witnessed an abandonment of the belief that it is possible to establish a global theory of development or underdevelopment. In consequence there is no dominant paradigm at present and sociologists studying development are adopting a variety of analytical approaches. This has meant that in this book we utilise a number of different conceptual frameworks depending on the topic that is being examined and its context.

Although the sociology of development has never been a pure sociology it is now, more than ever, a hybrid creature drawing on political science, social anthropology, economics and other disciplines. The work of sociologists is the central focus of this book, but the reader will find that the multi-disciplinary nature of development studies is reflected in the ideas and writings on which we have drawn.

In the later chapters we examine an issue which increasingly

confronts the discipline: should sociologists be purely students of
social change or should they become actively and practically involved in attempts to induce social change? As this decade has
proceeded, the call for the adoption of a more applied sociological
stance has gathered in strength. A growing number of sociologists
believe that they must not only seek to explain development but also
roll up their sleeves and become involved in the day-to-day business
of formulating development policy, designing social organisations
and planning and evaluating development projects. We anticipate
that in the 1990s the debate over whether or not the sociology of
development should, and can, become more applied will become a
major concern for sociologists.

Finally, we wish to offer our thanks to all those who have assisted
us in the preparation of this book. Paul Cook gave us a valuable
criticism of our writings on industrial policy; Michael Cernea provided advance copies of chapters of the second edition of his
excellent volume *Putting People First*; and Leslie Sklair, initially
acting as an anonymous reviewer, provided us with many useful
suggestions as to how the original draft could be improved. In
particular, the word-processing prowess of our secretaries – Bev
Fraser in Canberra and Bridget Sutton in Manchester – merits
comment. Bev and Bridget have diligently, and with great good
humour, turned our drafts into a manuscript and spent many hours
despatching papers and floppy discs between the hemispheres. At
Harvester Wheatsheaf we thank John Spiers for encouraging us to
get down to writing the book and Peter Johns for nursing the project
through to completion. Our greatest debt, however, is to our wives
and many children who have missed barbecues, evenings at the
theatre and trips to the seaside because of the time devoted to writing
this book. Many thanks for your patience and support . . . and for
keeping the lawns cut!

David Hulme   Mark M. Turner
Manchester   Canberra

                                                    October 1989

ACKNOWLEDGEMENTS

The authors wish to acknowledge the following publishers and publications for permission to reproduce materials in this book: Methuen & Co. Ltd, *Bulletin of Concerned Asian Scholars*, *Asian Wall Street Journal*, Penguin (Australia) Ltd and New Internationalist Publications.

TABLES AND FIGURES

TABLES

FIGURES

1

AN INTRODUCTION TO DEVELOPMENT

Few people in the North have any detailed conception of poverty in the Third World . . . many hundreds of millions of people in the poorer countries are preoccupied solely with survival and elementary needs . . . permanent insecurity is the condition of the poor . . . flood, drought or disease affecting people or livestock can destroy livelihoods . . . the combination of malnutrition, illiteracy, disease, high birth rates, under-employment and low income closes off the avenues of escape; and while other groups are increasingly vocal, the poor and illiterate are usually and conveniently silent (Brandt Commission, 1980, p. 49).

If economics is dismal, development studies are morbid (Chambers, 1983, p. 32).

. . . there will be no time for idle academicism, to which the social sciences are particularly prone (Hunter, 1969, p. 27).

. . . a truncated and warped modernization – it has spread throughout the Third World. The modernization of under-development is forced to build on fantasies and dreams of modernity, to nourish itself on an intimacy and a struggle with mirages and ghosts (Berman, 1988, p. 232).

Technological advances in transport, the media, communications and trading systems, allied to sentiments of concern and responsibility, have made those who live in the advanced economies of the North increasingly aware of the differences between their living conditions and the living conditions prevalent in the nations of the South. Images of the problems and poverty of the inhabitants of poorer countries have become part of the daily experience of northerners through television, newspapers, education and the activities of voluntary organisations eliciting support for their programmes to assist the poor. Similarly, in the nations of the South, images of the relative affluence of life in the industrialised nations are reinforced on a day-to-day basis.

This increasing public awareness of the disparities in living conditions in different parts of the world is occurring at a time when the economic, social, cultural and political linkages among rich and poor nations are becoming more apparent. There is a growing realisation that conditions in rich countries are not only different from conditions in poor countries but are inextricably related to them. The citizens of industrialised nations wear shirts manufactured in Bangladesh, drink coffee from Kenya, eat burgers produced from Brazilian beef, dine in restaurants run by Vietnamese refugees, play radios assembled in Taiwan, holiday in the Gambia or Indonesia, have jobs dependent on the sale of military equipment to India, operate personal accounts with banks financially threatened by default on loans made to Third World nations and watch popular music extravaganzas to help feed the destitute in Africa. Those in the poorer countries work on equipment imported from rich industrial nations, drink Coca Cola or Guinness, watch 'Dallas' on television, depend on the prices that the crops they grow fetch in London and New York, apply for scholarships to study in Manchester or Canberra, take communion from Irish priests and experience declining levels of public service provision as their governments strive to meet the conditions of foreign aid packages.

For many in the North a popular image has arisen of the problems facing poorer countries – poverty, ill-health, famine, population growth, drought, indebtedness and political instability. But the Third World is not simply one vast morass of poverty, exploitation and degradation. There is an extraordinary diversity of characteristics and problems among developing nations (try comparing Brazil with Bhutan), and within developing nations (contrast the lifestyle and concerns of a Fulani herdsman with those of a successful Nigerian businesswoman). Notwithstanding this diversity, a common cry for the solution of Third World problems has arisen in both rich and poor nations and is on the lips of all, from urban bureaucrats to agricultural labourers: *development*.

Development is the subject of this book, in which we review the efforts of sociologists and other social scientists to understand and explain the variation in conditions among different groups of people and among nations, especially with regard to the incidence of poverty and powerlessness. We also examine the opportunities for social scientists to contribute to the achievement of developmental goals through practical involvement in development policy and programme design and evaluation.

TERMS AND DEFINITIONS

Constant attention to the meaning of terms is indispensable to the study of human affairs because in this field powerful social forces operate which continuously create verbal confusion (Andreski, 1972, p. 60).

Unfortunately, the meanings attributed to many of the terms and expressions used by students of development are a source of confusion. As a consequence it is necessary to consider in some detail the ways in which a number of common terms are used.

Development

Development is the leading objective of many governments. State bureaucracies are oriented to its achievement. Multilateral agencies spend huge sums of money trying to produce it. Non-governmental organisations are set up to deliver it. Millions of people eagerly await its arrival. Some worry about its adverse consequences. Development policies are formulated and development plans are drawn up. There are development programmes and development projects. Industrial development, rural development, urban development, institutional development, social development and a host of other developments are in evidence. There are developing countries, less developed countries, least developed countries and underdeveloped countries. Academics write countless words on it, run courses about it and advise governments on it. This book focuses on it. An enormous amount of energy and resources are devoted to development. But what is development? Does it in fact mean different things to different people? Unfortunately, it appears that development is at

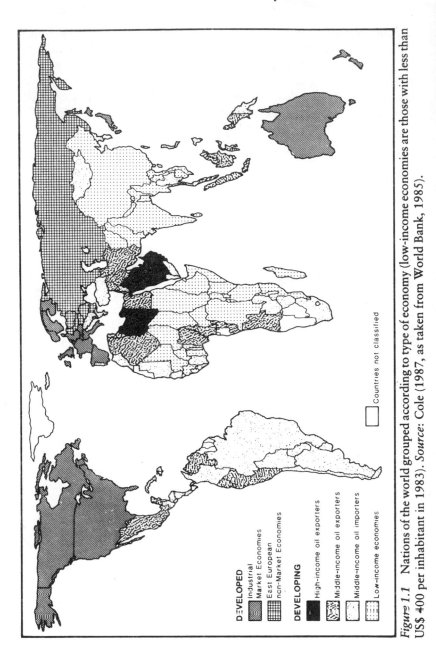

DEVELOPED
Industrial
Market Economies

East European
non-Market Economies

DEVELOPING
High-income oil exporters

Middle-income oil exporters

Middle-income oil importers

Low-income economies

Countries not classified

Figure 1.1 Nations of the world grouped according to type of economy (low-income economies are those with less than US$ 400 per inhabitant in 1983). *Source:* Cole (1987, as taken from World Bank, 1985).

once the most fundamental and elusive of concepts. Perhaps it is as Welch (1984, p. 4) suggests, 'the lazy thinker's catch-all term'. But as it is such a central concept we must follow Seers's (1977, p. 2) advice and try to 'brush away the web of fantasy we have woven around development and decide more precisely what we mean by it'. Such spring cleaning is not easy to accomplish.

Since the Second World War, development has been synonymous with economic, social and political change in the countries of Africa, Asia, Latin America, the Caribbean and the South Pacific (see Figure 1.1 for a classification and geographical distribution of developing countries). At first, definitions of development focused on economic growth and the replication of the economic, social and political orders found in the Western industrial nations. When it became evident that the developing countries were not modernising as anticipated a rethink of the meaning of development occurred. Social scientists redefined development in terms of progress towards a complex of welfare goals. For example, Seers (1977, p. 2) saw development as 'the realisation of the potential of human personality' allied to three specific goals – guaranteeing the provision of basic needs, the creation of full employment and the reduction of inequality. Related definitions of development in terms of the pursuit of a variety of basic needs have dominated the academic and government literature into the 1980s (Streeten *et al.*, 1981). Initially, such definitions were based on the provision of the minimum needs for physiological well-being (food, shelter, clothing) and basic services (health, education, clean water). Subsequently, they were extended to include access to employment opportunities, personal security and civil rights.

Variations between specifications of basic needs packages serve to highlight the fact that definitions of development and development objectives are grounded in the personal values of those involved in the activity and this has led in recent years to concern about who should define development rather than what it is. One forceful argument is that development must be defined by those whose lives are to be improved, rather than by technical experts or politicians, and must incorporate an explicit recognition of the need for the empowerment of the poor. For example:

Rural development is a strategy to enable a specific group of people, poor rural women and men, to gain for themselves and their children more of what they want and need. It involves helping the poorest among those who seek a livelihood in the rural areas to demand and control more of the benefits of development (Chambers, 1983, p. 147).

However honourable such definitions, they frequently bear little resemblance to the perceptions of those in power and to the practice of development. The notion of development derives from the nineteenth century idea of progress but unlike its evolutionary predecessor, development places emphasis on conscious action to bring about the desired transformations in society. Development policies, plans and programmes are designed to interrupt the free play of social, economic and political forces. Development is thus induced or imposed. This is such a gargantuan task that only governments are seen as being capable of organising and co-ordinating it. Development thus becomes the responsibility of government. The centrally-planned economic development and modernisation of the Soviet Union has provided a model for both communist and capitalist states. In order to support their claims to determine and guide the development process, governments have vigorously promoted an ideology of developmentalism. The frequent gaps between the rhetoric associated with such ideologies and the reality of actual conditions has done nothing to stem the ideological production and propagation. Populations may, however, be more cynical about developmentalism's promised land than in earlier years. There is a greater recognition that developmentalism is an elitist ideology, as it is governments which set up the developmental goals and pledge to achieve them on behalf of the governed. Seldom do the people frame the objectives for the government to pursue.

So what conclusion can be reached about the meaning of development? For most writers authentic development is perceived as being broadly concerned with the improvement of the conditions of existence of the majority of the population and particularly of the poorest. It is supposed to be a beneficial process which 'carries with it not only the idea of economic betterment, but also of greater human dignity, security, justice and equity' (Brandt Commission, 1980, p. 48). Any attempt to be more precise than this, in terms of specifying and prioritising the conditions to be ameliorated and indicating the means of attainment, must be seen as a personal preference reflecting the individual's values, and is unlikely to meet with general approval. The recognition that development has multiple meanings and applications is important but it does not make the subject an easy one for study. In Chapter 3 we shall investigate competing meanings and uses of development when we look at the ways in which different theoreticians have employed it.

Third World

The term Third World is now widely used as a synonym for developing countries. It features in journal titles and a multitude of academic books, the mass media routinely employ it, while even the *Oxford English Dictionary* has accepted it. Despite its apparent precision, there is some confusion about the meaning of this expression. In particular, does it refer to different types of political system or to different levels of economic production, or to both? When it was first coined in France in the 1950s political aspects were stressed. There was a perceived need for a third force between the opposing Cold War power blocs of the West and East. This was the Third World of uncommitted, non-nuclear and non-aligned nations, mainly comprised of newly-independent nations such as Nigeria, Ghana, India and Indonesia. With the lessening of Cold War tensions and the proliferation of new and independent sovereign states, the term became more strongly associated with 'neglect, exploitation and revolutionary potential' (Wolf-Phillips, 1987, p. 1313). The First World referred to the advanced market economies (e.g. the United States and France), the Second World to centrally-planned economies (e.g. the Soviet Union and Hungary) and the Third World referred to all other nations. Whether poor centrally-planned economies – China, Vietnam, Cuba, Ethiopia – fit into the Second or Third World or not has been a source of confusion. Worsley (1984, p. 311) has pointed out that while such an issue might appear purely academic, these labels and their usage are not without influence on events. In this book we have elected to use the term Third World as a convenient shorthand to refer to all low- and middle-income countries, regardless of their political system. The reader should be aware that there are dangers in using this term, most especially that it may create an image of Third World nations as being a homogeneous group with similar circumstances and problems. While Third World countries can be viewed as exhibiting some common features, such as relatively high rates of population growth and significant proportions of their populations having low incomes, sight must not be lost of the considerable economic, social and political diversity that exists both among and within such nations. One severe critic (Naipaul, 1985) seized on this diversity to denounce the concept of the Third World as 'myth . . . [which] despite its congenial simplicity is too shadowy to be of any use'. Another commented on an 'irreducible untidiness about the term' (CARTW, 1979, p. 196). Still others have suggested that the diversity problem can be solved by subdividing the nations that are generally held to comprise the Third World into more than one category. For example, Wolf-Phillips (1987, p. 1320) proposes limiting the Third World to 'developing countries' and classifying the 'least developed countries' as the Fourth World.

North–South

This has become a fashionable classification since it was popularised in the report of the Independent Commission on International Development Issues (usually referred to as the Brandt Commission 1980). The expression was selected by the Commission to emphasise the economic divide between the North (rich nations) and the South (poor nations) and to highlight the presumed desirability of a North–South dialogue grounded in a common concern for global problems and freed from the complications of East–West political interests. Although the division is inaccurate in cartographical terms (given that the majority of the population of poorer countries live in the Northern Hemisphere and the location of Australia and New Zealand in the Southern Hemisphere), it is a significant proposal in terms of the geopolitical regrouping that is suggested. The Commission regarded the diverse nations of the South as possessing a highly-developed awareness of a common predicament – being dependent on the North, being unequal with the North and often being former colonies of the North. This self-awareness apparently led to Southern solidarity in global negotiations with the North. As with much writing on development it is necessary to distinguish between desirability and feasibility. High levels of Southern solidarity are often illusory, while the envisioned dialogue between North and South has yet to take place.

THE SOCIAL SCIENCES AND DEVELOPMENT

Change, progress and development have been constant themes of the social sciences since the last century. Up until the Second World War, however, the geographical focus of such work was essentially Europe and the United States. The bulk of theoretical and empirical study concerned industrialisation and the rise of modern man in Northern Europe. The United States increasingly came under analytical scrutiny as its economy and power grew to unprecedented heights. Building on the foundations laid by the fathers of modern social science – Marx, Weber and Durkheim – writers sought to identify and analyse the processes of modernisation operating in these geographical areas. This has had important repercussions for subsequent work on development in the Third World, as the major theoretical constructs utilised in development studies in the post-war period have their roots in the work of Marx, Weber and Durkheim. To characterise things rather crudely, one could say that much of the thinking on developing countries in recent decades is a reinterpretation of elements of the earlier theories about economic and social change in Europe. This will be seen when we examine the competing theories of development in Chapter 3.

Prior to the Second World War, the only group of social scientists demonstrating a sustained interest in the countries now referred to as the Third World were social anthropologists. Much of the initial work of this small band of academics examined primitive societies from the perspective of societal evolution, but that paradigm was replaced by a funtionalist approach in the early decades of this century. The functionalist frameworks were not directly concerned with the subject of change. Rather, they sought to analyse non-European societies in their own terms as viable and internally consistent social and cultural formations that permitted their members to meet their physical and spiritual needs. The vast majority of social anthropologists working during this era actively sought to study what Margaret Mead termed 'untouched societies'; that is, groups that had not been modified by contact with the Western world and the intrusion of the missionary, the planter, the prospector and the colonial administrator. This was not always possible and some social anthropologists studied societies that had been 'touched'. They often earned a reputation for being troublemakers and 'reds' from European settlers and civil servants while in later years they were abused as 'apologists for colonialism' and 'instruments of imperialism'.

The situation changed dramatically after 1945 as the colonial era drew to a hasty close and scores of newly independent states came into being. As the cohorts of colonial administrators returned to Europe they were replaced by a new army – Western academics, fired by the prospect of analysing what was happening in these new nations and, commonly, employed in the numerous universities and tertiary education institutes established around the time of independence. Sociologists started to look at emergent class structures, changing value systems and the influence of social and cultural factors on economic development. Political scientists, who had found little of interest in colonial administration, took a keen interest in the political structures, processes, parties and politicians of these nascent states. Social anthropologists continued with their emphasis on the study of more remote groups, although some began to observe induced change in rural societies and started to report and analyse the social consequences of development strategies.

Among the social sciences, however, economics took (and has retained) the dominant position in relation to its influence on the practice of development. Independence in Asia and Africa was closely identified with comprehensive national economic planning and the preparation of voluminous five-year plans intended to direct scarce resources towards those sectors which were believed to be of the highest priority if rapid economic growth was to be achieved. Market institutions within the new states were held to be so poorly developed that they were not an efficient mechanism for resource allocation. In the early years there was considerable optimism about the ability of economic planning to foster rapid economic growth, modernise economic, social and political institutions and improve living standards. These plans required the creation or expansion of ministries of finance and planning, often staffed by expatriate economists while indigenous counterparts were being trained. Back in Europe and the United States, theoretical development economists devised models for understanding and forecasting economic growth (these included the Lewis Model, the Harrod Domar Model, Ros tow's Stage Theory, Rodan–Rodensteins's 'Big Push', Scitovsky's work on externalities, and many other models). Their colleagues in the field and in international development agencies used these various, and often conflicting, constructs to determine sectoral priorities, recommend appropriate macroeconomic policies and appraise and select public sector development projects that would help to achieve the projected growth rates. Despite concerns from within the discipline about the appropriateness of theoretical models, especially about the limits to planning, and outside the discipline from political scientists, sociologists and social anthropologists (Hill, 1987; Robertson, 1984; Hall and Midgley, 1988), economics has remained the most influential discipline. The baton has been passed on, however, from the interventionist development economists of the 1960s and 1970s to adherents of the new orthodoxy of li' eralisation, deregulation and the rolling back of the state. In this text we necessarily make reference to the work and contribution of economists as they have dominated both theoretical and practical aspects of development. However, our major concern is with the non-economic social sciences and the contribution that they might make to the understanding and practice of development.

Despite investing so much time and effort in the study of development, sociology (and most of the other non-economic social sciences) have exerted a minimal impact on the practice of development. A number of factors explain this apparent paradox (Hall and Midgley, 1988). Many sociologists have inherited a strong distaste for anything that smacks of social engineering. They suggest that their professional integrity might be compromised and that they would only be used to clear the way on behalf of powerful institutions, elites and classes. Some argue that sociology's practical role is to disseminate its findings in a generalised way to policy-makers and planners, who are thus enlightened and take the insights into account as they go about their business. Although there is some justification in this view it leaves much to chance and assumes that what sociologists have produced is of interest to the development practitioner. This is frequently not the case. Vagueness and abstraction characterise much sociological output and severely limit its practical relevance. Even where sociologists are well-equipped with useful skills there is a widespread ignorance in aid agencies and government departments about what technical abilities sociologists might possess and the ways in which they can contribute. But much tertiary-level sociological training in both the developed and developing worlds does not prepare graduates for making significant and influential contributions to development. A disdain for practical matters has left sociologists without both a body of normative theory which they can apply and a clear idea of their practical task.

The blame for sociology's peripheral position is not entirely self-induced. Sociologists have often been excluded from policy-making and planning on suspicion that they are all left-wing ideologues. While this allegation is untrue, sociologists and anthropologists are certainly more likely to express criticism and dissent on development initiatives than the representatives of other disciplines. The economists, agriculturalists, engineers and assorted technical personnel who populate planning offices place their faith in their quantifiable terms and remain sceptical of the imprecise and less easily manipulated social parameters of development. Sociologists may even be viewed as hindrances to the smooth implementation of development plans, and when project personnel must be sacrificed because of financial constraints it is the lone sociologist who is invariably viewed as the most, dispensable person. Finally, institutional obstacles are seen to obstruct the advance of sociologists in the world of development. For example, aid agencies may lack adequate mechanisms for recruiting sociologists or they may be perceived as a threat to the power balance between departments.

Despite these handicaps and problems there is a growing body of opinion that one of the principal tasks of a sociology of development should be to get involved in the practice of development. One World Bank sociologist puts the case as follows:

sociology and anthropology have primarily endeavoured to explain and describe past or existing social structures, rather than to look toward the future and project change . . . [they] have to face the nuts and bolts of development activities, to roll up their sleeves and deal with the mundane, pragmatic questions of translating plans into realities in a sociologically sound manner. They need to link data-generation, action-oriented research, social analysis, design for social action and evaluation into a continuum, and thus stretch sociology's contributions far beyond simple pronouncements (Cernea, 1985, pp. 9–10).

Hall and Midgley (1988, p. 5) echo these sentiments and argue that sociologists have an important practical contribution to make to development. There are equally persuasive advocates promoting the same line among anthropologists (Grillo and Rew, 1985). Chambers (1983) has posed the question of whether sociologists (and other non-economic social scientists) have the right to criticise development plans and policies if they are not prepared to get practically involved in their formulation. He contrasts these 'negative academics' with the 'positive practitioners'. But sociologists may legitimately ask whether what they do has to be useful. The answer to that must surely be no, and who, anyway, decides what is useful? However, if the sociologist takes the option of non-involvement then he/she must be prepared to play the role of a permanent but potentially ineffectual critic of development. The problems do not disappear even when social scientists opt for involvement. There is disagreement over what should be done and how it should be done. Ethical dilemmas constantly arise. Also, is it possible to employ sociologists in formulating a plan of action when 'usually [they] have a hundred "don'ts" for every five "do's" ' (Cernea, 1985, p. 8). Some progress has been made, however, and this is the subject of later chapters of this book.

AIMS OF THIS BOOK

One of the few clear lessons of the study of development in the last two decades is that no individual discipline can adequately deal with the complexity of the topic, and indeed that some form of multi-disciplinary approach is necessary if our present understanding is to be deepened. This book attempts to incorporate such a perspective, although it must be understood that we make no claim to a balanced multidisciplinary text. Such a goal has remained elusive for the present generation of textbooks. While the book emphasises the contribution of sociologists it also draws on the work, ideas and data generated by economists, social anthropologists, political scientists, geographers and many others who are not easily pigeon-holed.

The basic aim of this book is to provide students of social science with an overview of the major issues surrounding development, with a particular emphasis on social change and social action. We range more widely than most sociology of development texts in an effort to provide an introduction to the multiple facets of development. Thus, we move from description of conditions in the Third World to global theories of social change and from policy considerations to the modes of social organisation required for development. In the short space allowed we cannot hope to cover everything in detail but from the references provided all subjects can be followed up by the interested student. The book is written at the undergraduate level but it will also be of use as a preliminary text for postgraduates who are new to the topic or who wish to sample work outside the confines of a specific discipline.

In this opening chapter we have explored some of the fundamental problems of concept and orientation in the study of development. Chapter 2 provides background on the conditions of life in developing countries, using both statistical measures and personal case histories. The diversity of the Third World will be very apparent from the data presented. In Chapter 3 we switch our attention to the various approaches used by theorists to explain the nature and course of development. Our survey takes us from the modernisation school of the 1950s to the neo-Marxists, populists and counter-revolutionaries of today. The subject of Chapter 4 is sociological aspects of change. Obviously there are many, but we have only space for a few of the more important ones – class, ethnicity and family, kinship and gender. At this point we move to more applied matters. Chapter 5 looks at some of the major policy concerns of developing countries. What are the major issues and how have countries attempted to solve them? Chapter 6 examines the proposition that sociologists concerned with social change in developing countries should involve themselves more directly in development policy-making and planning. Using case studies we investigate the role that sociologists can play in the design of development projects. In Chapter 7 we look at the role of social organisation in development. Again employing case studies we look at the different forms of social organisation which can be used to bring development, paying particular attention to the matter of popular participation. In the final chapter we try to make some general observations from our developmental survey and address the central problem of power and its relationship with development.

2

LIFE IN THE THIRD WORLD – DEVELOPMENT STATISTICS AND PERSONAL HISTORIES

Before examining differing theoretical perspectives on development it is necessary to ensure that the reader has a knowledge of some of the available evidence on the conditions of life in developing nations, how they vary among nations and social groups and how they compare with the conditions of life in developed nations.

As we noted in the first chapter, development is an elusive, abstract and multifaceted concept and as such is not easily amenable to direct measurement. In practice it is only possible to present indicators of the level of development of a nation, region or group of people using such statistics as per capita income, health standards, life expectancy, literacy, malnutrition or indices which incorporate several such surrogate measures. All such figures are crude indicators, not accurate measures, of the levels of development. Their purpose is not to show that one nation, region or group is more or less developed than another. Rather, those indicators provide a rough idea of the differences and similarities in the living conditions of the units that are being compared.

Caution over the interpretation of development statistics is not only necessary because of their surrogate nature. It must also be recognised that many of these statistics, and particularly those relating to the rural areas of poorer countries, are of limited reliability. The World Bank (1987, p. 197) in its authoritative, annual *World Development Report*, advises that many of the statistics it publishes (and which most teachers and commentators on development are content to use) 'are subject to considerable margins of error . . . [and] should thus be construed as indicating trends and characterising major differences among economies, rather than taken as precise quantitative indicators of those differences'. Even the most

Table 2.1 Development statistics

	GNP per capita 1987 (US$)	Average annual growth rate of GNP per capita 1965–87 (%)	Average annual population growth rate 1980–7 %	Total fertility rate 1987 (births)	Average life expectancy 1987 (years)	Contribution of agiculture to GDP 1987 (%)	Population living in urban areas 1987 (%)
LOW-INCOME COUNTRIES							
Ethiopia	130	0.1	2.4	6.5	47	42	12
Zaire	150	– 2.4	3.1	6.1	52	32	38
Bangladesh	160	0.3	2.8	5.5	51	47	13
Tanzania	180	– 0.4	3.5	7.0	53	61	29
China	290	5.2	1.2	2.4	69	31	38
India	300	1.8	2.1	4.3	58	30	27
Kenya	330	1.9	4.1	7.7	58	31	22
Pakistan	350	2.5	3.1	6.7	55	23	31
Nigeria	370	1.1	3.4	6.5	51	30	33
Sri Lanka	400	3.0	1.5	2.7	70	27	21
Indonesia	450	4.5	2.1	3.5	60	26	27
LOWER MIDDLE-INCOME COUNTRIES							
Philippines	590	1.7	2.5	3.9	63	24	41
Egypt	680	3.5	2.7	4.8	61	21	48
Ivory Coast	740	1.0	4.2	7.4	52	36	44
Thailand	850	3.9	2.0	2.8	64	16	21
Turkey	1210	2.6	2.3	3.8	64	17	47
Columbia	1240	2.7	1.9	3.2	66	19	69
Malaysia	1810	4.1	2.7	3.8	70	–	40
Mexico	1830	2.5	2.2	3.6	69	9	71
South Africa	1890	0.6	2.3	4.5	60	6	57

UPPER MIDDLE-INCOME COUNTRIES						
Brazil	2020	4.1	2.2	3.5	65	11	75
Argentina	2390	0.1	1.4	3.0	71	13	85
South Korea	2690	6.4	1.4	2.1	69	11	69
Libya	5460	– 2.3	4.3	6.9	61	4	67
HIGH-INCOME OIL EXPORTS						
Saudi Arabia	6200	4.0	4.3	7.2	63	4	75
Kuwait	14610	– 4.0	4.5	4.8	73	1	95
INDUSTRIAL MARKET ECONOMIES						
United Kingdom	10420	1.7	0.1	1.8	75	2	92
Australia	11100	1.8	1.4	1.9	76	4	86
Japan	15760	4.2	0.6	1.7	78	3	77
United States	18530	1.5	1.0	1.9	75	2	74

Source: The World Bank (1989) *World Development Report*

basic of all such statistics, population, i.e. the number of people living in a defined area, is unreliable for many developing countries (Hardiman and Midgley, 1982, p. 63), where birth and death registration is an administrative luxury that cannot be afforded and censuses may be non-existent (Ethiopia), outdated (Egypt) or declared void (Nigeria). Different estimates of the population of China varied by as much as 164 million people in the mid-1970s (Kirk, 1979). Clearly, development statistics must be treated with caution and the arguments of those who assume that statistics are accurate must be closely examined. In a recent work, the economic anthropologist Polly Hill (1987, pp. 30–50) has accused the majority of development economists of utilising statistics which they know, or should know, are of a very poor quality and are unsuitable for sophisticated quantitative analysis. She records twelve reasons for this state of affairs and cynically postulates 'that as the sophistication of "data processing" increases, so the quality of the finished statistical product declines'. Robert Chambers (1983, pp. 51–5) has reported and provided examples of the 'pathology of rural surveys'. Many sociologists and anthropologists who have worked at the village level in developing countries would confirm these critical comments about official statistics. Duly warned, let us examine some of the available information (Table 2.1).

GROSS NATIONAL PRODUCT PER CAPITA

The most commonly cited statistic in the study of development is gross national product (GNP) per capita. It is calculated by estimating the money value of all goods and services produced in a country in a year, plus net factor income (from labour and capital) from abroad, and dividing by the estimated mid-year population, although for technical reasons it is often based on a three-year period. (Details of how the calculations are made are available at the back of the *World Development Report*.) This statistic is one of the most widely used tools in social science and is not only used by economists but by the majority of social scientists as a crude means of comparing levels of development. There are, however, considerable problems in the use of GNP per capita as an indicator of development or of welfare, particularly when it is used for comparisons over time

(Abramovitz, 1959) and comparisons of countries (Kuznets, 1953). It is worth considering some of the weaknesses and shortcomings associated with the calculation and use of GNP per capita as, despite criticisms, it remains the most widely cited development statistic and is used in this volume:

1. Apart from general problems relating to the collection of data, the estimation of GNP for developing countries is made especially difficult because of the importance of economic activities, the products of which are used for subsistence, or exchanged through non-monetised transactions. The valuation of subsistence agricultural production remains as much an art as a science, with little known about the physical volume of production in many countries, let alone its financial worth. Even in more urbanised developing countries the data available on the production of goods and services in the large urban 'informal' sector is very limited, and considerable assumptions are made when placing values on informal products.

2. So that comparisons can be made, GNP per capita is usually converted from the local currency to a common unit, most often the US dollar. This requires a number of assumptions to be made about exchange rates. Variations in these assumptions can lead to significant differences in the final figure which is computed.

3. GNP per capita produces an average of the value of production (and by inference, income) for each person, but it provides no indication of the distribution of income among a population. For example, a country such as Mexico has a relatively high GNP per capita of US$1830 in 1987. However, around 58 per cent of national income accrues to the wealthiest 20 per cent of the population, while the poorest 20 per cent of the population receives around 3 per cent of national income. There is a danger that the average figure disguises the reality that a significant proportion of Mexico's population have per capita incomes of only US$300 or US$400 per annum.

4. GNP per capita is not an accurate indicator of general levels of welfare in terms of such factors as malnutrition and health status, employment, personal security and literacy. Indeed, given the nature of the calculation of GNP per capita, it is conceivable that a country with a stagnant economy and a population being decimated by famine, ill-health and refugee

outmigration could record an increase in its annual GNP per capita because of declining life expectancies.

The shortcomings of GNP per capita as a means of estimating progress towards the achievement of developmental goals have long been recognised. In consequence, there has been extensive research to design an alternative yardstick, a social indicator, by agencies such as the United Nations Research Institute for Social Development (UNRISD) and the World Bank. A number of composite indicators have been proposed including Drewnowski's 'welfare index', McGranahan's 'development index' and Morris's 'physical quality of life index' (PQLI).

Morris, whose proposed index is the least complicated of these three, sought out indicators of socio-economic performance that did not reflect the values of specific societies, did reflect the distribution of social results and could be easily calculated and understood. The only indicators that met these criteria were infant mortality, life expectancy and the level of basic literacy (Morris, 1979). Morris scaled each of these indicators, combined them in a simple arithmetic fashion and computed PQLI scores for 150 countries. Correlations between GNP per capita and PQLIs for these countries yielded interesting results, with notable deviations from linearity at the upper and lower ends of the per capita GNP range. The high income oil producers had relatively low PQLIs, while a number of countries with low per capita incomes – Sri Lanka, Cuba, Guyana and South Korea – had high PQLIs. These findings provide a clear indication of the dangers of treating GNP per capita as an indicator of a nation's level of development. However, the PQLI has not been generally accepted and critics have pointed to the narrowness of the indicators that are used to compute the index and have questioned the rationale for treating each indicator as being of equal importance. The search for a yardstick for development now appears to have lost its momentum, although the US Population Crisis Committee is currently busy promoting 'the international human suffering index', which is compiled by adding ten measures of human welfare to create a single figure which claims to measure differences in living conditions among countries (Camp and Speidel, 1987). Most students of development are agreed that something less crude and more reliable than GNP per capita is desirable, but in the absence of general agreement on the nature of an alternative measure, they continue to rely heavily on GNP per capita.

BACKGROUND DATA ON DEVELOPMENT

Later chapters assume that the reader has a general understanding of social and economic conditions in the Third World and of the contrasts between developing and developed countries. Readers who wish to acquaint themselves with some of the basic information should make a study of Table 2.1. Brief comments on some of the most salient features of the table and its indicators are provided below.

GNP per capita

Although developing countries are often referred to as poorer nations, there is a wide range in GNP per capita from US$130 (Ethiopia) to US$3230 (Venezuela) and US$7940 (if, in 1987, one regards Singapore as developing). In the widely used World Bank classification, countries are ranked as low-income (GNP per capita of less than US$480 in 1987), lower middle-income (US$480–US$2000), upper middle-income (US$2000–US$6000), high-income oil exporters and industrial market economies. It must be noted that GNP per capita provides no indication of how income is distributed. The available evidence suggests that in many developing countries income distribution is highly skewed towards the wealthy. However, such data is sporadic, often out of date and should be treated with caution.

Poverty

None of the major publications of development statistics provides regular estimates of the numbers of people living in absolute poverty in different countries. This is partly because of technical difficulties in defining poverty but also because of the lack of reliable data. The World Bank's 1978 *World Development Report* estimated that in 1975 around 770 million people in developing countries lived in absolute poverty. Fields (1981), using US government information, suggests a figure of around 800 million. Despite these problems of estimation it is evident that a significant portion of the world's population live in conditions of abject deprivation.

Population growth rates

In almost all cases, developing countries have higher population growth rates than industrialised nations. These range from China's relatively modest 1.2 per cent per annum to Kenya's extraordinary 4.1 per cent per annum (which suggests that its population could double in the next 17 years!). While the world's largest nations, China and India, have lowered their population growth rates over the last two decades many other nations, particularly those in sub-Saharan Africa, have witnessed accelerating rates of population growth.

Fertility

Total fertility rates, that is the average number of children that would be born per woman living to the end of her childbearing years if existing age-specific fertility rates continue, are relatively high in most developing countries. For 1987, they range from 2.4 live births per woman in China to 8.0 live births per woman in Rwanda. Cross-national changes in fertility patterns in recent decades have been very complicated, and fertility is clearly a variable that is influenced by a complex web of social, cultural and economic factors.

Life expectancy

Life expectancy at birth is lower in almost all developing countries than in developed countries. However, there are wide variations between countries. At very similar levels of per capita income the poor countries of Sierra Leone and Sri Lanka have life expectancies of 40 years and 70 years respectively!

Structure of economic activities

For most developing countries agriculture has a more important economic role, in terms of its contribution to gross domestic product (GDP), than in developed nations. This is particularly the case of low-income nations where agriculture may dominate the economy. In 1987, approximately 57 per cent of Nepal's GDP was accounted for by agriculture and only 14 per cent by industrial activities. Generally, the industrial and manufacturing sector is better developed in middle income countries. For example, in 1987, 38 per cent of Brazil's GDP accrued from industry and only 11 per cent from agriculture.

Urbanisation

The definition of what is or is not an urban centre varies greatly from nation to nation. However, broadly speaking, urbanisation is at lower rates in the lower-income countries than in the middle-income countries, and is highest in the developed nations. There is a marked contrast between the nations of Africa and Asia, where the majority of the population are rural dwellers, and Latin America, where the majority of people are usually living in urban areas. In almost all developing countries the annual growth rate of the urban population exceeds the natural population growth rate.

CASE STUDIES

A consideration of the types of data presented in Table 2.1 helps to give the student of development a fuller understanding of the social and economic conditions prevalent in developing countries. However, there is a danger that a concern with statistical averages and aggregates depersonalises the development challenge and leads the reader away from the need to recognise that development is about improving the living standards and life chances of individual men, women and children. One may be concerned about statistics on poverty, infant mortality and nutrition, but these anxieties are nothing alongside examples of what conditions are like for individuals and families in developing countries. In this section a few brief accounts are presented in the form of case-studies to help deepen the reader's understanding of what life is like for the poor. The accounts are personal, being direct extracts from verifiable sources, each of which is gratefully acknowledged. They have been selected subjectively and present qualitative information. Nevertheless, they can make a vital contribution to the reader's appreciation of the problems that development projects and policies are meant to be tackling. While conceptualisation and abstraction are essential for an understanding of development processes it is equally important to relate elegant theories to ugly facts.

Case study 1: who works, who eats in a Bangladesh village?

Sharecroppers cultivate about a quarter of Bangladesh's farmland; wage labourers apparently cultivate an even larger percentage. Sharecropping is most widespread in the north-west, where the village of Katni is located. For example, Nafis, a landlord who together with his younger brothers owns 60 acres of land in Katni's vicinity, cultivates three-quarters of this land by means of sharecroppers and the remaining quarter with hired labour. The landowner and the sharecropper generally split the crop equally, but in some districts the landowner takes two-thirds. In Katni the costs of seed and fertilizer are usually deducted before the division of the crop, but an AID study reports that in most cases the sharecropper bears these costs alone.

Poor peasants generally prefer sharecropping to the alternative of wage labour. The rewards of sharecropping may be meagre, but the rewards of wage labour are even less. The rich peasant Kamal estimates that hired labourers cost him only a quarter to a third of his crop, whereas a sharecropper receives one half. The standard wage for male labourers in Katni is about 33 US cents per day;

women labourers who process the crops earn even less. Sharecropping not only pays better than wage labour, but also offers more security. The sharecropper is in effect hired by season. Although he has no permanent claim to the land, at least he doesn't face the uncertainties of the wage labourer, whose plight was summed up by Dalim: 'I can't say today where I'll work tomorrow'.

Sharecropping does have its drawbacks, however. The sharecropper needs oxen and plough, and he pays dearly if he must rent them. He cannot reap the rewards of his labour until the harvest, and in the meantime he may have to borrow money to feed his family. If the crop is damaged by floods, drought or pests, the sharecropper might end up earning even less than a wage labourer. The cost and risks of sharecropping, and the delayed rewards, make it almost impossible for the totally landless families of Katni to sharecrop. Instead, they earn their living by wage labour.

In Katni a day's work earns two pounds of rice, one *taka* (16 *taka* = \$1US) and a morning meal. The labourer Dalim explains: 'With that *taka* I used to be able to buy two more pounds of rice, with a little left over for oil, chilis and salt. But today one *taka* won't even buy a single pound of rice. Employers used to give their workers a few free vegetables when they went home in the evening, but nowadays they aren't so generous. I tell you, times are getting harder for men like me.'

At times of peak agricultural activity – the weeding of the spring rice, the transplanting of the rainy season rice, and the rice and jute harvests – wages for hired labourers sometimes rise slightly. Strong young men like Dalim will often work on a contract basis, agreeing for example to harvest an acre of rice for a set fee. During the slack seasons, however, many landless labourers face unemployment. Some turn to petty trade, buying vegetables in the villages and selling them at the local markets or in the Lalganj bazaar. In the dry winter season, the younger men sometimes find work at a nearby brickworks or at construction sites in Lalganj, but we often heard the complaint, 'No work, no rice'.

'Today I've gone to three villages looking for work,' Ameerul, a landless laborer, told us one morning. 'I found nothing. No work means no rice. Yesterday I couldn't find work, and I ate nothing all day. Finally in the afternoon I ripped three bamboo poles out of the wall of my house, chopped them up and sold them in town as firewood. With the money I bought three pounds of wheat flour. I had half a *taka* left over, so I bought a cup of tea and a handful of puffed rice. Last night we ate the flour. I have six mouths to feed. Even when I find work, I only earn two pounds of rice and one *taka*. Two pounds of rice won't even fill the stomachs of two people – for six it's nothing. And what can you buy today with one *taka*? Each day I ask myself: how will I live? How will my children live?'

This case study was taken from a longer article: James Boyce and Betsy Hartmann (1981) 'Who works, who eats?', *Bulletin of Concerned Asian Scholars*, vol. 13, no. 4, pp. 18–27.

Case study 2: Mexican families surviving – together

The burden of a $104 billion foreign debt has jolted Mexico's development course into reverse, forcing more and more Mexicans to rely on the world's most basic economic unit: the family. With real wages set back to the levels of the early 1960s, families make do by combining their diminished resources, 'putting more water in the soup', as the Mexican adage goes. With no economic growth for the past six years and a sharp recession unfolding, the family has acted as a cradle for small, subsistence enterprises that take the place of vanishing farms and factories.

A recent study of 95 urban working-class families showed how families were banding together to cushion the blow of the crisis. The average size of households in the study grew by more than 10 per cent as they incorporated more wage-earning cousins, uncles and in-laws. At the same time, the number of adult females and young males pushed into the work force rose by 25 per cent.

Here is how two working-class families, one from the countryside and one from the inner city, have confronted hard times.

The Avinas   It's as though the economic crisis has set time back many years in the tiny central Mexican farm community of Barrio de Guadalupe de Mezquitillo. Traditional rope sandals are making a comeback, replacing more costly factory-made shoes. Donkey carts appear more frequently on the one paved highway. Animals are all bones. 'The crisis is forcing us to return to the old way of life, when we depended on the land and the family,' says Manuel Avina, the 76-year-old patriarch of a huge clan living here. Mr Avina never earned much farming this dusty plain. Now he and his family barely subsist. With little money to invest in his crop, he can't raise much more corn than that he, his wife and three grandchildren consume. The grandchildren were left to him by a son who emigrated to the United States. Mr Avina loads his harvest's small surplus onto a cart and tries to sell it for cash in a nearby town, but he must increasingly resort to bartering it for other staples.

Mr Avina is thankful he lives near a vast and supportive family – 10 children, 70 grandchildren and a host of other relations. When he needs groceries, he goes to the general store owned by a son, who often won't accept his payment. When his animals get sick, he takes them for treatment to a grandson, who hasn't charged him since the crisis began. Now that he can't afford to buy new clothes, a cousin makes them for him. Even the one son who left Mexico for the United States contributes to his father's welfare. When Mr Avina didn't have money to repair his tumbledown wooden shack, the emigrant son returned to the village and used the money and skills he had obtained working in the US construction industry to build his father a new brick home.

Mr Avina's children also look out for each other. Last year, when Antonio Avina's corn crop failed and he could find no work in the city, his brothers supported his family for several months. 'When it doesn't rain in my land, it will rain on my brothers,' says Antonio Avina. 'If there is something for one, there is something for all.'

The Ravelos Armando Ravelo's family has had to battle a natural disaster as well as an economic one. A severe recession caused Mr Ravelo to lose his job as a cook in a Mexico City restaurant in 1985. Shortly after, one of the most devastating earthquakes in recent history destroyed the family's rattletrap apartment building. Mr Ravelo, his wife and three children were crammed into a one room emergency shelter with their son-in-law and seven grandchildren, who also had lost their home. Struggling to support the enlarged household, Mr Ravelo and his wife got jobs as servants. An uncle arranged a job for one son in a brewery, and another son pitched in what he earned at a factory. The grandchildren salvaged and sold whatever they could from the wrecked buildings around them.

When the Ravelos were finally relocated in a new apartment complex a year later, the grandchildren and son-in-law stayed with the family. The addition of one new worker barely compensated for all of the new mouths to feed. Mr Ravelo worried he would soon be cast out on the street again. So last year, Mr Ravelo and his wife quit their servant jobs and gambled that their extensive family contacts could earn them a living as vendors in Mexico's thriving black market. 'All of the money now is underground – if you know the right people,' he says.

Mr Ravelo's best contacts are members of his family. A nephew who lives along the US border ships him smuggled electronic products. A brother-in-law from southern Mexico sends clothing from other Latin American countries. A network of cousins, uncles and nephews in the capital supplies him with everything from American-made boxing gloves to Japanese-made electric knives. Aggressively hustling their wares, the Ravelos have been able to support their enlarged household. Mrs Ravelo sells door-to-door during the week and operates a booth at an open-air market at weekends. After finishing their factory shifts, his two sons go to work selling smuggled radios in the plant car parks.

This case study was taken from a larger article of the same name: Matt Moffett (1988) *Asian Wall Street Journal*, 3 August, pp. 1–7.

Case study 3: life on a sugar hacienda in Negros Occidental, the Philippines

For over a million of Negros Occidental's 1.8 million people, the sugar hacienda is a total life support system. Although sugar farms come in all shapes and sizes, most of the province's sugar land, about 70 per cent, is occupied by larger farms of over 50 hectares. And there is a certain uniformity to the layout and life of the haciendas, of which Hacienda Esperanza is a fair sample. Lying at the centre of 1,000 hectares planted largely with sugar, the hacienda compound is a self contained community with its own school, stores, chapel, clinic, housing tract and central administration. The hacienda's 858 residents live in two clusters of small, wooden houses, the larger group separated from the administrative compound only by the width of a narrow cane field. Although these tumble-down shacks offer only 25 square metres of floor space for families with as many as 10 members, water, electricity and primary education are all free, courtesy of the hacienda. Furnishings consist of sleeping mats, worn cooking utensils, a few plates and spoons, and, among the more fortunate, a wooden wardrobe. Most workers own only the clothes on their backs and have four to ten malnourished children. Jerry de la Cruz, for example, is the eldest of six children dependent during most of the year on their father's daily wage as a tractor driver, P21 or about A$2.30. Like all workers they survive on endless loans from the hacienda. When the hacienda manager cut the family's credit two years ago, before his death, three of the children, Jerry included, had to drop out of school.

A hundred metres and a world away lies the administrative compound. Past the galvanized iron cluster of equipment barns, through the tall, cast iron gates opened by shotgun guards, and down the long gravel drive that cuts across manicured lawns, rises the Spanish colonial Big House, with the manager's residence above and offices below. For the manager or his children, occupancy can be a stepping stone to a brilliant career in Manila. Aurora Pijuan, daughter of the hacienda's manager during the 1960s, broke into the headlines with her selection as Miss International and has continued to make them as movie starlet and ex-wife of the man who dared to marry President Marcos's eldest daughter.

A dozen domestics staff the Big House and wait on its long dining table that serves as meeting place for corporate executives and visiting sugar barons. My first week back in 1981 coincided with a luncheon for fifty in honour of a parochial visit by the Bishop of Bacolod. Seated opposite the young manager, I noted his table conversation was interrupted several times by hacienda workers in tattered clothes shoving bits of paper before him and muttering into his ear. Whether lunch, dinner or corporate conference, the workers came constantly, I later learned, to borrow money against next month's or next year's wages for every imaginable need – a child's visit to the doctor, a mother's burial, a baby's baptism, or a daughter's high school tuition. The ritual was always the same. As soon as each one ascended the grand staircase into the dining room, these grown men would hunch their shoulders, curl their bodies to an adolescent's height and shuffle haltingly towards the manager, who stiffened slightly in sternness. 'Please sir, it is my second child. Three days' fever. I wouldn't trouble you but . . .' With a glance at the paper but without making eye contact, the manager flicks his signature across the debt voucher. Shuffling backward in the same posture of dependence, the worker mutters, 'Thank you, sir, many thanks, sir, we won't forget this, sir . . .' while the manager continues his dinner-table conversation. Most workers carry debts equal to three or even six months' wages, and repayment is impossible since about 90 per cent of household income goes for food alone. 'They are born in debt, live in debt, die in debt,' said the hacienda manager.

This case study was taken from Alfred McCoy (1984) *Priests on Trial*, Ringwood, Australia: Penguin, pp. 54–6.

Case study 4: a Bissa woman from Burkina Faso

The wife My name is Zenabou Bambara. I'm 28 and I have four children. My husband's name is Adama Mone and my co-wife is called Mariam. Mariam was in labour last night – there is a new baby in the household. Until yesterday she worked with me in the fields, but now she will have six days' rest until the naming ceremony – in that time all she has to do is fetch water and cook.

This means more work for me in the fields. It's the third time we've planted but there is no rain. I'm tired, my back aches. But there is nothing to show for my work. Look at the earth. See how dry it is? The millet should be one foot high by now, but this dry ground yields only dust.

A woman's work in the fields is important. But it is not her only work. In the morning I get up and prepare the meal, and if I have no flour I pound the grain. After that I walk to the fields which are 14 kilometres away and join my husband who has ridden there on his bike. I work the land with him until two o'clock, and then I fetch firewood to carry home. Sometimes I sell this wood to other people and get a little money for myself – then I buy something for the sauce to go with the tô (millet porridge). In the afternoon I have to make four trips to the well to fill the storage jar in my compound.

This work is woman's work, and it's because of this that a woman has more to do than a man, that she gets more tired. I would like it very much if my husband helped me, but he will not because he is the one who holds the authority. The man cannot help the woman – it is not his role. He can demand anything of his wife but she cannot ask anything of him.

A man only has to worry about the family's land. But I have my own field to weed too, on top of all my other work – I have to organise myself to find enough time to cultivate my own land, because every bit of food counts.

After the harvest last year my husband gave my co-wife and me some millet to keep in our huts as an emergency store. But we have used it up and have to rely on what he gives us every four days. If only it would rain we could pick leaves to make a thick sauce and make the millet stretch further.

The husband I'm the one who gives the orders concerning our work and our food. With this calabash I measure out the millet to my two wives – it is up to them to make it last.

Actually, it's true – women do work more than men. The woman works with us in the fields. Then she has to go back to the house to fetch water and firewood, grind millet into flour and cook the *tô* and sauce. She also has to wash the children. I can see for myself that she is tired, that she works too hard. But tradition and habit stop me from helping her. It is a woman's place to do that work. I don't see why I should help her.

This case study appeared in *New Internationalist* (1985), vol. 151 (September), p. 20.

Case study 5: a labourer in Sri Lanka

Emmanuel, aged 55, supports his wife and five children by sorting fish. When the boats come in he helps the fishermen by disentangling fish from the net. For this he is given a parcel of fish which when sold earns him Rs.10–15 per day. Work is not available every day, and all earnings are spent on day-to-day consumption. The house in which they lived was only partly constructed of bricks and cement with a *cadjan* thatched roof. It had been financed by selling a small portion of the crown land on which they were squatting at Rs.10,000. The extent of the land sold was unknown. Once this money had been spent no more was available to complete the work. The walls were only three-quarters built and the windows and doors were only openings. The 10 perches of land on which they lived was going to be legally handed over to them shortly.

There were no items of furniture or any consumer durables. The few cooking utensils were stacked on an old packing case. When we visited the family, Emmanuel's wife aged 42 was in hospital, having given birth to their youngest child two days ago. The eldest daughter was aged 17. None of the children attended school although sometimes the younger children attended a free kindergarten organised by the voluntary agency Sarvodaya Sharamadana.

The only assistance received by this family was Rs.110 worth of food stamps. The six coconut trees in the garden only provided enough coconut for their day-to-day consumption. As this house was located on the beach, no other cultivation could be practised. Although there were many pigs being reared in the area, this family did not raise any.

No debt had been incurred due to the fact that present income was insufficient to repay it and to the lack of assets which could serve as collateral.

This case study was taken from the files of the Federation of Thrift and Credit Cooperatives, Colombo, Sri Lanka.

3

APPROACHES TO DEVELOPMENT

The concept of development is essentially concerned with social change and human progress in a group of countries, mostly former colonies, which are lumped together under convenient but increasingly misleading collective titles such as the Third World or the South. Since the Second World War the explanation of development or the lack of it has been a major academic growth industry. Before that time, students of social change and social scientists in general focused their attention on the dynamic West, as had the founding fathers of the social sciences like Durkheim, Marx and Weber. Non-Western societies were regarded as the academic territory of social anthropologists. But they were few in number and their self-appointed task of studying the primitive, the exotic and the untouched involved a functionalist perspective in which social change was of minimal concern. There was no research programme or paradigm identifying developing countries as a major object for scientific explanation. The Third World had not yet been invented. The radically changed political climate of the post-war years altered that. Colonies began to achieve independence in a world where the capitalist West and the communist East were engaged in a cold war. Part of this war was the struggle to acquire allies from the developing countries. Meanwhile the United Nations had been established and had broadly delineated the field of study – the disparity in socio-economic conditions between the developed and underdeveloped nations. Social scientists were thus allocated the task of generating explanations of the causes of underdevelopment and of pointing to ways of curing it. A broad theoretical consensus in the 1950s gradually fell apart as Third World realities failed to match First World expectations. Radical new theories emerged, the proponents of the various schools of thought each claiming that their theory held the key to understanding development and underdevelopment. In this chapter the major approaches to development will be described and assessed. Then the thorny question of the relationship between theory and practice in development will be discussed.

MODERNISATION

In the 1950s and 1960s thinking and action on development were dominated by the modernisation approach. Economists were in the vanguard, promoting simple models of development which focused on the problems of how to secure rapid economic growth and capital formation. Their models were derived from the experience of Western countries and were soon found lacking when faced with Third World differences and complexity. This necessitated interdisciplinary co-operation with sociologists, political scientists, public administrators and other social scientists, and the modernisation paradigm became the intellectual property of all the social sciences. It was, however, very American. The United States had assumed leadership of the 'free world' and was engaged in a cold war with the forces of evil. Following the demise of Hitler, this evil was seen to be represented by communism. It was necessary to save the world from these unspeakable forces of communist darkness and to ensure that the world remained ordered according to the best political and economic interests of the United States. Academic help was required for an understanding of what was happening in the Third World and for suggesting how these countries could be persuaded, lured or cajoled into remaining in the capitalist free world camp. Destabilising nationalist and revolutionary movements in the context of decolonisation gave greater urgency and larger resources to the academic task. Given this environment, where the specifications of the academic task were determined by political, military, administrative and business elites in the United States, it is not surprising that modernisation theory commenced with and maintained a conservative, pro-capitalist ideological framework.

To Wilbert Moore (1963, p. 93), 'modernization is a "total" transformation of a traditional or pre-modern society into the types of technology and associated social organization that characterize the "advanced", economically prosperous, and relatively politically stable nations of the Western World.' The 'effective political authorities' are to decide the policy priorities from their assessment of the multitude of developmental problems which require resolving. A slightly different definition is provided by Cyril Black (1967, p. 7), who sees modernisation as 'the process by which historically evolved institutions are adapted to the rapidly changing functions that reflect the unprecedented increase in man's knowledge, permitting control over his environment, that accompanied the scientific revolution.' Although there is some confusion and disagreement about the meaning of modernisation (Smith, 1973, pp. 61–2), the two definitions above are representative and enable us to make several generalisations. First, the world is said to consist of the traditional and the modern. Each of these dichotomous components is seen to possess certain distinct qualities, for example different economic structures, values and family organisation. Second, the transition from one historical period to the other is facilitated by the process of modernisation. Third, this process is directed by national elites through policy initiatives. They engineer the changes necessary for achieving modernity. Finally, the modernisation paradigm is a celebration of Western civilisation, a proclamation of the 'self-confidence of ethnocentric achievement' (Tipps, 1973, p. 206). The West is seen as superior to the Third World in all social, political and economic aspects. The scientific revolution which has permitted Western mastery of the environment must be adopted by the underdeveloped nations if they are to achieve the privileged status of being modern. Modernisation thus becomes synonymous with Westernisation. Any claims to value neutrality in modernisation theory thus disappear in the implicit assumptions that what is Western is good and desirable and that a replica of Western society is the promised land to which the underdeveloped nations must aspire.

The dichotomous view of societies as being either traditional or modern was not new to the social sciences. Such a perspective was being vigorously promoted in the nineteenth century. Maine furnished a contrast between societies or ages resting primarily on ascribed status and tradition and those resting on 'contract' and achieved status. More important for later generations of sociologists was Durkheim's work. He classified societies according to the opposing concepts of mechanical solidarity and organic solidarity. Mechanical solidarity characterised traditional societies where individuals differed very little from each other. They shared the same values, believed in the same sacred objects and performed similar economic tasks. Traditional societies held together because individual members were not yet differentiated. Such mechanical solidarity gave rise to small, relatively self-contained groups, which Durkheim called 'segments'. For example, a simple peasant farming community could be described as a segment. A few or perhaps a great many of these similar but largely unrelated segments comprised a 'segmental society'. A country with an undifferentiated peasantry scattered over many villages and mainly devoted to subsistence production would qualify as a segmented society. Increases in the density of social interaction sound the death knell for mechanical solidarity. The division of labour becomes more specialised and complex. Agreement on beliefs and moral ideas declines while differentiation grows. The consensus of mechanical solidarity is lost but a reformulated consensus emerges from the organic solidarity of the new order. The units of the new and modern society are interdependent. People recognise the need for this interdependence and agree that a high level of differentiation is required to maintain the relative equilibrium of the modern society. This theme of increasing differentiation accompanied by a reintegration of the new units is common in the writing of the modernisation school. Smelser (1963), Hoselitz (1960) and Parsons (1951) are leading exponents of this line of argument. Although criticised by Durkheim, Tönnies also utilised a compelling dichotomous model to explain the development of European society, or indeed for the analysis of any society past or present. Tönnies identified two types of social organisation, *Gemeinschaft* or community and *Gesellschaft*, which is commonly translated as society. *Gesellschaft* is perceived as a human relationship 'characterized by a high degree of individualism, impersonality, and proceeding from volition or sheer interest' (Nisbet, 1970, p. 74). Noncommunal modes of law, organisation and polity were, according to Tönnies, busily replacing those of the community in Europe. The dichotomous typology of Tönnies obviously influenced Weber in his account of the change from traditional to rational authority. The whole historical process of rationalisation as described by Weber is akin to Tönnies's transition from *Gemeinschaft* to *Gesellschaft*. The dichotomous Weberian ideal types of communal and associative social relationships closely resemble the distinctions drawn up by Tönnies.

The *Gemeinschaft/Gesellschaft* dichotomy was prominent in the theory of culture change or acculturation which absorbed social anthropologists in the 1940s and was then incorporated into the sociological paradigm of modernisation. The most famous figure in the culture change debate was Robert Redfield (1941, 1947) who postulated a continuum from 'folk' to 'urban' on which communities can be placed. Folk society was 'small, isolated, non-literate and homogeneous, with a strong sense of group solidarity' (Redfield, 1947, p. 293). Urban society was the antithesis of this and so was large, non-isolated, literate, heterogeneous and lacking a strong sense of group solidarity. Change from folk to urban occurred largely through contact with influences and agents coming from the urban society. This acculturation results in the disappearance of the ideal type folk community.

The heritage of the above thinkers is clearly expressed in the traditional/modern dichotomy that pervades much of modernisation theory. The proponents of the latter have certainly extracted this notion from these earlier works and recast it for their own purposes and time. One outstanding difference between the modernisation theorists and their forefathers is in the moral judgement of modernity. As we have seen, the modernisation paradigm rejoices in the arrival of modernity and points to Western society as the most advanced and desirable form of social, political and economic existence. Their predecessors were less enthusiastic. Durkheim pointed to the anomie evident in the transformation from mechanical to organic solidarity and showed that social problems and human distress resulted. Tönnies demonstrated a certain nostalgia for communal forms of organisation while Weber was pessimistic about the future of political power in the West.

The dichotomous view of societies obviously ran hand-in-hand with the evolutionary perspective of societal development. In the nineteenth century the doctrine of evolutionism guided almost all social, philosophical and historical thought. The fundamental idea is that 'societies like organisms can grow, flourish and decline' (Smith, 1973, p. 26). Different nineteenth century theorists stressed different factors in their evolutionary schemes. Thus, the stages of societal development which they all identified varied from one writer to another, according to the classificatory criteria employed. But all schemes of evolution could be presented as a sequence of ideal–typical discrete stages. The classical evolutionary theories all focused on drawing up these stages for the history of Western societies. Nobody then had much interest in the Third World. But this was the specific task adopted by the modernisation theorists, the exponents of neo-evolutionism. Their problem was to explain and predict how these Third World countries were going to 'replicate the transition' (Roxborough, 1979, p. 13) already experienced in the West. The stages of development device was enthusiastically adopted from the evolutionists and applied to the new situation.

The most famous and influential sequence of modernising stages was provided by Walt Rostow (1960). He saw 'self-sustaining economic growth' as the economic distinction of modern Western society. To achieve that distinction was what modernisation was all about. However, societies had to pass through five stages in order to get there: traditional society, the preconditions for take-off, the take-off, the drive to maturity and the age of high mass consumption. Technological constraints limited production in the first stage. Many of these constraints were removed in the second stage when rational scientific ideas, infrastructure and an orientation to business assumed importance. These changes resulted not endogenously, as had been the case in Western Europe, but from external intrusion which shocked the traditional society into change. During the brief take-off period (a few decades at worst), the share of net investment and saving in national income rose from 5 per cent to 10 per cent or more. This applied to Great Britain 1783–1802, Japan 1878–1900 or even India post-1950. A process of industrialisation could be discerned but modern technology was confined to the leading sectors. The drive to maturity saw investment rates of between 10–20 per cent of national income and modern technology diffuse through the entire economy. The mature economy had now arrived and its leaders could opt to use its resources for high mass consumption, but other possible scenarios included the welfare state and the pursuit of external power. This five-stage growth model of Rostow's has received enormous attention over the years. One attraction was the simplistic but captivating imagery of developing countries taking off into self-sustaining growth. Another factor was the book's sub-title, 'non-communist manifesto'. This naturally appealed to the American elites responsible for designing policy and to a generally conservative Western political consciousness. It also provoked considerable hostility from Marxists and, some years later, from liberal academics. It did, however, give further support to the view that 'for the first time in history, a universal pattern of modernity is emerging from the wide diversity of traditional values and institutions' (Black, 1966, p. 17).

Modernisation had cast off parts of the unilineal model of the older evolutionists by admitting that there were diverse paths to development. While the ultimate goal might be identical, starting points and the ways to get to the one destination could differ. Greater knowledge of history and the obvious empirical diversity of developing countries necessitated and enforced this view. Thus, Steward (1955) proposed a theory of multilinear evolution where similar societies could move in different directions. Sahlins and Service (1960) distinguished 'general' and 'specific' evolution. This separated two levels of adaptive development, that of a particular culture or society, and that of culture or civilisation generally. Thus general evolutionary breakthroughs could be identified while the varied histories of specific societies could also be contained in the theory. Other writers looked more to complex typological classification for their neo-evolutionary paradigms. Parsons (1966), for example, provided a five-category typology: primitive societies (Australian Aborigines), archaic societies (Mesopotamian Empires and Ancient Egypt), historic intermediate empires (China, India, Islamic Empires and the Roman Empire), seed-bed societies (Israel and Greece), and modern societies (the United States, the Soviet Union, Europe and Japan). The societies at each stage possess a similar degree of social differentiation and had evolved or imported comparable integrative solutions.

It is apparent from the discussion so far that while there are common strands within the modernisation perspective there is no monolithic structure. There is variation created by differences of stress, specificity and interest. In the rest of this section on the modernisation approach we shall look at several of these variations.

A popular and persistent model of the modernisation approach was that of the dual economy. The basis for this lay in the assertion that many developing countries were characterised by two economic sectors. The massive contrasts between low technology agriculture in rural areas and modern industry and infrastructure in the urban areas could not escape even the most casual observer. Lewis (1954) suggested a macro model consisting of an agricultural and an industrial sector. He saw the former as a labour reserve for the latter. The disguised unemployment of the agricultural sector would enable the transfer of labour resources to the dynamic industrial sector without affecting agricultural output. Lambert (1967) proposed that in Latin America a dual structure predominated in Brazil, Mexico, Colombia, Venezuela and Chile. The populations of these countries were divided between archaic and developed forms of social organisation which roughly coincided with the categories of rural and urban. The archaic forms were rapidly shrinking under the onslaught of modernisation. The all-conquering developed sector would soon be triumphant. A final example of dual sectors was provided by Boeke, a former Dutch colonial administrator. Although writing earlier in the century, Boeke's translation into English coincided with the onset of modernisation theory. His thesis is neatly summed up in Kipling's lines: 'East is East and West is West, and never the twain shall meet', approvingly quoted by Boeke (1953, p. 12). A precapitalist rural social system is contrasted with an imported capitalism. The two are engaged in a spiritual clash which finds expression in economic, social and political life. Furthermore, Western economic theory was totally inappropriate for the analysis of rural subsistence agriculture. While sharing the modernisationists' faith in the dichotomy model, Boeke differs from his fellow-travellers in his pessimistic view of the future. Changes in the village economy would lead to social and economic retrogression for the rural masses. While this interpretation could be seen to support certain colonial policies aimed at 'keeping the villagers in their place', it does contrast with the modernisation school's generally optimistic outlook. In retrospect this optimism about the outcome of development seems quite astonishing but it reflects the modernisation school's naive confidence about the accuracy of its method and the efficacy of its prescriptions.

The focus of concern for many sociologists of the modernisation school lay in the study of changing values. In its most simple formulation writers argued that the change from traditional to modern society required a corresponding transformation of values. Talcott Parsons (1951) led the way with his pattern variables. These were alternative or conflicting value orientations found in the role expectations of people: self-orientation/collectivity orientation, particularism/universalism, ascription/achievement, functional diffuseness/functional specificity. Different combinations of pattern variables lead to different role relationships and different social structures. The first parts of each of the above pairs is indicative of the traditional while the second parts are associated with modernity. Hoselitz (1960) applied Parson's pattern variables to the development process and found that the developed countries were characterised by universalism, achievement orientation and functional specificity. Underdeveloped countries displayed the opposite variables. Thus, Hoselitz was able to claim that the transition from traditional to modern society was essentially a matter of changing pattern variables. The association of modernity with modern values was vigorously promoted in Lerner's (1958) famous study of the Middle East. He looked to a 'characterological transformation' through 'psychic mobility', or, alternatively phrased, a change in personality and values from the traditional to the modern. McClelland (1961) saw the key to being modern in the transfer of the 'mental virus of n Ach' (need for Achievement). This would especially stimulate capitalism, hence modernisation, and to ensure that the n Ach entrepreneurs of the Third World did not become too rapacious a sense of public responsibility was also prescribed. Moore (1963, p. 98) summarised the thinking of many in his statement that 'extensive value changes are the most fundamental condition for economic transformation'. Like others he pointed to the modern values of merit in individual performance, personal autonomy in decision-making, a belief in social mobility, faith in the ability of modern science to shape the world and support of the modes of political participation found in Western democracies. These attitudinal changes worked in tandem with institutional changes in order to produce modernisation.

By the 1960s it was quite clear that, in many instances, modernisation was not a smooth ride along the road from tradition to modernity. There were discontinuities and breakdowns, rebellions and social protests along the way. In sociological terms this was described as a problem of integrating the newly differentiated structures of modernity. According to Smelser (1963), the disturbances arise because the differentiation progresses faster than the integration. Also, the forces of tradition are still trying to hold their own. There is a three-way tug-of-war. Political scientists moved into the debate anxious to prevent the disintegration or diminution of control by the formal political institutions. Transplanted Western democratic institutions did not necessarily flourish and in some cases could experience an early demise. The Congo in 1960 and the Nigerian civil war a few years later violently and graphically demonstrated how far modernisation disturbances could go. Thus, Huntingdon (1968) declared that the political institutions of developing countries, whether traditional or modern transplants, often proved too inflexible or too weak to withstand the growing pressure for political participation. Breakdown or 'political decay' resulted. This problem could be solved. The promotion of political order should be the primary goal of political modernisation. It was not the form of government (i.e. not the Western democratic ideal) which was the major political distinction between nations but their degree of government (i.e. their ability to maintain order and so promote and control the modernisation process). In this formulation, the differences between democratic and communist states were less than between both of these and many Third World states, where 'governments simply do not govern'. This approach provided an analytic justification for American support of authoritarian regimes, as the latter could be described as strong in their degree of government. Eisenstadt (1970) drew on both Smelser and Huntingdon in his gloomy analysis of the failure of modernisation to proceed as had been initially intended and prophesied. He noted 'continuous internal warfare . . . extreme antagonism and cleavages' (1970, p. 427) with economic crises fanning the flames and making a way out look almost impossible. There was a failure to establish organic solidarity. Social mobilisation or differentiation had occurred but the anticipated reintegration of the newly differentiated groups had not taken place as anticipated. The elites on whom so much depended had failed to perform their roles in the prescribed manner. Some squandered the state's resources while others, lacking any clear principles of regulation or priorities, exacerbated conflicts between various groups whose aspirations continued to rise. Policy could also oscillate between attempts to control all power positions and giving in to the demands of various groups.

Eisenstadt's work (1970) was an appropriate obituary for the modernisation paradigm. The miraculous transformations of traditional societies into modern ones had not taken place. Increased poverty, growing indebtedness, political repression and stagnating economies were all too evident – and they were not supposed to happen. More radical theories were already being advanced and the modernisation school reeled under a barrage of criticism. The radical theoreticians utilised competing frameworks to understand underdevelopment in the Third World, but all owed a debt to Karl Marx. It was from Marx's work that many of the new insights were drawn. However, the modern neo-Marxists of development studies did not reproduce the classic Marxian viewpoint.

KARL MARX – THE CLASSIC VIEW

Like Durkheim and Weber, Marx also engaged in the construction of grand theories of societal development. His distinctive and enduring contribution to social science was to focus on the economic aspects of man's activities. He argued that major historical changes (e.g. the transformation of feudalism into capitalism) were caused by conflicts generated in the mode of production. The latter was comprised of the forces of production (raw materials, tools, machines and techniques) and the relations of production (relations between people in the economic processes of production, distribution and exchange). As the forces of production are developed so the relations of production must be altered. The alteration is achieved through struggles between social classes. Some classes will strive to maintain the status quo as they benefit from that social order but others will want to reshape the relations of production to bring them into line with the forces of production and to allow further development of the latter. Thus, old modes of production are overthrown, and replaced by higher modes of production. In Europe, feudalism gave way to capitalism, and Marx predicted it was only a matter of time before the proletariat would triumph over the bourgeoisie and usher in the epoch of socialism leading to communism, the highest stage of societal evolution.

Marx was writing in the late nineteenth century and concentrated on a theory of capitalism and of capitalist development. Although Europe was his major interest he was aware of non-European precapitalist societies. It could hardly have been otherwise. This was the zenith of European colonialism, the final scramble for colonial possessions. Thus, scattered through Marx's voluminous works are various observations on colonialism and the capitalist penetration of precapitalist societies. Many of his thoughts seem to have a closer affinity with other nineteenth century evolutionists and their successors in the modernisation school than with the neo-Marxists of recent years.

While recognising different precapitalist modes of production around the world, Marx nevertheless retained a rather unilinear view of history. All societies would eventually become capitalist. Marx contended that 'the country that is more developed industrially only shows to the less developed the image of its future' (Marx, 1967, pp. 8–9). However, the precapitalist modes of production found in the underdeveloped world were essentially static, and so ill-equipped to generate the transition to capitalism internally. For example, the Asiatic mode of production, according to Marx, was 'based on a village economy, characterised by a union, within the village, of agriculture, and handicrafts, a traditional, hereditary division of labour and an absence of private property in land' (Brewer, 1980, p. 56). The economic surplus was taken by the state and not by individual landlords. The producers' control of their own means of subsistence enabled the Asiatic mode of production to resist change and movement to a higher mode of production. Marx identified state power as the means of overcoming both this and other static precapitalist modes of production. In large part this seemed to mean colonialism by states possessing superior modes of production.

Colonialism, for Marx, was a necessary evil. It might have been brutal and immoral, but without it how could the static precapitalist societies be made to develop the essential forces and relations of production that bring capitalism and then socialism? Lacking dynamics, precapitalist societies had to be awakened by colonialism and its accompanying capitalist onslaught. Merchant capital was, however, only destructive and exploitative. The trade and plunder which characterised merchant capitalism did little to develop the productive forces. But industrial capital, while it was destructive of the existing order, also transformed that order. This was what the Third World required and it did not seem to matter to Marx how the colonial intrusion was perpetrated. Thus, with reference to China and the opium trade, Marx remarked that, 'It would seem as though history had first to make this whole people drunk before it could rouse them out of hereditary stupidity' (Marx and Engels, 1969, p. 20). Marx often treated the precapitalist societies with disdain and disapproval. Often he knew little or nothing about them. Even his Asiatic mode of production focused exclusively on India and even then it was ill-formulated. Marx's enthusiasm for India was for the modernising and integrating factors created by British rule – the railway system, the electric telegraph, the 'native' army trained by British drill-sergeants, the 'free' press, private property in land, and a class 'imbued with European science' and with the requisite qualifications for assuming government. All of these were pre-requisites for the inevitable rise of industrial capitalism in India. Such enthusiasm for those developments would be shared by some of the nineteenth century evolutionists and by the modernists of the 1950s and 1960s. From tradition to modernity was essentially the same as from precapitalist to capitalist.

Furthermore, this effort of the bourgeoisie to create a world in its own image was perceived to be progressive. Consider Marx's approval of the Mexican–American War of 1847 as a step forward for Mexico and in the country's best interests that it should be 'placed under the tutelage of the United States'. After all, Mexicans were repositories of regressive Spanish vices such as 'boastfulness, grandiloquence and quixoticism' (Aguilar, 1968, pp. 66–7). But for Marx such modernity was only progressive because it led to socialism. The unilinear historical view of the 'bourgeois' theories stopped at capitalism, believing that this was the highest stage of development.

The neo-Marxists of recent years have drawn heavily on ideas expressed by Marx but rarely his explicit statements on colonialism. Indeed, many must be severely embarrassed by these statements. Although there are a number of variations, most neo-Marxists have adopted an almost antithetical stance to the dogmatic Eurocentric views of the master. They have focused on the external relations of Third World countries with industrial capitalism and have concluded that exploitation and underdevelopment have resulted. Furthermore, since Marx's death, history has demonstrated the inappropriateness of the unilinear model. For example, the variations in socialist revolutions are enormous.

Occasionally there are contemporary versions of the classic Marxian theme. Bill Warren (1980) has been the most influential of recent writers in this regard. He notes various improvements in social and material welfare under colonialism. Better health, longer lives, education and more consumer goods are cited among the benefits. Warren dismisses the neo-Marxist reformulations and claims that they have created an 'illusion of underdevelopment'. The focus on dependency has obscured the further economic progress brought about under political independence. The Third World has developed in broadly the way which Marx predicted. For example, the post-war record of the Third World on the standard measure of growth in GNP per capita is judged by Warren to be 'reasonably, perhaps even outstandingly successful as compared *either* with their prewar performance *or* with whatever past period of growth in the developed market economies (DMEs) may be taken as relevant for comparison' (Warren, 1980, pp. 190–1). Other statistical information which purportedly demonstrates such things as growth in industrial output and the fuller integration of the population into the capitalist market are cited to show that advances have been made in the development of the forces of production. Thus, the working class may still play the role for which it is destined. The political agenda is clear. Eject the obfuscations of neo-Marxism and nationalism, encourage the more rapid development of the forces of production and generate a growing working class fully conscious of its revolutionary role.

NEO-MARXISM: DEPENDENCY

By the late 1960s the sociology of development was in a state of crisis. Neither the modernisation school nor classical Marxism could provide adequate explanations of what was happening in the Third World and of how development could be achieved. A new paradigm was urgently required. It was found in the neo-Marxist dependency approach and was popularised, at least in the English-speaking world, in the works of André Gundar Frank.

But it was in Latin America that this school of thought originated. Until 1929 Latin American nations followed a conventional export-led strategy of development. The economic depression of the 1930s drastically reduced Western demand for Latin American products and revealed to these countries the problem of relying on external trade as the engine of growth. Thus, countries began to design inward-looking development strategies which would leave them less vulnerable to the vagaries of world trade. But it was not until after the Second World War that coherent ideological support for the inward-looking development path was formulated. This support and the suggested programme of action came from the offices of the United Nations Economic Commission for Latin America (ECLA) established in Chile in 1948. Although judged to be radical 'in an international agency context, [it] nevertheless conformed to the UN style of analysis with its bland, apolitical language of the international bureaucrat' (O'Brien, 1975, p. 9). ECLA believed that the conventional economic wisdom emanating from the developed capitalist countries was inappropriate for Latin America. It had failed to produce the anticipated economic development. ECLA looked beyond the domestic economic structures of Latin American countries to explain the persistence of underdevelopment on the continent. The system of international free trade was immediately identified as the villain of the piece (Blomström and Hettne, 1984, p. 40). The terms of trade and income elasticity of demand for primary product exports were declining while Latin America's income elasticity of demand from the developed economies was increasing. This generated a balance of payments crisis for the Latin American economies. Furthermore, while productivity gains in the developed countries (the centre) resulted in higher wages and increases in other factor prices, the situation in Latin America (the periphery) was the reverse. Productivity gains there produced only a decline in commodity prices and stagnant wages (O'Brien, 1975, pp. 9–10; Prebisch, 1950). The solution to this problem was to industrialise, specifically aiming to substitute current imports with domestic production. High tariff protection was essential in the early stages. The state would necessarily play a larger role than previously in promoting economic development. Finally, the establishment of a Latin American common market would facilitate further industrialisation.

While this model of development (import substitution industrialisation) proved to be a failure, the ECLA analysis of Latin American development had brought two important observations into the spotlight. Firstly, that the world could be perceived in terms of a core of developed industrial nations and a periphery of underdeveloped nations. Second, the core and the periphery were closely linked economically, especially in trade and investment. However, these links prevented true development from taking place in the periphery as they were designed to work only to the advantage of the centre. The countries of the periphery had been made dependent on the economies of the centre. Inward-looking import substitution industrialisation strategies of development were seen as the way to break this inequitable relationship of dependence. Only then could real development take place.

These notions derived from ECLA were taken over by other Latin

American social scientists who refined, modified and radicalised
them. All, however, adopted the view that the underdevelopment of
Latin America and other peripheral countries could only be understood in the context of the world capitalist system. Unlike Marx, the
dependency theorists believed that the relations binding centre and
periphery worked against development, against the creation of a
flourishing industrial capitalism. The relations merely perpetuated
underdevelopment in the periphery. Definitions varied slightly but
dos Santos succeeded in incorporating the two major perspectives of
the paradigm in his formulation of the notion of dependency:

a situation in which a certain group of countries have their economies
conditioned by the development and expansion of another economy, to
which their own is subjected . . . . Dependency conditions a certain internal
structure which redefines it as a function of the structural possibilities of the
distinct national economies (dos Santos as quoted in Roxborough, 1979,
p. 66).

Thus, there is dependency as an international relationship where
the strong economy conditions the weak while there is also dependency as a structure distinct from the advanced nations. The dependency school is not monolithic, as Blomström and Hettne's (1984)
book clearly demonstrates. O'Brien (1975, p. 13) notes that 'each
author emphasizes different aspects of how and why the international economy and its changes, condition changes in Latin America'. However, one author, André Gunder Frank, has achieved the
greatest fame and widest influence of the dependency school with his
version of dependency, a version crystallized or synthesised from the
ideas of ECLA and Marxism (Booth, 1975).

Frank's position is that, 'it is capitalism, both world and national,
which still generates underdevelopment in the present' (Frank, 1971,
p. 11). He does not define capitalism but portrays it in terms of a
global system of exchange which is both monopolistic and exploitative. Capitalism has thus been responsible for 'the development of
underdevelopment' since the sixteenth century, when Spain and
Portugal commenced the conquest of Latin America. The continent
has never experienced feudalism. For example, when both bourgeois
and Marxist social scientists identify feudalism in Brazilian agriculture they are dealing with 'myths' (Frank, 1971, p. 249). Once
merchant capitalism touched the continent's shores capitalist underdevelopment commenced. The basic structure of this capitalism has

remained largely unchanged since that initial colonisation. Indeed capitalism has penetrated every nook and cranny on the continent, so much so that nothing, even seemingly precapitalist or non-capitalist structures, can be explained without reference to capitalism. For example, subsistence agriculture is 'commercially determined because [it] is residual to commercial agriculture' (Frank, 1971, p. 286). The so-called 'Indian problem' is not any lack of cultural or economic integration of the Indian into society. Quite the reverse, the Indian's problem is his integration into the exploitative capitalist system (Frank, 1971, p. 169). This aspect of Frank's basic thesis is intended to disprove the modernisation school's theories of dual societies where, in Latin America, feudalism and capitalism were seen as essentially independent co-existing sectors. Capitalism, the progressive modernising force for the proponents of dualism, was for Frank the regressive structure which prevented progress and development.

The structure of the world capitalist system was presented by Frank as one of metropolis and satellite. The metropolis exploits the satellite and appropriates some or all of the economic surplus. The satellite is impoverished by this exploitative relationship and it is reduced to a state of dependency on the metropolis. The basic metropolis–satellite relationship is between the industrial capitalist nations and the nations of Latin America or indeed any other similarly placed Third World country. However, Frank identified a chain of metropolis–satellite connections stretching from the boardrooms of New York to the tenant farmer in the remotest Andean valley. For example, in his explanation of the development of underdevelopment in Brazil, Frank wrote:

this model consists of a world metropolis (today the United States) and its governing class, and its national and international satellites and their leaders – national satellites like the Southern states of the United States, and international satellites like São Paulo. Since São Paulo is a national metropolis in its own right, the model consists further of its satellites: the provincial metropolises like Recife or Belo Horizonte, and their regional and local satellites in turn . . . a whole chain of metropolises down to the hacienda or rural merchant who are satellites of the local commercial metropolitan centre but who in turn have peasants as their satellites (Frank, 1971, pp. 174–5).

In fact the whole world was comprised of a series of such metropolis–satellite constellations. Each metropolis appropriated part or even all of the economic surplus of its satellites. Thus, landless labourers may be exploited by small landowners. But they too may have economic surplus appropriated by large landowners or provincial business classes. And so the chain continues until the top of the hierarchy, the world metropolis, is reached and there is nobody above this metropolis to appropriate from it.

It is not only the imperialism of the world metropolis which has kept this basic structure intact over many centuries. The co-operation of dominant classes in the satellites has also been necessary. The dependency structure has permitted domestic ruling classes to appropriate part of the surplus. Consequently, they have little incentive to change the structure. They have benefited from under-development. According to Frank the bourgeoisie use government cabinets and other state instruments to 'produce a *policy of under-development* in the economic, social and political life of the "nation" and the people of Latin America' (Frank, 1972, p. 13). But the strength of dependency varies from time to time. Depressions and wars, the 1930s and the Second World War, for example, can result in the weakening of dependency ties as the world metropolis is unable to maintain its full hegemony over the satellites. This may enable the national bourgeoisie to engage in more or less auton-omous industrialisation as happened in Brazil, Mexico, Argentina and India during the 1930s depression and the Second World War. But such active capitalist involution, characterised by metropolis–satellite relations of internal colonialism or imperialism is not the only course. The alternative, passive capitalist involution, occurs when a satellite moves towards or into an isolated subsistence society of extreme underdevelopment. The history of north-east Brazil with its wildly fluctuating sugar industry is cited as an exemplar of this.

Finally, it is important to appreciate the practical political implica-tions of Frank's dependency model. As his analysis claimed that there were no feudal, semi-feudal or other precapitalist modes of production in Latin America there was no reason to support a bourgeois democratic revolution. Frank rejected the traditional Marxist view of the Left which called for such an event in order to develop further the forces of production and prepare for the pro-letarian revolution at some indistinct future date. He believed that the bourgeoisie had been in control of Latin America since the sixteenth century. Capitalism was well established everywhere and given the prevailing metropolis–satellite structure could not do other than generate further underdevelopment. Thus, all political efforts should be directed towards socialist revolution. The influence of Castro and the Cuban Revolution comes through strongly in Frank's works. In some ways, his theory of dependency is a vindication of the Cuban Revolution, a critique of Stalinist orthodoxy and a theoretical justification of immediate socialist revolution (Booth, 1975, pp. 65–6).

Although a short account such as this cannot do justice to all of the varieties of dependency that have been advanced, it is necessary to make brief mention of one more figure from the dependency hall of fame, that of Immanuel Wallerstein. While much of his argument coincides with the thoughts of Frank, Wallerstein has some additional insights and has built up a loyal following for world-system theory, his version of dependency. The subject of analysis for Wallerstein is the social system. This should not be confused with the nation-state. The social system is a 'totality' which transcends such political boundaries. It is defined as:

a division of labor, such that the various sectors or areas within are dependent upon economic exchange with others for the smooth and continuous provisioning of the needs of the area. Such economic exchange can clearly exist without a common political structure and even more obviously without sharing the same culture (Wallerstein, 1979, p. 5).

There are only three types of social system. The first, the 'mini-system', is essentially that of simple agricultural or hunting and gathering societies. But they are now defunct everywhere having been drawn into, modified, subjugated or destroyed by the two other social systems, both of which are world systems. The 'world empire' is defined according to the extraction of tribute by a central authority, and premodern civilisations such as China, Egypt and Rome are cited as examples. The final category is that of 'world economy', a system connected by market exchange. It should be noted that a world system does not have to spread over the entire globe, although the contemporary world system would appear to do just that. A single division of labour and multiple cultural systems define something that is called a world system.

According to Wallerstein, the late fifteenth and early sixteenth century saw the emergence of a European world economy, a completely new type of world system. It was economically unified, with a single division of labour, but politically diverse, with multiple polities. The division of labour was, and of course still is, that of capitalism. The essential feature of a capitalist world economy is production for sale in a market in which the object is to realise the maximum profit. The development of this system is inequitable. A three-tiered hierarchy of states is produced – the core, the semi-periphery and the periphery. Strong state mechanisms in the core (industrial capitalist nations) and weak ones in the periphery (the Third World) enable the core to enforce relations of unequal exchange over the periphery. 'Thus capitalism involves not only appropriation of the surplus value by an owner from a laborer, but an appropriation of surplus of the whole world-economy by core areas' (Wallerstein, 1979, pp. 18–9). Wallerstein would thus concur with Frank that the core is actively underdeveloping the periphery. In fact, it has been keeping the periphery weak since the dawn of agricultural capitalism. Conquest, threat, market restriction and industrial protection are among the tactics employed by the strong states to maintain the weakness of peripheral states.

The middle stratum of the international hierarchy, the semiperiphery, is apparently vital for the smooth running of the capitalist world economy. The semiperiphery prevents the polarisation of core and periphery. The core has created the semiperiphery in order to forestall political instability and the overthrow of the core's system of unequal exchange by the exploited majority in the periphery. The mechanism of this process is unclear in Wallerstein's work. The semiperiphery can both exploit and be exploited from its intermediate location while nations can over time be relegated from core to semiperiphery or in fact be promoted. This contrasts with Frank's metropolis–satellite relationship where it is difficult to see how the underdeveloped satellite can possibly change its underdeveloped status. Wallerstein's semiperiphery encompasses a bewilderingly wide range of countries in terms of economic strength and political background. Brazil, Mexico and Argentina rub shoulders with Portugal, Spain, Italy, Norway and Finland. Arab states such as Saudi Arabia and Egypt are ranged alongside Nigeria and Zaire while Canada, Australia and 'possibly' New Zealand are also located there. And there is still room for the socialist states of Eastern Europe and Vietnam (Wallerstein, 1979, p. 100).

The dependency paradigm took the world of development theorising by storm. It hastened the demise of modernisation theory and provided a more convincing and politically acceptable explanation of the Third World than the classical Marxian perspective. The major achievement of the dependency school was to redefine the object for study. Under the modernisation approach the academic focus had been fixed on happenings within the boundaries of the developing nations. The dependency approach broke out of this strait-jacket and identified the world economy as the principal object of analysis. The relations between nations determined developmental status. No longer could the blame for underdevelopment be placed exclusively on those who were underdeveloped. Poverty, economic stagnation, failure to industrialise, the absence of take-off and poor project performance now became more explicable. But, like its predecessors, the dependency paradigm did not have the answers to everything. After a brief honeymoon period in which it was rapturously received, dependency theory came under more systematic scrutiny and the criticism began to flow thick and fast. The wellspring of this criticism was largely from within the Marxist tradition, from a revitalised and reformulated debate about modes of production. This debate is the subject of the next section.

NEO-MARXISM: ARTICULATING THE MODES OF PRODUCTION

An early and highly influential critique of the dependency perspective came from the Latin American Marxist, Ernesto Laclau. His main target was Frank but Wallerstein was also included in a postscript to the reissue of his original essay (Laclau, 1971, 1977). Laclau's basic objection was to Frank's view that Latin America was entirely capitalist and had been so since the early days of Spanish and Portuguese conquest. In order to argue his case Laclau relied heavily on that elusive Marxian concept, the mode of production.

For Frank and Wallerstein, capitalism is a system of exchange relations. This abstraction, according to Laclau, enables these dependency theorists to include an extraordinary range of 'exploitative relations' under capitalism – Chilean *inquilinos*, textile workers in Manchester, even serfs of the European Middle Ages and slaves on a Roman *latifundum*. Indeed, so all-encompassing is Frank's perception of capitalism that 'we could conclude that from the neolithic revolution onwards there has never been anything but capitalism'

(Laclau, 1971, p. 23). Laclau returns to the Marxian concept of mode of production – 'an integrated complex of social productive forces and relations linked to a determinate type of ownership of the means of production' (Laclau, 1971, p. 34). Only two modes of production are of interest to Laclau for the Latin American case. These are feudalism and capitalism. In both modes the economic surplus is appropriated by dominant classes but under capitalism the labourer is 'free' to sell his labour-power while ownership of the means of production is severed from ownership of labour-power. Laclau continues by defining something called an 'economic system', that is 'the mutual relations between the different sectors of the economy, or between different production units, whether on a regional, national or world scale (Laclau, 1971, p. 35). Thus, in direct opposition to Frank, Laclau observes that a given economic system might be comprised of different but co-existing modes of production with one mode of production assuming a dominant position.

In Latin America, while capitalism was dominant, there had been feudal structures throughout the continent while today 'semi-feudal conditions are still widely characteristic of the Latin American countryside' (Laclau, 1971, p. 32). Laclau was anxious to distance himself from the dualism thesis of the modernisation school. In the latter there was no obvious connection between the modern progressive sector and the closed traditional sector. By contrast Laclau argued that feudal-style exploitation was accentuated and consolidated by capitalist activities in Latin America. Peasants subjected to servile obligations and servile exactions in order to maximise profits are cited as examples. The survival of the feudal mode or even re-feudalization occurs as an integral and structured part of the larger economic system which is dominated by the capitalist mode. Laclau concurred with Frank that the economic surplus was being transferred from the periphery to the centre. However, whereas Frank believed this transfer to be the cause of underdevelopment, Laclau held it to be the result of more basic relations. Ownership of the means of production, that fundamental Marxian concept, formed the core of these basic relations which determined 'the forms of canalization of the economic surplus and the effective degree of the division of labour, the basis in turn of the specific capacity of the productive forces for expansion' (Laclau, 1971, p. 34). Laclau's explanation of the necessity of underdevelopment to development has been accused of being unconvincing, both theoretically and in practice (Brewer, 1980, p. 170). Focus on the relations of production is certainly useful but it almost appears that Laclau has done this more for purposes of demonstrating Marxian authenticity than for explanatory enlightenment. One cannot, however, accuse Laclau of merely reiterating the classic Marxian position as he does not share the optimism of Marx concerning the development of the productive forces in a capitalist Third World. Laclau's work may even be viewed as a critique of the classic Marxian perspective.

Working simultaneously but independently of Laclau on the mode of production issue was a group of French anthropologists, Meillassoux, Godelier, Terray, Dupré and especially Rey (Clammer, 1975, 1978a). Their writings represent a synthesis of Marxist principles, the inspiration coming by way of the dense and difficult prose of the Marxist theorists, Althusser and Balibar. The new economic anthropology eagerly adopted Althusser's distinction between a mode of production and a social formation.

The mode of production is an abstract concept which appears to include 'forces and relations of production, and must include mechanisms of distribution' (Clammer, 1978b, p. 12). It should be noted that conceptual disagreements and ambiguity about what constitutes a mode of production and uncritical usage of the concept, especially for all manner of explanatory purposes, has weakened the case of this version of neo-Marxism. The social formation is a more concrete concept in that a real society may be thought of as a social formation. It contains several different modes of production and as such has obvious affinity with Laclau's notion of the economic system. The modes of production are articulated, that is they co-exist or interact, with one mode of production dominating over others in the social formation. This differs from classical Marxism, where modes of production are seen as successive stages of development. For example, capitalism replaces feudalism. In the anthropological reformulation it is well appreciated that the transition between modes is an extremely long affair, so long in fact that transition is the normal state of affairs. Thus, the major analytical task is to understand the ways in which the different modes affect each other. The modes are in contradiction in that one must replace the other and it is necessary to identify how each is reproduced during the transition from dominance by one mode to dominance by another. A brief account of Rey's work should help to clarify matters (Rey, 1973; Foster-Carter, 1978; Brewer, 1980, pp. 183–207).

Rey's principal objective is to construct 'a single analytical framework that will comprehend both the European transition from feudalism to capitalism and also the latter's articulation with other precapitalist modes' (Foster-Carter, 1978, p. 218). Rey identifies three stages of articulation. The first interaction involves capitalism reinforcing the precapitalist mode. For example, in West African lineage societies the trading of slaves and goods actually strengthened the existing mode of production. In the second stage the capitalist mode of production establishes its dominance over the co-existing modes. For example, wage labour will be recruited (if necessary by force) and inculcated with the labour relations of capitalism. Simultaneously, the agricultural subsistence economy will be allowed to persist or to resist capitalist encroachment. Even when cash cropping is introduced it may only make a partial penetration of rural areas. Traditional and capitalist modes of production will interact. Capitalist penetration of agriculture is a slow process. The third stage represents the total disappearance of the precapitalist mode. This has not yet occurred in the Third World.

Rey believes that, with the exception of feudalism, all precapitalist modes of production are hostile to and so resist the spread of capitalism. In order to implant capitalism violence is needed. The state promotes colonialism for this civilising mission, and Rey does recognise something called a colonial mode of production, defined by the forced recruitment of labour and the forced sale of products. Once the dominance of the capitalist mode is established then the colonial troops can withdraw, political independence may even be granted and capitalism can be reproduced in what is now the neo-colony by purely economic means. While the precapitalist mode is still in evidence (e.g. in post-independence political groupings or traditional agriculture), metropolitan finance capital is the dominant force, especially in the export sector. The underdevelopment of an indigenous capitalist class under the colonial mode of production necessitates the massive intrusion of this type of capital.

As Brewer (1980, p. 198) has observed, we arrive, by a completely different route, at similar political conclusions reached by Frank. The exploitation suffered by Third World populations can only be ended through the direct confrontation of a socialist revolution. For Frank, an actively underdeveloping capitalism is in every nook and cranny of the Third World and will not fully develop the productive forces. For Rey (1971, p. 463, as cited in Brewer, 1980, p. 198), 'Throughout the world, capitalism to-day plays a fundamentally counter-revolutionary role: it keeps the most archaic forms in existence; it restores them when they are threatened.' Capitalism will only remove 'archaic forms' at a very slow pace because it suits capitalism to do just that. If necessary, old precapitalist modes will be revitalised. The analysis is in great contrast to Frank but the prescriptions for political action are similar. As with all schools of development theory, that of the 'articulation of modes of production' fraternity has encountered stiff criticism. The elusiveness of the basic mode of production concept and its loose application have been considerable stumbling blocks to its wider acceptance. Foster-Carter (1978, p. 224) has aptly noted that some writing (though not Rey's) 'seems to be a ghostly *pas de deux* performed by modes of production apparently conceived as Platonic ideas'. In such instances, allegations of academic isolation in ivory towers away from the reality of development are well founded. Indeed, the decline of the mode of production approach may have much to do with the fact that people saw it becoming increasingly a matter of semantics and not about what was actually happening in the Third World. A further problem with the approach was that in some hands there seemed to be an infinite number of modes of production. As one crossed every mountain or swamp in Papua New Guinea, for example, a new language group, culture and mode of production could be encountered! Some have asked whether the colonial mode of production is a legitimate concept. What is its precise relationship to capitalism? The defining characteristic is forced recruitment of labour, yet many examples could be cited where there were no shortage of willing precapitalist applicants for admission to the world of capitalist labour relations. Perhaps Rey's generalisations on this matter result from his utilising only one case study, that of lineage societies in Congo-Brazzaville. Other criticisms abound (see Foster-Carter, 1978; Booth, 1985; Roxborough, 1979).

Other neo-Marxists also abound. For example, Arghiri Emmanuel (1972) proposed a theory of 'unequal exchange', in which he extends Marx's theory of prices of production to the international economy. Froebel and his associates (1980) identified qualitative changes in the world economy leading to a 'new international division of labour'. Commodity production was being subdivided into fragments and assigned to whichever part of the world had the most profitable combination of capital and labour. This meant that, for the first time, manufacturing could be profitably pursued in developing countries. Samir Amin (1976) has appropriated just about every concept in the neo-Marxist armoury and created a theory focusing on capital accumulation. There are others in the neo-Marxist camp with less ambitious theoretical programmes. We have only provided a sample of some of the major debates and issues in the enormous and often stimulating theoretical literature which neo-Marxists in the 1970s and early 1980s have provided.

NEO-POPULISM

While the neo-Marxists were arguing over modes of production and world systems another group of writers were drawing inspiration from a different source. This was the tradition of populist thought. Since the early nineteenth century, Europe had regularly produced writers who criticised large-scale industrialisation on the grounds that the social and human costs of this process by far outweighed the benefits (Kitching, 1982). They generally wished to erect barriers to prevent the destruction and depredations of industrialisation. The period after the First World War saw Russian writers, especially Chayanov (1966), take the populist view beyond criticism and into questioning the economic rationale for large-scale production in both agriculture and industry, while simultaneously suggesting an alternative development strategy. This vision of development is still with us today in the works of the contemporary neo-populists and focuses on 'small-scale enterprise, on the retention of a peasant agriculture and of non-agricultural petty commodity production, and on a world of villages and small towns rather than large industrial cities' (Kitching, 1982, p. 98). The present-day neo-populists are not, however, incurable romantics pursuing some rural idyll. They know rural life is hard and characterised by poverty. They are familiar with and use the science of economics far more than their predecessors, they accept partial industrialisation and are intent on modernising (i.e. making more productive) peasant agriculture. Their overriding moral concern is still that of inequality and the principal problem which they address is how to distribute wealth and income equitably. Their proposals for small-scale production and other related policy innovations are generally made with this consideration to the fore. The neo-populists are a varied group according to the names cited in Kitching's book. Julius Nyerere, E.F. Schumacher, Michael Lipton, the International Labour Organisation (ILO), the World Bank (!) and, we would add, the ecodevelopers are all neo-populists. It is apparent that their names are better known than many other writers we have encountered in our survey of development theory. Many people have heard of and maybe even know a bit about Julius Nyerere, the former president of Tanzania, or E.F. 'small is beautiful' Schumacher, or multinational organisations such as the ILO. By contrast, only the select few know of and even less understand those who theorise on articulating modes of production, whatever the intellectual merits of this approach. As one might expect from the name-tag we have allocated, neo-populist ideas are more accessible and have a fairly wide currency and appeal. They also seem to be practically-oriented, especially when compared to neo-Marxist theories or Parsonian pattern variables.

Julius Nyerere had plenty of appeal in the second half of the 1960s when he elaborated and then attempted to implement his version of African socialism. Both liberals and revolutionaries joined in the initial applause. Nyerere believed that a surviving traditional form of African socialism could be utilised as a basis for immediate socialist development. The need to pass through a fully developed capitalism in order to attain socialism was denied and soundly criticised as an ethnocentric device of European thought. Pre-colonial Africa was socialist, and even if African families were politically unconscious of this, they lived according to the basic principles of *ujamaa* – mutual respect, sharing of property and income, and the obligation to work. Weaknesses were admitted. Women were subordinate and exploited while material poverty was evident. Colonialism had introduced corrupting elements, such as economic individualism and class conflict. But all was not lost. A revitalised and improved African socialism could be mobilised to produce equitable social and economic development.

Nyerere assigned a central role to agriculture. For purely pragmatic reasons this was inevitable. Tanzania was a country largely comprised of poor peasant farmers. Rapid industrialisation was out of the question as domestic capital was scarce and, lacking infrastructure and skills, multinationals would hardly view the country with relish, whatever the dependency theorists might say. Nyerere's vision was of a Tanzania made up of self-reliant *ujamaa* villages producing and consuming co-operatively. Any industrialisation should be labour intensive, technologically appropriate and geographically dispersed. Towns and cities were exploitative and parasitic and did not have central roles in the nation's essentially agricultural future. Middle-men and moneylenders, domestic or international, also displayed these unsavoury characteristics and were not to be trusted. Co-operation, co-operatives and hard work were more than adequate as substitutes. Finally, as Kitching (1982, p. 69) observes, 'it is not too much to say that socialism, for Nyerere, *is* equality or at least "fairness" in the distribution of society's wealth.' While increasing production was undoubtedly important, it had to be undertaken in conjunction with steps to ensure 'fairness' in its distribution.

The implementation of the *ujamaa* philosophy did not quite work in the expected manner. While services certainly improved and equality was at least maintained, economic growth did not occur as hoped (see Table 2.1). Slow production increases in food crops were particularly worrying. The forced 'villagisation' often proved unpopular while administration left much to be desired. Communal agriculture was neglected by the people while drought did nothing to help (for detailed evaluations see Kitching, 1982, pp. 104–24; von Freyhold, 1979; Mwansasu and Pratt, 1979).

According to the academic economist Michael Lipton (1977, p. 13), 'the most important class conflict in the poor countries of the world today is not between labour and capital. Nor is it between foreign and national interests. It is between rural classes and urban classes.' These do not appear to be classes in the Marxian or even Weberian sense but seem more akin to interest groups. Whatever their precise delineation they are in conflict and the urban variety has been consistently winning. In order to forestall organised rural opposition, urban elites have been kept busy buying off leading rural classes. The outcome of these conflicts and political manoeuvres is a development policy biased in favour of urban areas. Poverty, which is heavily concentrated in rural areas, is maintained and developmental progress prevented.

The urban bias policy regime includes the promotion of capital-intensive industrialisation, spatially concentrated in urban areas and inefficient. The domestic terms of trade are loaded against the rural producers. They must suffer overpriced farm inputs while simultaneously accepting government initiatives to keep food prices low for urban consumers. Too little is invested in rural education while too many of those acquiring skills migrate to the cities. But urban bias is not only evident in resource allocation, it is also a state of mind. The skewed resource allocation is linked to a prevailing disposition towards urban bias among decision-makers and persons of influence. Not only do they make inequitable resource allocations in favour of urban areas, they also find intellectual justification for them.

The tragedy for Lipton is that he believes peasant agriculture to be highly efficient. Capital/output ratios are lower for peasant agriculture than for other economic activities – 'the impact on output of $1 of carefully selected investment is in most countries two to three times as high in agriculture as elsewhere' (Lipton, 1977, p. 16). His remedy is to redirect capital into agriculture and away from inefficient urban activities and overprivileged urban classes. If the 'price twists' (e.g. government measures to keep food prices cheap, subsidies for imported industrial capital goods) were removed then the whole urban bias conspiracy would be exposed. Then equitable development based on the efficient peasant farmer could take place. Eventually, industrialisation may be permitted, but 'A developed mass agriculture is normally needed before you can have widespread successful development in other sectors' (Lipton, 1977, p. 23). Many did not believe him and there was much debate and criticism. For example, on empirical grounds his assertions were questioned about the one-way flow of resources from rural to urban areas, whether taxes actually did penalise agriculture more heavily than industry or whether intra-rural income distribution was less unequal than intra-urban income distribution. On conceptual grounds his notion of class came under strong fire while the short-run nature of his economic analysis was also found to be wanting (for critical comments see Byres, 1979; Corbridge, 1982; Kitching, 1982, p. 84–92). Even Lipton (1984, p. 139), in a forceful defence of his thesis, admits that 'urban bias does not apply to all less developed countries, for example some very open economies'.

A final contender for inclusion in the neo-populist category is ecodevelopment, a word coined in 1972 by combining ecology and development, meaning 'an ecologically sound development' (Glaeser and Vyasulu, 1984, p. 23). The origin of this approach lay in the late 1960s when pollution control necessarily forced itself on to the political agenda in industrial nations. This encouraged a wider concern with the physical environment. Soon alarm bells were ringing, warning that the planet was in peril (e.g. Dasmann, 1972). Rapidly increasing pressure on the world's resources could not be sustained. 'Eco-doomsters' predicted disaster ahead. Mankind stood 'on the brink of extinction' (Ehrlich, 1970, p. 1), 'the present course of civilization is suicidal' (Commoner, 1972, p. 294). Something had to be done to save 'spaceship earth'. It was necessary to promote a harmonious relationship between society and the physical environment, a relationship which would ensure the health and longevity of both.

Central to the ecodevelopment case was the critique of economic growth. In addition to the environmentalists, many economists were questioning whether development could be equated with constant expansion of the GNP or whether such expansion could be maintained. Didn't more production mean more pollution and environmental degradation? And what was the cost of remedying these catastrophes? The British economist, Mishan, waged a long war against economic growth (Mishan, 1967, 1977). He argued that the uncritical acceptance of economic growth as being good overlooked the enormous costs of that growth. He also weighed in with support for the environmentalists, saying that they did not want a 'no-growth economy *per se* much less a recession in a growing economy. . . . [They wanted] the public at large to accept a steady state economy as a desirable norm of social policy' (Mishan, 1977, p. 108). Schumacher (1973, p. 28) worried that the pursuit of unlimited economic growth had adversely affected 'the self-balancing system of nature [which was] becoming increasingly unbalanced.' He went on to bemoan the fact that there was an uncritical acceptance of the notion, propagated by economists and politicians, that growth of the GNP must be good 'irrespective of what has grown and who, if anyone, has benefited. The idea that there could be pathological growth, unhealthy growth, disruptive or destructive growth is . . . a perverse idea which must not be allowed to surface' (Shumacher, 1973, p. 46). Even the staid Club of Rome commissioned a report entitled *The Limits to Growth* by scientists from the Massachusetts Institute of Technology (Meadows *et al.*, 1972). This was followed by a further report which concluded that man's focus on growth must give way to equilibrium (Forrester, 1971).

Ecodevelopment claimed to have the answers to the impending environmental disasters which threatened earth. At first ecodevelopment was supposed to be 'a development strategy based on the judicious use of local resources and small farmer know-how, applicable to the isolated rural areas of the Third World' (Sachs, 1971, p. 1). However, the concept was soon expanded to mean:

an approach to development aimed at harmonizing social and economic objectives with ecologically sound management, in a spirit of solidarity with future generations; based on the principle of self-reliance, satisfaction of basic needs, a new symbiosis of man and earth; another kind of qualitative growth, not zero growth, not negative growth (Sachs as quoted in Glaeser and Vyasulu, 1984, p. 25).

According to Sachs ecodevelopment entails the following types of policies:

- harmonisation of consumption patterns, time use, life styles;
- appropriate technologies, ecologically-based designs;
- low energy profile, promotion of renewable energy base;
- new uses for environmental resources, careful husbandry of resources, recycling;
- ecological principles to guide settlement patterns and land uses;
- participatory planning and grass-root activation.
  (after Glaeser and Vyasulu, 1984)

Sachs and his contemporary ecodevelopers are at pains to point out they are not advocating a type of regression towards some idealised pastoral life-style, which anyway never actually existed. They also say that they don't necessarily aim to halt growth but to find 'methods and uses of growth which make social progress and sound management of resources and environment compatible' (Sachs, 1977, p. 1).

These conciliatory remarks towards the idea of growth may reflect the efforts of the ecodevelopers to placate Third World mistrust and, in some cases, downright hostility towards ecodevelopment. First, the Third World reaction to escalating global pollution problems in the 1970s was that they had been created by the industrial nations who should therefore assume the responsibility of solving them. Second, there was the suspicion that anti-growth, anti-industrialisation talk was part of a conspiracy to keep the Third World in a perpetual state of underdevelopment. Considerable production increases were necessary even to supply basic needs in many countries. Discussions which cast doubt on the merits of growth were a luxury of industrial nations. The ecodevelopers have since stressed their support for industrialisation through an alternative industrial strategy, arguing that it is a key element of development (e.g. Vyasulu, 1984). This is in line with all of the neo-populists of development. Thirdly, the ecodevelopment movement has been keen to promote appropriate technology in agriculture and manufacturing. This was originally small-scale, simple, easy to maintain, labour-intensive, non-polluting and simple to replicate. Third World governments were once more suspicious of a First World plot aimed at fobbing off the Third World with second-rate technology in order to protect First World privileges. Thus, a more recent reformulation of appropriate technology is that it is 'any technique, intermediate or advanced, large-scale or small, simple or sophisticated, that uses science in a way suited to the requirements of a given situation – defined by the concept of ecodevelopment – and therefore including economic, socio-cultural ecological and political factors' (Glaeser and Vyasulu, 1984, p. 31) – not the clearest of definitions! Perhaps governments, or at least pressure groups, in Third World countries are increasingly aware of environmental matters as forests are removed, watersheds denuded, soil erosion flourishes, urban pollution accelerates and, they realise, some of the most unpleasant industries and toxic wastes of the First World have been relocated to the Third World. International agencies and Western political lobbies continue to broadcast their concern about the urgency of the problems. Ecodevelopment is, thus, very much alive.

CONCLUSION

In this chapter we have reviewed some of the major post-war approaches to the sociology of development. No theory has achieved and maintained explanatory dominance. At present, some Marxists have identified an impasse in Marxist-influenced approaches to the sociology of development (Booth, 1985). They see no clear way forward but have argued that certain metatheoretical problems require solution before further advances can be made. But others are not so encumbered. Dependency theory refuses to go away and is subject to regular reassessment (e.g. Seers, 1981). There is even a body of literature referred to as dependency reversal, in which writers attempt 'to establish the events, processes and phenomena which exemplify the breaking out from dependency' (Sklair, 1988, p. 702; Doran *et al.*, 1983). A further suggestion is that the 'left-Weberian tradition' will furnish the most useful insights for the sociology of development (Vandergeest and Buttel, 1988). There is even a revitalised modernisation perspective in which some of the errors of the past are acknowledged and efforts are made to deal in new ways with the unfinished agenda of modernisation (Nash, 1984). This approach shares with a new interpretation from the Left (Worsley, 1984) a concern for culture, especially the way in which culture may influence the development process.

Despite all this activity there is some doubt about whether sociology of development theory has made any significant contribution to the practice of development. Some would say that a predilection for abstraction and theories of the grander kind make it difficult for sociology to connect with the real world of development. The distinctive features of countries and regions disappear in terminologies of modes of production or pattern variables, which seem to be of no use to those formulating and implementing development policy. Discussions of broad societal processes may provide few concrete suggestions to those whose task it is to bring about development.

One of the major problems of the sociology of development has been whether much of it is in fact sociology. It has been alleged that in the 1950s sociology relegated concern with social change to a minor disciplinary role and abandoned pre-war interventionist principles (Midgley, 1988). This abdication of responsibility facilitated the rise of economics both in the theory and practice of development. Acceptance of development as an essentially economic process was easily obtained. Sociology played a supporting role. Economists (e.g. Hoselitz, 1960) even became their own do-it-yourself sociologists. The leading figures of neo-Marxist sociology of development have been economists or writers of political economy and social economics (e.g. Frank, Warren, Wallerstein). Even when such social phenomena as poverty and basic needs were thrust to the forefront of developmental concern it was writers grounded in the traditions of neo-institutional economics (e.g. Myrdal, Seers and Streeten) who led the way (Midgley, 1988, p. 21). At present the ideas of a group of

economists, known collectively as the counter-revolutionaries
(Toye, 1987), seems to hold sway in the world of development. In
contrast to most sociologists, but like many of their disciplinary
predecessors, these economists (e.g. Bauer, Balassa, Little and Lal)
have demonstrated how theory can easily be translated into practice
by policy-makers. Indeed, they believe that poor development performance is primarily the result of poor policy-making and have
identified three major problems in contemporary development policy – the over-extended public sector, the over-emphasis on physical
capital formation and the proliferation of distorting economic controls. While many believe that the application of their 'new vision of
growth' is both blinkered and myopic, influential figures in the
political and financial media, the New Right, Western governments
and multilateral economic agencies such as the World Bank are
highly receptive to the counter-revolutionary ideas. It is even possible to see some sociological support in the form of a strategy called
institutional development, 'the process of improving the ability of
institutions to make effective use of the human and financial resources available' (Israel, 1987, p. 1). But sociology is still only
managing to squeeze in as second fiddle. Bauer (1984) returns to the
economist's do-it-yourself sociology in his explanations of how
culture affects economic performance.

Despite the problems of subordination, abstraction and grand-
ness, the theoretical enterprise in the sociology of development has
not been a waste of time and its future is potentially bright. Firstly,
the days of grand theory seem to have passed. No longer do we find
eager advocates of theories which claim to explain everything. In
part this is due to the realisation that heterogeneity is one of the
leading characteristics of the Third World. Thus, instead of search-
ing for regularity and generalisable features of development which
cause the constituent parts of the Third World to look alike, sociologists now seem willing to address a very different problem – what
are the forces which have led to such dramatic variation in the third
World Formation? (Vandergeest and Buttel, 1988, p. 692). As
Boudon (1986, p. 78) has noted, development theorists have shared
a predilection for conditional laws of the type 'if A then B'. This has
proved to be an exercise of doubtful validity, as for every law
formulated a counter-example can be produced from the heterogeneous Third World. Boudon's (1986) pertinent advice is that 'such
so-called laws are in fact *ideal models* which can be more or less

realized in *certain cases*, but whose area of validity cannot be exactly defined'.

The appreciation of some or all of these shortcomings in sociology of development theory has led to a diminution of the abuse-hurling and vitriol-pouring which characterised earlier theoretical debate. What is now emerging is a retreat from dogmatic ideology and an acceptance that 'there is a limited commensurability across perspectives' (Harrison, 1988). The way forward in the 1980s has been through more theoretically-informed empirical work. Sociologists have become wiser because of the theoretical debates of the 1970s. They have learned from questions asked, mistakes made and assumptions disputed. They no longer feel the need to provide readers with a theory. In Walton's (1987, p. 200) words, the trend is toward explaining 'rich and unruly experience'. With that as the principal objective it is therefore permissible to utilise appropriate theoretical components drawn from a variety of perspectives. It is also true that sociologists have indicated their willingness to utilise their theories in the service of problem-oriented research. And where once there were Marxists calling for political strategies to accelerate socialist revolutions which never came, there are now theoreticians advocating a 'revitalized interest in the real-world problems of development policy and practice' (Booth, 1985, p. 777).

4

SOCIOLOGICAL ASPECTS OF
CHANGE IN DEVELOPING
COUNTRIES

Since the early days of sociological enquiry the study of social change has been a major concern. Indeed, this entire book is about social change. As we have seen, when people talk of development or of the Third World they are invariably speaking about such change. Often the images of the changes are rapid and sometimes dramatic. Governments are overthrown with regularity, populations expand at high rates, large cities become vast metropolises, modern export industries record rapid growth, technological breakthroughs lead to huge increases in rice production and literacy becomes more widespread. Paradoxically, some of the images of change point to its slowness and the continuity with the past. For example, some wonder whether rural life has changed that much while others argue that the structures of inequality and exploitation have altered little. Other images portray the negative elements of change such as environmental destruction, the pervasiveness of political violence and the loss of identity and culture. Obviously change has many aspects but in this chapter we have space for only a few. We have selected three basic areas of social change and will examine the ways in which sociologists have interpreted those changes.

CLASS IN THE SOCIAL STRUCTURE

Any sociological discussion of social structure cannot avoid the notion of class. It is one of the most fundamental concepts and is probably represented in more sociological literature than any other concept. Although its major application has been in the study of the development of industrial capitalism it has occupied a prominent place in the analysis of social change in the Third World. In both cases disagreement is rife about the definition, configuration, role and importance of class. It belongs to the family of essentially contested concepts where there are endless disputes about the proper usage of a term among those who employ it. The problem is compounded in the Third World by the weaker development of classes as compared to the industrial nations. Also, Third World class structures display far greater diversity and complexity than those of the First World.

For the modernisation theorists the passage to modernity required the destruction of pre-industrial stratification systems and their replacement with those found in contemporary Western society. The sharp polarity of social strata in traditional society and the ascriptive norms which supported them would be swept away. Achievement norms would come to dominate as the division of labour became more complex and the stratification pyramid would be far more gradual with a greatly enlarged population in the middle areas. Economic growth would be the engine for this social transformation (Hoselitz, 1964). Orthodox Marxists shared the modernisers' view that capitalism would destroy traditional social class structures and establish classes normally found in the capitalist mode of production. There would, however, be no burgeoning middle class to stabilise society. Rather, the Third World would witness the polarisation of bourgeoisie and proletariat which inevitably accompanies industrialisation.

But neither perspective provided an adequate explanation of what was actually happening in the Third World. This led to a rethinking and revitalisation of class as an analytical tool. Elements of Marx and to a lesser extent Weber were the basis of this new movement. In the 1950s and 1960s classes had been conceptualised in a rather static way. Sociologists ordered populations into strata according to variables such as wealth, income, education and race or explored the functional complementarity of different classes. Among a multitude of problems which afflicted these functionalist-inspired stratification schemes were their inability to incorporate change and their denial of class conflict (for a full critique see Turner, 1978). The new perspective perceived classes as relationships between large groups of people who shared similar positions in the economic system. Conflict between classes was seen to be a vital element of all class systems.

Class analysis was thus an aspect of the study of power. Third World class systems were seen to be complex and getting no simpler. Finally, the world economic system was recognised as a major determinant of the class systems of Third World nations. The renewed interest in class in the 1970s did not produce a unified product. Disagreement was still rife but more imagination, more conceptual rigour and more informed analysis resulted in better sociological explanation that addressed both history and contemporary conditions in the Third World. In the remainder of this section we shall examine a few strands of this rich literature.

With class conflict, and hence the political struggles between classes, being placed in the forefront of class analysis in the Third World the matter of class consciousness has become a major sociological concern. Just because a class can be identified 'objectively' according to its members sharing similar locations in the productive processes of society, this does not mean that they will act as a class to pursue class interests. Marx was well aware of this when he likened the French peasantry to a sack of potatoes, alike but unrelated, and made the distinction between class *in itself* (the politically undeveloped sack of potatoes) and class *for itself* (the class which is self-consciously aware of its role in societal development). Nobody would deny that the objectively defined classes exist in the Third World today. Although it is difficult to generalise, a hypothetical country might have an urban bourgeoisie and possibly a separate class of big rural landowners. A middle class of white collar workers, often state employees, would be in evidence. A class of petty-commodity producers working in the informal sector could be found in all urban settlements – market and street vendors, small repair shops, motorised tricycle drivers. A wage-earning proletariat would be employed in the modern sector of the economy, especially in manufacturing. In the rural areas a differentiated peasantry would dominate but there would also be a growing class of landless labourers. Note the complexity and multiplicity of classes in this simple hypothetical model. But having identified the classes we are left with the problem of whether they are self-conscious political actors – is there class consciousness? A straightforward yes/no type answer would be misleading.

Class consciousness and class alliances for the achievement of political goals are certainly present in the Third World. The most graphic examples are to be found in the twentieth century revolutions in countries such as China, Cuba, Vietnam and Nicaragua. In some of these cases (e.g. China and Vietnam) one can find an intelligentsia leading a disgruntled peasantry. Eric Wolf (1971) has convincingly argued the case of the political importance of the peasantry as seen in the peasant wars and rebellions of the present century. Working class consciousness has been seen to be of vital importance in other revolutionary contexts. Thus, Petras (1981) champions the role of the working class in both Cuba and Nicaragua and attests to the health of working class consciousness in much of Latin America. For example, the capacity of the Argentine working class to mount highly successful nationwide general strikes demonstrates 'the extraordinary degree of class solidarity and organization' of that class (Petras, 1981, p. 260). But class consciousness need not be so dramatic. James C. Scott (1985) has argued that although formal organised political activity is largely the preserve of the middle class and the intelligentsia, peasant class consciousness can be seen in everyday forms of resistance. Such resistance takes the form of 'foot dragging, dissimulation, desertion, false compliance, pilfering, feigned ignorance, slander, arson, sabotage and so on' (Scott, 1985, p. *xvi*). Others have followed Scott by identifying numerous modes of everyday peasant resistance in a range of countries. But one should be careful not to overstretch the notions of class and class consciousness and to make them account for every act of defiance, protest, conflict or obstruction. Also, the search for class consciousness should not only focus on the underprivileged and the exploited. The wealthy and powerful provide many examples of class consciousness. They are always active in defending their own interests. The sorry history of cosmetic land reforms in the Philippines or of brutal and repressive military counter-revolution against a socialist regime in Chile are examples of this. Sometimes, the bourgeoisie will secure a populist alliance with other classes and so preserve its interests. But the upper or ruling class may itself be riven with splits and conflicts. Thus, Zeitlin *et al.* (1976, p. 1009) have analysed the dominant class in Chile in terms of 'class segments', a segment being a section of the class having 'a relatively distinct location in the social processes of production'. Such distinct locations give segments distinct interests and awareness and the potential for political action in pursuit of the segment's interests. In Chile, Zeitlin explored the relative political power of the landed and non-landed segments of the capitalist class and found that 'the landed capitalist, who personified the coalescence of large agrarian property and corporate capital, played a disproportionate role in the political leadership of their class' (Zeitlin *et al.* 1976, p. 1027). Using a similar approach Hawes (1987) identified four major segments of the bourgeoisie during the Marcos era in the Philippines. Crony capitalists, state capitalists, producers for the local market and producers for the international market competed in the policy-making arena to further the interests of their particular segments. But one should not assume that the segments of dominant classes are clearly defined. Multi-sectoral business interests within one family, intermarriage, ritual kinship ties, friendship, membership of the same clubs and attendance at the same educational institutions make the distinction between segments blurred and work against the single-minded pursuit of segmental interests.

For many writers it is not the existence of class consciousness which is their main concern but its periodic nature or apparent absence. A rise in the price of a staple product can forge temporary class alliances between the urban working class, the petty commodity producers and even the salaried middle class. Street demonstrations, even riots, can rapidly ensue and the stability of a government can be undermined. Riots over attempted increases in the price of bread in the Sudan and Egypt are good examples of this process. When the immediate objectives have been achieved, then the class alliance will disappear as fast as it arose and political action on a class basis may well be abandoned. Sometimes an absence of class action among the underprivileged masses can be explained in terms of the need of this population to direct almost its entire attention to earning the basic necessities for survival. The time, the energy and the resources for class-based political organisation and action are lacking. The problem is compounded by the lack of approval of such independent action by government and the dominant classes. The fact that the poor are comprised of various class positions and are not some homogeneous mass can also work against concerted and organised class action by the poor. For example, if the price of corn or rice is raised then peasant farmers should benefit. It is even conceivable that agricultural wage labourers could get an increase in pay. However, poor urban classes will suffer from increased food prices and hence suffer from a decline in living standards.

It is clear that there are competing modes of group formation and group identification which can determine social action. They are not vestigal remains of some prior mode of production. Available evidence indicates that factors such as race, ethnic identity, kinship, religion and gender are important bases for collective and individual action throughout the Third World; and they are by no means absent from the First World! In a study of rural class relations during the push for 'authentic' African socialism (*ujamaa*) in Tanzania, Feldman (1975) noted the existence of rural classes which might be expected to be engaged in antagonistic relationships. However, between landlords, employers of labour, lessees and labourers there was no apparent conflict of interests despite the 'objectively' antagonistic nature of their class positions. Also in Africa, Kilson (1987) has noted the difficulties of developing class consciousness. The widespread African populism is 'intricately atavistic' with political leaders relying on traditional authority. The push for modernisation may paradoxically be accompanied by efforts to restore certain cultural forms (e.g. to purify Islamic practices). Peel (1980) has forcefully argued that in contemporary Africa, 'non-class modes of consciousness and action' have been extremely important. For example, religious beliefs may determine action more than economically-defined class position.

Patron–client relations have been identified as an institution that works against the development of class consciousness. They are vertical linkages which cut across social class divisions. Patrons from one class provide services to clients from another class. The patron may lend money, sponsor a wedding, contact an official on behalf of the client who reciprocates by undertaking some manual work or political promotion for the patron. Usually, patron–client relations are portrayed as rural phenomena but they can also be observed in urban areas (Turner, 1988). The patron often provides 'subsistence crisis insurance' (e.g. help following a poor harvest) and 'life crisis insurance' (e.g. payment of funeral bills) for the client. Perceptions of the social structure may well be determined by the vertically-oriented dyads of the patron–client structure rather than by any model based on class, however obvious it may appear in objective terms. If the patron–client ties are eroded or removed then the potential for and likelihood of class action by the clients is greatly increased. Scott and Kerkvliet (1973) have argued that the decline of patron–client ties in south-east Asia removed subsistence insurance for the peasantry. This situation provided the basis for a sense of exploitation and the moral basis for action. Agrarian unrest, even revolution, followed.

A final viewpoint on the absence of class consciousness is that of containment. Obstructions are deliberately placed in the way of the full development of a class and so contain that class, thus preventing the full realisation of class consciousness and postponing class action until a more suitable future occasion. In Papua New Guinea, it has been alleged that the state has consistently worked to contain the emergence of a working class (among other classes) by legal control (Fitzpatrick, 1980). In the pre-war colonial period the indentured labour system ensured that the male plantation workers were re-patriated to their home villages after their spell on the labour lines. Thus, wage labour was only an occasional experience and people remained firmly tied to their traditional mode of production. In the post-war era, the state introduced trade union and industrial rela-tions laws to promote class containment. The persistence of circular migration supported the maintenance of the traditional mode of production. While the notion of containment does provide some useful insights into why class consciousness is so poorly developed in much of the Third World, it too has many problems. The principal problem is to identify exactly what is being contained. Also, the proponents of containment seem to have acquired some prophetic knowledge about what should happen in the future. Containment supports the primacy of class explanations for sociology. If classes are not being formed and becoming conscious then they are being contained. Other bases for group action are banished to explanatory insignificance. This seems highly contentious.

Also contentious is the role of the middle class. In the first half of the nineteenth century, the Russian thinker Belinsky announced that 'countries without a middle class are doomed to eternal insignifi-cance' (Berman, 1988, p. 191). Modernisation theorists reiterated this message more than a century later in their view that the rise of a middle class was a major indicator of development and political stability. Marx did not see capitalism's progress requiring any great expansion of such a class. Some neo-Marxists identify international conspiracies holding back the development of a middle class. Others point to international capital creating a middle class to service its interests and to act as a buffer between it and the teeming masses. But foreign businessmen often complain of inefficient and overgrown bureaucracies packed with middle class state functionaries obstruct-ing economic advancement. As you can see, the notion of middle class is certainly problematic. Sometimes this is due to conceptual confusion. For some writers the term middle class is coterminous with that of the bougeoisie. In this case the middle class becomes the progressive national bourgeoisie eager to lead the rapid development of the forces of production. But at the other extreme the middle class can be portrayed as some residual hotch-potch of clerks, business-men, army officers, professionals, shopkeepers and others seeking classification between the poles of the bourgeoisie and the pro-letariat. The problem of vague definition was raised in the 1950s. Terms such as 'middle sectors', 'middle elements', 'middle segments' vied with or were used interchangeably with 'middle classes'. J.J. Johnson (1958, 1964) argued that 'the middle sectors' were anything but a compact layer. They were not tightly organised. Also, members lacked a common background of experience and were not fully self-conscious. The absence of these features precluded the middle sectors from qualifying as a class.

In more recent work, Roxborough (1979, p. 78) has rejected such reasoning. He asserts the existence of a class-type object occupying the middle ground of the stratification system and identifies the conceptual problem as one of whether the middle class is one class or several. He has identified at least four fractions or classes which could be labelled middle class – the lower ranks of the bourgeoisie, urban professionals, managers and those occupying 'political roles', and a petty bourgeoisie. White-collar workers are banished to the working class, a move that would be questioned by some sociologists and perhaps by the white-collar workers themselves. Roxborough contends that the relative size of such classes will vary from one country to another but that they will frequently be found in political alliance with one another, 'and many of their responses will be sufficiently similar to justify treating them as an undifferentiated bloc' (Roxborough, 1979, p. 79). He does, however, warn against losing sight of the heterogeneity of the middle class which he has identified.

Most would now agree with Roxborough that the middle class has played and continues to play a central role in the development of Third World societies. The role is not that of the middle class in industrial societies. Furthermore, there is not one standard political role played by the middle class in every Third World society. There are a multiplicity of roles. The one selected varies according to interaction with other classes, the nature of colonial development and the historical experience of any one country or region. Thus,

Cardoso and Faletto (1979) have observed a range of middle class participation in Latin America during the first three decades of this century. One of the leading features of this transition period was the diversification of export production leading to the appearance of a middle class. In pre-war Brazil, Vargas incorporated a few sectors of the middle class into power alliances in support of his industrialising policies. Meanwhile in Colombia the oligarchic bourgeoisie blocked middle class access to power. In Chile the middle class was incorporated as an ally of a fraction of the upper class while in Peru the middle class went to the other end of the social spectrum to join up with the revolutionary peasant movement. Finally, in the enclave mining economies of Mexico, Bolivia and Venezuela the only way for the middle class to participate in the exercise of power was to enlist the support of the peasants and popular masses for revolution.

Recent studies of the middle or intermediate class locate their analyses in terms of the changing dimensions of state power. The state is generally perceived as an institutional expression of class relations. The dominant classes control the state, attempt to pursue their own interests and keep the dominated in their place. Thus, analyses of African class formation have increasingly pointed to the role of the modern state as an autonomous force in class formation. Drawing on the elite theories of Pareto and Mosca it has been demonstrated how political power creates economic opportunity and determines the configurations of the class formation (e.g. Sklar, 1979; Diamond, 1987). The swollen state serves as the basis of dominant-class formation. The state is the major employer and it has become directly involved in many aspects of economic development and production via the parastatal organisation. Patronage systems abound while corruption is endemic. The post-colonial dominant classes have established their position by parasitism and they have been busy in securing the inter-generational transmission of class status (e.g. by favoured admission to elite schools, by acquiring large landholdings which can be passed on to heirs).

For Bangladesh it has been argued that the classes relating to production (the bourgeoisie, the working class and the peasants) were unable to attain strong positions because colonialism placed the productive processes under the control of metropolitan capital or made those processes subservient to the interests of that capital. The British created an indigenous administrative class to run the state on behalf of Great Britain and its commercial interests, primarily the production and export of jute. With decolonisation and incorporation into Pakistan the country became an internal colony of the new state. But eventual independence has not altered the basic structure of relationships. An intermediate class under the direction of the military still mediates between international centres of power and capital and the 'pauperised' masses (Shahidullah, 1985). Arguing from a similar perspective, Ahmad (1985, p. 44) contends that 'the intermediate and auxiliary classes of the periphery occupy a strategic field in the economy and politics of their countries, thus obtaining powers and initiatives which make it possible for them to struggle for political dominance over other classes, including the bourgeoisie'. He illustrates his point through studies of several Middle East and Near East countries where he notes the 'overdevelopment' of the state. By this he means the overwhelming role of the state in all aspects of these societies. The apparatuses of the overdeveloped state are heavily populated with the intermediate classes, which are thus able decisively to influence the direction which these societies take. Nationalism is seen to be 'the classic terrain' for the politics of the intermediate classes. It takes a myriad forms – from a petty-bourgeois led communist revolution in Afghanistan to the installation of Khomeni's clerico-fascism in Iran.

As we have seen from the observations above, the middle class should not be characterised merely as a class which keeps the lid on things on behalf of the bourgeoisie. While it is undeniable that the middle class does perform important control functions on behalf of capital it is also active on its own behalf in the process of development. But returning to our original problem with this middle area of the social structure, what are we actually talking about? The difficulties of definition and classification have not gone away. There is still no consensus on who or what constitutes a middle class. Are there middle classes or just a middle class? Is it acceptable to lump the petty bourgeoisie in with state employees? Are we really dealing with one or more status groups and not classes at all? There is still much to clarify and to learn. And this applies to all aspects of discussions of class in the Third World.

ETHNICITY

While an appreciation of the role of class is vital for understanding change in the Third World, class will not reveal all. There are other modes of group identification which have been around for considerably longer than the youthful classes of Africa and Asia and which continue to provide a basis for social action and political mobilisation. One of the most enduring modes of self-identification is that of ethnicity. Like class it is a boundary phenomenon delineating groups and cleavages within society. Ethnic identity may be perceived in various ways – according to race, culture, religion, language or place of origin. A unique combination of such items differentiates the ethnic community from the rest of society and provides the basis for self-consciousness among members of the ethnic community. The self-identification may even be encouraged by the discriminatory policies of ruling classes and dominant groups. Alternatively, members of indigenous ruling classes or aspirants to that status may base their claims to power on the mobilisation of an ethnically-based consciousness. In urban situations, the importance of ethnic identity is not some particularly tenacious remnant of rural life but is 'a direct response to the exigencies of survival in a competitive urban economy where economic opportunities are scarce' (Roberts, 1978, p. 141). Ethnicity can be used to monopolise occupations or places of employment and clients, and generate a climate of trust. Thus, ethnic identity can assume greater importance and intensity in urban rather than in rural areas. Ethnic identity is not something hard and fast with its own immutable rules. It is flexible. Politicians, colonial classifications, urban poverty and other exogenous factors can promote the development of ethnic self-identification and associated social action.

Although ethnic communities are evident and increasingly assertive in industrial societies, it is in the Third World that ethnic divisions abound. Furthermore, there is no rule about scale. Ethnic communities can be any size. In Papua New Guinea, with a population of approximately 3.5 million, there are more than 700 language groups, some of which number no more than 300 people. In India, by contrast, the Sikh minority is comprised of up to 20 million people. In most cases, the ethnic diversity of Third World nations derives from the experience of Western colonialism, although countries such as Iran, Thailand and Afghanistan, which never came under formal European control, also harbour a multitude of ethnic divisions. The colonial powers grabbed territory, made treaties among themselves and drew lines on maps which showed scant regard for the communities living there. When decolonisation came the governments of the newly-independent states found themselves in charge of ethnically diverse nations where people's commitment to nationalism was often minimal.

The most obvious result has been an epidemic of mininationalism (Snyder, 1982). This occurs when ethnic communities become alienated from the nation-state or feel oppressed by it. They then assert their identity and aspirations in demands for greater freedom. Such demands vary in intensity from requests for more autonomy to declarations of independence. The reaction of the state also varies and can take the form of accommodation and negotiation through to military suppression. A few examples will illustrate these points. In the 1970s as independence approached in Papua New Guinea the ethnic patchwork quilt which Australia had sewn together seemed in danger of coming apart. Micronationalist movements proliferated. These were spontaneous local movements which aimed to achieve development through communal action (May 1982). Most possessed a loosely defined ethnic base although membership could cut across tribal and linguistic boundaries. An integral tendency of the programmes of these micronationalist movements was towards withdrawal and disengagement from the larger national community. They were, however, short-lived and as members lost interest, expectations remained unfulfilled and leaders moved on, so the threat of national fragmentation declined. Violence was rare both on the part of the state and of the micronationalists. The state generally eschewed violence for more traditional Melanesian negotiation and compromise. This was also the case when the rich island of Bougainville attempted to secede from Papua New Guinea. The islanders shared a distinctive black skin colour and like everywhere else in the country had particular items of culture which set them apart. They resented a lack of consultation about the political future and their role in an independent Papua New Guinea. Colonial officials had often displayed insensitivity while the administration's neglect in previous years had not been forgotten. The development of a massive copper mine was undertaken with contempt for the villagers. A group of eloquent, highly-educated and able leaders was thus able to gain the support of the majority of Bougainvilleans for secession. Concessions by the national government, such as a provincial government and the payment of mining royalties, eventually secured Bougainvillean co-operation and kept the Papua New Guinea state intact. But micronationalist sentiments were not destroyed. Over a decade later they have resurfaced, and this time with violence to both people and property.

Events in Lebanon show how a state can simply fall apart due to 'religious separatism, splintered ideologies, and squabbling clans' (Snyder, 1982, p. 173). Bitter struggles between the constituent elements of the pluralistic communal structure have resulted in the deaths of thousands of people as rival militias shoot it out on the streets of Beirut and elsewhere. Various Muslim militias, the Palestine Liberation Organisation, Christian Maronites and the rightist Phalange struggle for control. The armed forces of Israel and Syria also pitch in. The Lebanese state seems powerless and is unable to restore any semblance of order. Meanwhile Kurdish nationalists have taken advantage of the war between Iraq and Iran to press for greater autonomy from the Iranian government. The fiercely-independent Kurds have fought for independence against Turkey, Iraq and Iran for many years. The cost has been high. However, in order to devote its full military power to defeating Iran, Iraq created an autonomous region for the Kurds and granted them their own national assembly. Baghdad then offered both material and spiritual backing to the Kurdish autonomy movement inside the borders of Iran. Following the 1988 ceasefire with Iran, Iraq turned a significant proportion of its military might on to the luckless Kurds. Chemical warfare by Iraq was alleged and a horrified world watched thousands of Kurdish refugees stream into camps in neighbouring Turkey.

Sometimes mininationalist movements can achieve their ultimate goal – independence. Bangladesh is the most celebrated case. British decolonisation left the state of Pakistan physically separated into two parts, West and East. The only unifying factor was a common dislike and fear of the Hindu majority in India. The Bengali-speaking majority in East Pakistan felt that they were being treated as second-class citizens by the dominant groups in the West. Secession was demanded and a bloody struggle followed. Up to a million Bengalis were slaughtered before the independent state of Bangladesh was established. Ironically, the new country of Bangladesh now has its own ethnic separatist movements among the tribal minorities who resent Bengali hegemony and the encroachment of lowland populations on to their traditional lands. At the other end of the mininationalist scale was the miniscule British protectorate of the Gilbert and Ellice Islands. With decolonisation the people of these South Pacific atolls decided through a referendum to split into Tuvalu (Ellice Islands) and Kiribati (Gilbert Islands). There was no conflict and certainly no violence as Kiribati (population 56,000) and Tuvalu (population 8,700) went their own independent ways.

But ethnicity in the Third World is not all mininationalism. Each ethnic group is not seeking its own separatist path. If this were the case, anarchy would probably reign supreme. The ethnic cleavages are certainly there and are potentially sources of conflict and social disruption. In such circumstances, the struggle for development can become even more difficult than it already is. Governments are often aware of this and strive to maintain ethnic balance. For example, cabinet posts may be allocated on the basis of ensuring an equitable regional distribution. Expenditure on development projects may be more linked to satisfying competing regional demands than to fulfilling declared developmental objectives. Such expenditure patterns may be viewed as economically inefficient but politically expedient. Armies may be recruited on an ethnic basis which ensures that no single ethnic group dominates. Representatives of troublesome minority groups may even be sought for military service in an effort to defuse ethnic tension. Recruitment of Muslims into the Philippine military is done with this in mind. Thus, the state retains control. The same principles may be introduced into recruitment for the massive government bureaucracies which characterise the Third World.

Sometimes it is impractical for conflicting ethnic groups to strive for separatism. In Malaysia there has been a long history of tension between the Malay community (currently 59 per cent of the population) and the large Chinese minority (currently 32 per cent of the population). The Chinese-dominated state of Singapore seceded from the federation in 1965 but serious riots between the ethnic groups occurred in Malaysia in 1969. The Malays have used their political ascendancy to challenge the Chinese domination of the economy. By mobilising state resources the Malay community, or a highly privileged section of it, has succeeded in securing control over more than the officially-targeted 30 per cent of the economy. The state has also moved to promote certain Malay cultural elements such as the use of the Malay language in formal education. The Chinese are not regionally concentrated and so have no territorial base for separatism, if indeed they wished to pursue such a policy. But the Malay-dominated government must also move carefully as the Chinese minority is not small, while an all-out attack on Chinese interests could result in unwanted international repercussions for Malaysia. In contrast, some ethnic groups may be so weak that they are unable to defend themselves against the depredations of stronger ethnic groups, the state and the representatives of capital. The exploitation of natural resources provides many examples of this. As the developmental frontier moves westward across Amazonia so the indigenous inhabitants are displaced, their traditional habitats destroyed, their cultures lost and their lives sometimes sacrificed.

In the previous section on class, we warned of making sociological explanations in terms of one variable. Class could not reveal all things about Third World societies. The ethnic dimension should be treated in a similar manner. Society is extremely complicated. Some writers portrayed the 1966–7 civil war in Nigeria as a communally-inspired affair – the Ibos versus the rest. Recent interpretations show that matters were not that simple. Biafra's (the Ibos's) attempted secession was a strategy that every other major ethnic group had toyed with at one time or another. Furthermore, the Biafran version was designed specifically to allow the Ibo bourgeoisie re-entry into the larger Nigerian community on terms set by themselves. The Federal side (the rest) was far from unanimous in its stance while 'co-operation across ethnic lines of the avant-garde and the army radicals with their supporters in the trade unions, shows that Nigerian politics is not only about communal conflicts, as the ethnic theorists would have us believe' (Cohen, 1987).

FAMILY, KINSHIP AND GENDER

While sociologists have awarded great importance to classes and ethnicity in analysing the organisation and development of Third World societies, the study of the family will produce an equally rich source of sociological explanation – and dispute! In the institutions of family and kinship one encounters cultural diversity at its greatest.

Societies have evolved a multitude of different rules and regulations concerning marriage, divorce, control of property, inheritance, household formation and size, the roles of men and women, child-rearing practices and the tracing of descent. Anthropology is built on the study of such manifestations of kinship, while the Bible is full of genealogies and kinship obligations. This is because, in pre-industrial societies, the family and kinship lie at the core of most social, economic and political relationships. Roles and functions which modern societies would allocate to specialised institutions, such as schools, the army, the workplace, hospitals, trade unions and churches, would be performed under the all-encompassing web of kinship. A person's obligations in pre-industrial societies are largely framed in terms of kinship. For example, among the people of the Plateau Tonga, which lies in present-day Malawi, it was 'the kin-group which acts in inheritance, which owns joint property, which provides and receives bridewealth, which demands compensation for injury to its members and is held responsible for its members' actions . . . [and] which is involved in feuds' (Colson, 1962, p. 211). To this list can be added the fact that the family is the unit of economic production and consumption. The family and kinship are the prime reference points for social organisation and action. They must be, as competing institutions are few and far between. In some small-scale pre-industrial societies, alternative institutional structures are virtually non-existent. But what happens when colonialism and development come along? We shall examine some aspects of this by posing – and hopefully answering – three basic questions. First, does development inevitably produce patterns of family and kinship like those in Western society? Second, if we turn this question around then we can ask whether it is necessary for Third World societies to mirror Western family and kinship patterns before development can take place. Finally, we must investigate changes in gender roles; specifically, how have women been affected by the process of development?

In the cruder versions of modernisation theory it was assumed that under the beneficial aegis of development the multitude of archaic kinship patterns of Third World societies would be swept away. They would be replaced by the nuclear family household of modern Western society and its associated kinship model. As institution-building progressed so the complex modes of extended family and kinship practices would fade away into history. Doubts about progression along such a simple unilineal path were first raised in the West, where post-war sociological studies consistently uncovered vital patterns of enduring extended family relationships. While they may not have been as intense and extensive as those in developing countries, they were none the less alive and well and evident across a range of social classes. In addition, an American survey in the late 1970s revealed that the nuclear family household (i.e. married couple with or without children under eighteen years of age), although considered typical, constituted only 40 per cent of 'all families' in the United States (Goode, 1982, p. 94). Other surveys showed that extended family households were statistically uncommon in the world. They were certainly not the norm of peasant society. However, this latter discovery did not mean that extended family relationships were unimportant, merely that extended families tended not to live under the same roof. Studies of developing societies were consistently attesting to the strength of extended family relationships, despite the alternative institutional structures being erected by colonial and independent governments. The mode of production theorists latched on to this. They linked the uneven penetration of capital in Third World societies to a concerted effort, on capital's behalf, to preserve certain traditional modes of production. A central component of these traditional modes was traditional kinship. Thus, Rey (1971) identified the preservation of the lineage mode of production in West Africa while Fitzpatrick (1980) has argued that the colonial maintenance of traditional rural forms in Papua New Guinea was designed to control labour and prevent class formation.

Empirical studies reveal that there have been important and widespread changes in family and kinship relations in the Third World. However, they have not been along the idealised and ethnocentric lines prophesied in the modernisation theorists' nuclear family dream. Extended family relationships have retained considerable importance although they may be modified and recast to cope with the changing conditions brought about by development. The Mexican case study in Chapter 2 illustrates the vital role of the family in combating adverse economic circumstances. Béteille (1974, p. 97) has convincingly argued that, 'In agrarian societies one counts many people among one's relatives and it is considered both natural and proper to support and exact support from one's kinsfolk in every sphere of activity'. A person cannot deny obligations to kin without offending deeply-rooted values. Among rural populations the nuclear family household is the dominant form and acts as a production and consumption unit. When further labour is required then the extra hands are often mobilised along kinship lines even if cash payments are made for that labour. When marriages need financing, school fees require payment, bureaucratic services are required, medical bills need meeting and favours and help of many kinds are needed, then rural people turn first to their extended families. You will note that modern institutions (schools, colleges, government agencies, doctors and hospitals) may be providing the service. But in order to secure that service the support and intercession of kinsfolk may be necessary. The traditional idiom is invoked in the modern context and is adapted in the process. However, one should not run away with the idea of some rural idyll in which kin are selflessly devoted to meeting their obligations to each other and everybody is consequently happy with the world. Conflict is also evident as is the breakdown of kinship structures. For example, in Hausaland there has been a tendency for the traditional farm labour organisation (the *gandu*) to collapse with the weakening of obligations (Mabogunje, 1980, pp. 87–8). Under the *gandu* a married son works in a subordinate capacity on his father's farm for a variety of benefits. Sometimes, cousins were involved. But fragmentation of landholding and the increasing scarcity of land have caused the *gandu's* collapse. Such partial breakdowns in the traditional order have been reported throughout the Third World.

Another typical scenario could be as follows. The demand for labour may be reduced by mechanisation (e.g. threshing machines, mechanical ploughs). A growing labour surplus combined with the increasing role of cash in rural economies may weaken kinship bonds and push labour relations between kin towards those of an employer/employee type. There may be conflicts between kin competing for limited work opportunities. In some cases a family household may prefer to hire non-relatives as they have no obligations to them beyond a market payment. Expenditure for kinsmen doing equivalent work could be greater.

The most obvious manifestation of change in tight-knit rural societies is the massive migration to urban areas. Millions have left their rural homes in search of better opportunities in the towns and metropolises of developing countries. In this novel and dynamic urban environment one would expect to encounter the greatest breakdown of the extended family and the triumph of its nuclear relative. However, the extended family has remained as a prominent and essential feature of life for most urban residents. The majority of people in towns are poor and have no government social security to fall back on. To survive in the city they need to mobilise the meagre resources at their disposal. Kinship is one of these resources which enables them to cope with urban life. Through kinsmen they may find jobs, obtain accommodation, get advice, and obtain support in times of unemployment and severe economic hardship. Urban kin will often provide the rural migrant with his or her introduction to city life. But people will construct social networks which transcend kinship in their efforts to gain economic and social security in the urban setting. The strength of kinship will vary with the urban situation of the individual and the family. For Latin America, Roberts (1978, pp. 142–4) has reported that among small-scale entrepreneurs operating 'extended domestic enterprises', kinship relations are important. Workers who are relatives are trustworthy. Family events are celebrated and there is intensive interaction between kin members both within the city and outside it. People whose jobs do not require high levels of trust with others are less likely to maintain strong kinship ties. Where high degrees of poverty and job instability exist, even the nuclear household may come under threat.

Studies of the Caribbean and Central America where these sorts of conditions prevail have identified the prevalence of single-parent families and unstable households. Men lack the economic security to take on family obligations, while women are unwilling to take on the liability when the man may prove to be a drunkard, unable to earn a regular living and prone to violence. In Latin America's urban middle classes, extensive usage of non-kin friendships have been reported. In the Philippines such friendships are easily and frequently converted into ritual kinship relations through the institution of *compradazco*. Baptismal sponsors (godparents) enter into a range of mutual obligations with the child and its parents. Poor families might also attempt to obtain persons of higher socioeconomic status (e.g. employer, supervisor, politician) as *compadre*, as a strategy to improve their own economic and social security. Among upper income groups in Third World countries, kinship solidarity has been important for ensuring business success. Roberts (1978) has noted the use of kinship ties among recent immigrant groups in Mexico (e.g. peninsular Spaniards) for building substantial economic enterprises. In a Nigerian study it was found that the more educated and higher income groups spent proportionately the same amount of income on extended family members as the less educated and lower income groups (Obikeze, 1987). The strong commitment of the upper groups to the ideology of the extended family was explained in terms of reciprocity, repayment of debts, social respect and securing the social and political support of the extended family. Thus, urbanisation has not brought about the destruction of the extended family although it has provided a very new setting and circumstances for the operation of kinship ties.

As a final comment on our first question, the relationship between the family and kinship and development, we should refer to Goode's (1982, pp. 182–7) comprehensive surveys of major trends in world family patterns. He was trying to discover whether there was a convergence of family patterns towards the conjugal type. He observed such things as a decrease in marriage between kin, a movement to medium or high divorce rates, a decline in matrilineal kinship structures, and a lessening of the power and inclination of the wider kin group to interfere in, or share the benefits of, the nuclear family household. Goode did not pretend that in some relatively early future all families would be exactly alike. He remarked on the unevenness and slowness of change. But the important point of Goode's amassed evidence was that where changes were taking place they were not in the direction of divergence. Societies might not be rushing headlong into convergence with their family patterns but development was certainly not generating any greater differentiation.

Our second problem is whether a particular family structure is a prerequisite for development. Does the family system have 'an independent facilitating effect on the modern shift toward industrialization' (Goode, 1982, pp. 190–1)? Evolutionary theory, the source of inspiration for some development theory, produced a number of unilineal models purporting to chart the development of the family from a mythical state of promiscuity to the monogamous ideal of Victorian England. Some sociologists have subsequently taken up the task and although demonstrating greater rigour and empirical awareness they have been unable to present any convincing sequence of kinship structures culminating in a type which fits industrial societies (e.g. Murdock, 1949). While we can dismiss the sequential stages of evolutionary theories, this does not necessarily invalidate the claim that a particular type of family structure is needed for industrialisation to take place. Clark Kerr *et al.* (1973, p. 94) have argued that the 'composite or extended family is, more often than not, unfavourable in some respects to economic growth'. While there is a guarantee of social security, 'the extended family tends to dilute individual incentives to work, save and invest'. They note the demands of industrialisation (e.g. loyalty to the enterprise, selection and promotion on the basis of competence) require the weakening or destruction of extended family ties. This happened in the West, while in Japan the traditional family system was altered during the course of industrialisation further to facilitate that industrialisation. Even in revolutionary Russia and China deliberate steps were taken to weaken loyalties and obligations to the extended family in order to secure loyalty to the state, the principal instrument of industrialisation.

Goode (1982, pp. 190–3) offers a few suggestions which give qualified support to Kerr *et al.*'s enthusiastic claims. He believes that the family systems of the West have been different from those of other major civilisations for over a thousand years and by the time factory jobs opened up in late eighteenth century England, changes in the family had made at least some of the population in harmony with the demands of the new industrial system. 'Their extended kinship ties and obligations, and their links with family land, did not interfere with the new type of work obligations' (Goode, p. 191). Turning his attention to Japan and China, Goode identifies comparative elements of family structure which facilitated Japanese industrialisation and handicapped pre-revolutionary Chinese efforts in that direction. For example, equal inheritance in China meant that family capital could not usually be kept intact, unlike in Japan where one son inherited all the property. Nepotism was far less prevalent in Japan while the socially mobile were far less obliged to help the undeserving members of their family. But as Goode himself emphasises, these cases are extremely complex and 'family variables cannot be said to be the prime creators of the dramatic contrast'. More recent but equally spectacular industrialisation in South Korea, Taiwan, Singapore and Hong Kong only adds to the complexity and urges greater caution before making sweeping generalisations.

One should also keep in mind that the development strategies of some countries may not be attempting to emulate and replicate the Western, Japanese, Korean or Soviet models of industrialisation.

This is especially the case in poor countries which are predominantly agrarian. Here, rural development is necessarily the focus of the national development strategy. In populist models, such as that employed in Tanzania, the state may try to use the extended family as the primary instrument for development. The values of co-operation, mutual support and sharing as found in the extended family may be viewed as more worthy ideals for improving the world than a blinkered fixation with economic growth. Building development on traditional institutions such as the clan and the extended family was placed at the forefront of Papua New Guinea's first independence development strategy and was enshrined in the constitution. Dominant classes may not, however, approve of such radical development initiatives whose alternative visions of the future order threaten the status quo. Multilateral agencies, such as the World Bank, may add their technocratic disapproval on the grounds of inefficiency and inability to raise production. For most planners the independent nuclear family is the ideal. Both rural and urban populations frequently disagree.

We now turn to our final question, that of gender – how has development affected women? Development theory has shown little interest in socially-determined inequalities between men and women as the survey in our last chapter shows. Equally, the practice of development, in terms of national and international development agency policy, has neglected women until recently (Rogers, 1980). In the 1950s and 1960s, in the few instances when attention was devoted to women's role in development, some inequalities were acknowledged but it was assumed that as modernisation progressed the just and natural order of gender relations would be established (e.g. INCIDI, 1959). This just and natural order was in fact the unequal and unnatural gender relations which characterised Western societies and which came under strong fire from a revitalised feminist movement from the late 1960s onwards. While sociological interest and enterprise were awakened in the West, the radical dependency school of development theory still stood aloof from the question of gender and development. Anthropologists utilising the mode of production framework were not so circumspect and commenced thorough investigation of women's roles in both traditional society and in the development process. But the real impetus to the analysis of women and development came from the women themselves and a realisation that if development had not been a great success in general terms, then for women success was even more elusive. Compared to men, women always seemed to do worse. Commencing with Ester Boserup's (1970) pioneering work on women in agricultural systems in Africa, a host of studies has since been undertaken. All attest to the fact that women have consistently missed out in the process of development. We glimpsed this in our case study in Chapter 2 and as the International Labour Organisation succinctly put it:

Women and girls constitute one-half of the world population and one-third of the official labour force, perform nearly two-thirds of work hours, but, according to some estimates, receive only one-tenth of the world's income and less than one-hundredth of world property (as quoted in Hill, 1987, p. 340).

The transition from subsistence economies has been particularly severe on women. One cannot pretend that life for women was ever a bed of roses in such societies but in many cases the division of labour was more equitable and women appear to have held more power and rights in property. The latter came under assault during the colonial era when the imperial powers overturned communal systems of land tenure and introduced the Western notion of private property. Colonial officials often failed to register women's assets or usufruct rights and because of lack of cash women were largely excluded from purchasing land. Men increasingly owned the land although women still continued to farm it. Matrilineal systems of kinship also entered into decline and men assumed the power previously held by women. Simultaneously, men were entering an expanding cash economy by migrating to wage-paying jobs in mines, plantations and cities. Women were left behind to cope with the business of rural production, to provide the non-market agricultural base which subsidised the new industries of the cash economy. Tasks which were formerly performed by men now fell to women. When smallholder cash cropping opportunities arose they were invariably directed to men by both colonial and independent governments despite the fact that women played such a prominent role in agricultural production. In some cases the demand for land for cash cropping forced women to grow their subsistence crops on more marginal land – greater effort for less return. Technological innovations did not necessarily provide labour-saving relief for women. New hardware was generally appropriated by men and even if it was used for women's tasks this might merely entail women being allocated other work. While all these changes were often adding to women's productive labour, women still had to attend to domestic chores – cooking, collecting wood and water, cleaning and caring for the young and infirm. Such tasks could be particularly onerous if husbands were away as labour migrants or children were attending school. In traditional subsistence economies both husbands and children would have relieved the burden of some of these jobs. But colonial administrations and independent governments have promulgated the ideology of women's primary responsibility for non-productive work. The status of this work and of subsistence production (i.e. non cash-earning women's work) has been downgraded, while the status of male cash-earning activities has been elevated. Not only have women come to do more work but what they do is negatively regarded. Case study 4 in Chapter 2 provides a vivid illustration of the socially-defined double burden that many women shoulder.

The picture that we have drawn above reflects the experience of many African societies and has been reported, reiterated and elaborated in much writing (e.g. Boserup, 1970; Rogers, 1980; Nelson, 1981; Tinker, 1976; and Blumberg, 1981). The marginalisation of women has not proceeded at an equal pace and in the same manner everywhere. The surplus of agricultural labour in some Asian societies may entail men ousting women from certain jobs in order to secure cash income from those jobs. In such cases, the amount of time women invest in agricultural labour could fall. It seems possible that in some places a significant minority of agricultural households are headed by women who are widowed, divorced, or have very sick husbands. Women may then adopt the managerial role normally claimed by men. Barnard (1983, p. 131) estimated that 13 per cent of households in the Muda area of Malaysia were 'effectively headed' by women because of the reasons cited above. Buvinic and Youssef (1987) estimate that as many as 18 per cent of households in the developing world are officially headed by women. They further note that because of male migration in search of work, the unofficial figure is much higher – 63 per cent in one southern African country. Men may not always monopolise the ownership of land. Stivens (1985) has noted a 'reconstituted matriliny' leading to the 'feminization' of land in Negeri Sembilan, Malaysia. Malay women in the study villages owned the titles to almost all the ancestral rice land and orchards and half the smallholder rubber land. There has been a constant tendency for new land in Negeri Sembilan to end up in female hands. Finally, technological innovation (e.g. the installation of a village water pump) may sometimes relieve drudgery for women and need not always be seen as some instrument of male oppression.

Improved transportation systems in rural areas have had mixed effects on women. In Mexico such development apparently increased demand for locally-made ceramic animal figures, thereby increasing the earnings of rural women in some areas (Tinker, 1976, p. 27). Even in the smallest Mexican towns, manufactured fabrics have become available thus permitting women to make clothing without having first to weave the cloth. In many countries the development of rural markets has created numerous opportunities for women to participate in the cash economy. Markets in many parts of Africa, south-east Asia and the South Pacific are dominated by female vendors. Especially in West Africa, associations of such women traders may wield important political power. On the negative side, roads have allowed the products of urban industries to penetrate rural areas and displace the traditional manufactures of women. In Java, the import of Coca-Cola and Australian ice-cream ruined local soft drink manufacture and ice-cream production, both of which had been small-scale female ventures. Sago processing by women in Sarawak was replaced by machine processing run by Chinese men (Tinker, 1976, pp. 27–8).

Sometimes, it may be a matter of swings and roundabouts for the rural woman producer. For example, in Indonesia technological and oganisational change has meant that women have lost their former pre-eminence in cloth production (Price, 1983). Also, the labouring tasks assigned to women are generally the more menial, lower-paid ones. However, in hand-drawn batik, women still lead in terms of skill and expertise, while women play important roles in the management of the textile industry. Census data would appear to underestimate women's participation rates in textile manufacture, while 'at all levels within the textile industries women's contribution adds considerably to the families' ability to survive' (Tinker, 1976, p. 109). In a study of a poor village in Iran, it was found that women cultivated the household plot of herbs and pulses, tended the animals, made cheese, butter, ghee, yoghurt and bread, spun, weaved, sowed, cooked and did the housework (Afshar, 1985). Labour-saving devices had not reached them. If this were not enough, women also played a leading role in the production of carpets, although they owned neither their own produce nor the means of production. They could not even sell their labour. Women had become more enslaved to men and remained confined to the sphere of domesticity. However, the disruptions of the Islamic revolution have resulted in falling demand for carpets and a subsequent reduction in the amount of work done by women. The burden of work in livestock production has also been reduced while the departure of landlords has raised family income and hence the household's standard of living.

Has the urban experience been any better for women? Education is a critical variable, as through the acquisition of formal educational qualifications a person obtains the necessary credentials for formal employment. In rural areas educational opportunities are not only limited but they are also biased in favour of men. Illiteracy rates are higher among women while participation rates in the formal educational system are lower. For example, in the Iranian village mentioned in the last paragraph, 60–70 per cent of the boys but only 5 per cent of the girls attended first and second grades. No girls stayed up to fourth grade. Illiteracy or extremely low levels of educational attainment characterise rural women and disqualify them from the formal job market. Their backwardness can also be used to rationalise their exclusion from other new activities involving technological innovation (e.g. control of coffee grinders or threshing machines and exclusion from learning to drive motorised vehicles) and emphasises the process of domestication.

Where illiterate or semi-literate women do migrate to urban areas – and they have in their millions – openings in the labour market are severely restricted. There are opportunities in petty trading and home-based craft industries. The latter may suffer from competition with mass-produced items. The world-wide explosion in the ready-to-wear garment industry has drastically reduced the demand for clothes from small-scale tailoring establishments. Formal educational qualifications are necessary for factory employment in this industry. Even in petty trading, educational qualifications can be a distinct advantage. In a Nigerian case-study it was noted that 'without exception, the women in my sample who had been able to earn a substantial independent income had attended primary school. All of these women had learned to read, write and speak some English' (Remy, as quoted in Tinker, 1976, p. 29). Domestic service is a major option for the woman with low educational attainment. Ironically, it is the growth of the urban middle class which has increased the demand for this low-status, poorly-paid but frequently arduous labour. Middle class incomes, often obtained through both husband and wife engaging in cash-earning occupations, allow the hire of cheap domestic help. The middle class wife's escape from domestic drudgery is facilitated by the surplus of women's labour among the poorer social classes and the desperate need for money in those classes. There is even an international dimension. Relative affluence in the newly-industrialising countries such as Singapore or in cash-rich oil producers of the Middle East has led to a trade in female domestic labour from countries such as the Philippines, Sri Lanka and Bangladesh. In these cases it is not illiterate rural migrants who take up these low status opportunities but highly educated women whose own and whose families' prospects for capital accumulation and socio-economic advancement in their home countries are very limited. Another option is prostitution, and the major cities of the Third World house many young female migrants from rural areas engaged in this occupation. Often, they have responsibilities for providing for young children and other family members and may remit some of their earnings back to rural relatives.

Despite men generally having more privileged access to education, women have made significant inroads in many countries. But the crucial question is how far women have been able to translate their educational achievements into equality of opportunity in the formal labour market. In Latin America during the 1960s there was an annual increase of 12 per cent in the enrolment of women in intermediate-level schools (de Figueroa, 1976). By 1970, women comprised 48 per cent of the total primary school enrolment and exceeded male enrolment in higher education. They have subsequently entered such demanding occupations as law, medicine and dentistry in larger numbers than in the United States. In common with other countries, some occupations (e.g. nursing and teaching) become identified with women. Low status, indicated by poor pay and conditions of service, has often resulted whatever the skill and knowledge levels required. Even apparently contradictory evidence must be treated with caution. In 1980, women comprised 61 per cent of teachers in Singapore but accounted for only 26 per cent of primary and secondary school principals and 31 per cent of vice-principals (Inglis, 1983). Government moves to improve pay and conditions of service have been interpreted by Inglis as less an acknowledgement of women's vital role in and contribution to education but rather as a move to attract more men into teaching. Women are also much in evidence in the burgeoning state bureaucracies of developing countries. They are mostly found working as keyboard operators or in the lower clerical levels and are under-represented in middle and senior management posts.

A recent focus for much research has been the impact of the new international division of labour (NIDL) on women and gender relations. Increasingly transnational corporations (TNCs) have been locating parts of their manufacturing capacity in the Third World. Of the four million jobs that Lim (1980) estimates TNCs have created in developing countries, between one quarter and one third are occupied by women. These female employees are not evenly spread out, however, in terms of region or sector. They are concentrated in seven countries (Brazil, Hong Kong, South Korea, Malaysia, Mexico, the Philippines and Singapore) and are mainly employed in the rapidly-expanding clothing, toy and electronics industries. Three main reasons have been advanced to explain these concentrations. The first is that in these three industries there is a preference for women, as they are more skilful in manufacturing operations and hence more efficient. This is often referred to as the 'nimble fingers' argument (Elson and Pearson, 1981). Secondly, female labour is generally paid at lower rates than male labour. Humphrey (1985, p. 214), in a study of manufacturing industry in São Paulo, Brazil, found that even in 'multinational companies in dynamic industries' women were to be found 'in the lowest-paid dead-end jobs at the bottom of the job hierarchy'. Skilled manual jobs and supervisory positions were reserved for men. Thirdly, female workers are widely regarded as being more docile and manipulable than male workers. For example, in Asia 'their backgrounds – young, unmarried, with little education and coming from rural areas – make them ideal employees from the management's point of view' (Lin, 1987, p. 220).

While a hypothetical case could be made that the incorporation of women into the industrial sector will create new opportunities for women to improve their situation, there is much evidence that this is not happening. Women's part in the Asian economic miracle and the recent expansion of Mexican and Brazilian export manufacturing have been associated with heavy costs. Women are allegedly paid low wages for long hours and are expected to work rotating shifts and long overtime when required. They have long and tiring journeys to work, and at the factory are exposed to a variety of health hazards. They learn few skills and have little prospect of job advancement. Outside the factory, they frequently live in crowded conditions, share their wage with a large number of dependents, cannot afford to eat adequately and have little time for recreation or family visits.

Sklair (1988, p. 706) proposes that 'the NIDL operates to undermine certain traditional patriarchal relations while, at the same time, shoring up the supports of patriarchy in general'. Others urge caution in the interpretation of recent changes (Greenhalgh, 1985) and emphasise that they should be set in an historical perspective. For example, the Confucian traditions of China, Japan and Korea were based on the most patriarchal of family systems and elements of these systems are readily observable in those countries and in Hong Kong and Taiwan today. The family system can still be viewed in terms of sexual stratification that involves parental use of daughters to advance the fortunes of sons. The situation in Hong Kong, which is claimed to be remarkably similar to those in other East Asian countries, is described as follows:

Girls are socialized into filiality, inferiority, and indebtedness; discriminated against in schooling and skills; pushed early into the labour force, where because of lack of training, they find low-status, ill-paid jobs; pressured to live at home and give their earnings to their parents, who use them for family expenses and sons' tuition (Greenhalgh, 1985, p. 301).

The NIDL also has significant implications for family structure in newly-industrialising societies. In the seven countries referred to earlier it is becoming increasingly common for the major, or even the sole, wage earner in a family to be a young, unmarried woman. Evidence 'strongly indicates that most of their wages flow directly into the family where it often goes to support unemployed men or fatherless children' (Sklair, 1988, p. 707). In some circumstances the NIDL is held to be responsible for significant increases in the proportion of female-headed households in urban areas. While more research is needed on these issues it is clear that the impacts will vary with the specific cultural context. Safa, cited in Sklair (1988), argues that the disruption to family life occurring along the rapidly-industrialising Mexican border with the United States is much greater than that occurring in comparable Jamaican and Puerto Rican situations because of the lack of a tradition (and related social coping mechanisms) of female-headed households.

As a final comment on the disadvantaged position of women in development, it is obvious that inequities in the distribution of power are the root cause. While one can point to prominent women political leaders such as presidents Gandhi and Aquino and prime minister Bhutto, they tend to be the exception rather than the rule. Political elites are dominated by men. In a recent study of our own in Papua New Guinea, it was found that in successive elections for the 109-person national parliament, the number of women elected fell from a meagre three to a barely visible one to nil (Turner and Hegarty, 1987). In regimes which are dominated by the military – and these are numerous in the Third World – women are totally absent from the higher ranks and so are excluded from these important decision-making and decision-influencing positions. Surveys also reveal that leading entrepreneurs, trade union representatives and religious leaders are men. In short, elites, whether national or local, are generally male domains. This has allegedly led to the perpetuation of dominant ideologies which support the ascendancy of men. Patriarchy still rules in all social classes. Tradition (e.g. Muslim fundamentalism) and modernity (e.g. emphasis on women's domestic role) can both be manipulated to justify the subordinate position of women. Thus, for women to obtain full recognition of their role in the family and national development requires a fundamental shift in power relations

CONCLUSION

In this chapter we have utilised the major sociological categories of class, ethnicity, family and gender to describe and explain some of the major transformations and continuities in Third World societies. From our empirically-based survey it can be appreciated that we must observe extreme caution in making sweeping generalisations. The diversity of the Third World has been stressed in earlier chapters. Because particular conditions and explanations may apply to one country, this does not necessarily entail finding the same conditions and adopting the same explanations for other countries. This does not of course mean abandoning the search for explanations that have currency beyond the individual case.

There is also disagreement among sociologists about the processes operating in the Third World. While critics may identify this as evidence of sociology's scientific immaturity and thus dismiss its findings, such an attitude does not do justice to the discipline. Social life is inherently complex and constantly changing, and competing paradigms can furnish enlightenment, even if only the elimination of particular explanations of how things work.

But as we have demonstrated, sociological investigation has provided insights into the operation of Third World societies. Furthermore, much of the empirically-based work reviewed in this chapter can be useful to policy-makers and planners. For example, an understanding of ethnicity or gender roles cannot be dismissed as knowledge appropriate only for the ivory towers of academe. This is especially the case as the sociology of development seems to be moving away from blind adherence to ideology and grand theory and is increasingly concerned with problem-oriented research which is anchored in empirical investigation but remains theoretically grounded. It may be true that some of the analyses discussed in this chapter (e.g. those relating to class) cannot be directly transferred to government policy documents or development plans. However, the people responsible for such work would undoubtedly benefit from an awareness of the knowledge which sociology has generated. In particular, sociological analysis highlights the need, and provides potential guidelines, for appraising the likely distributional impacts of development policies and programmes on different social classes, different ethnic groups and between genders. Without such knowledge, policies and plans can be ill-informed, leading to failure, wastage of scarce resources, and social and political conflict. If the pursuit of development is to achieve success (or minimise failure) then an appreciation of the social context of development seems essential. And it is not simply a matter of waiting for economists, administrators, planners and other technical specialists to avail themselves of sociological products. Sociologists themselves should be actively engaged in demonstrating the worth of their wares and in communicating them in a comprehensible fashion to those who might use them.

5

DEVELOPMENT POLICIES

In the first chapter we noted that development is usually not seen as some naturally-occurring process of societal evolution. Conscious action is needed to bring about the desired transformations. Responsibility for this action is claimed by the organisations of the state. The relative size and importance of these organisations in Third World societies makes this assumption of responsibility inevitable. It also means that the major explicit orientation of the state in Africa, Asia and Latin America has been towards development. Parliaments, assemblies, juntas, central committees, revolutionary councils and bureaucracies all faithfully proclaim their commitment to development. They hope to achieve their developmental goals by a judicious choice of policy measures, followed by their effective implementation. In this chapter we focus on some of the major policy issues which confront Third World governments and examine the ways with which they have been dealt. Space does not permit us to cover all of the leading policy areas and problems. Thus, we have selected five major issues – industrialisation, agriculture, education, population and environment. In the following discussion we have attempted to show how these issues are perceived and the range of actions that have been taken, and to comment on the various outcomes. Although we do not take the policy-making process as a main focus we do indicate some of the major influences on policy-makers and policy-making.

As a preface to our review of these policy areas it is worth briefly noting the major shifts that have occurred in overall thinking about the form that policy should take and particularly about the relative importance of the state in planning and promoting development. In non-communist Third World nations, the early development decades were characterised by the pursuit of economic growth and a belief that this could be achieved by a relatively high level of government intervention in most spheres. National development planning was highly regarded and the public sector did not only assist in policy formulation, implementation and regulation but was often also directly involved in agricultural and industrial production and commerce. As the 1970s unfolded, concern grew that poverty was inceasing, even in countries that were achieving reasonable rates of economic growth, and a strong lobby developed for a policy orientation that pursued 'growth with equity'. While this often led to a changed emphasis in the policy mix, exemplified by the basic needs strategy popularised by the International Labour Organisation (ILO), it was still based on the tenet that state intervention in economic and social matters should be at a very high level.

In the 1980s the paradigm for policy-making has changed and an intellectual climate conditioned by the New Right has been on the ascendant, at least in theory if not always in practice. The fundamental premise of this new orthodoxy is that the state should be rolled back and that market forces should increasingly guide resource allocation and decision-making. While the government should take responsibility for constructing and regulating a macroeconomic framework that permits competitive markets to set prices and allocate resources, the private sector should play the dominant role in identifying and supplying public needs.

These new themes have informed domestic policy-makers in many developing countries. In the nations that have found it necessary to seek loans for stabilisation and structural adjustment from the International Monetary Fund (IMF) and World Bank, the creditors have insisted on the recipients accepting policy conditions that generally entail the liberalisation of markets, reductions in public expenditure and the size of the public service and associated institutional reforms. The market failure paradigm that informed the economists advising on development policy in the 1950s is vanquished and in the 1980s a state failure paradigm has predominated.

While this shift of paradigm is dramatic and has important implications for all areas of policy it must be noted that, to date, its impacts have not been as far reaching as might at first appear. Many developing countries pontificate about privatisation, but few have taken any major initiative (Cook and Kirkpatrick, 1988). India, under Rajiv Gandhi, has made pronunciations about economic liberalisation, but has made only faltering steps in that direction and now appears to be reversing some of these (Kohli, 1989). The high ground of development policy prescription remains with the economists, but an understanding of the factors that lead practice to differ so greatly from prescription requires sociological and political insights into the ways in which different actors and groups involved in policy formulation and implementation influence the decisions that are ultimately reached.

INDUSTRIALISATION

Industrialisation played a starring role in all of the competing theories of development which we encountered in Chapter 3. Developed countries possessed large, highly productive and technologically-advanced industrial sectors. Such industrialisation could be correlated with all of the benefits which development was supposed to bestow – high personal income and high levels of social welfare. By contrast, Third World countries had poorly-developed, badly-developed or completely undeveloped industrial sectors. Underdevelopment could be explained in terms of this vital missing or malformed component. Policy-makers agreed with this interpreta tion and naturally identified industrialisation as the key to development. Only through industrialisation could significant advances be made.

However, getting firmly established on the path to industrialisation is no simple matter. The process of industrialisation is neither magic nor a naturally-occurring phenomenon. There are enormous obstacles facing the would-be industrialisers which they must negotiate. This entails a host of policy decisions which must be made in order to commence and sustain the push for industrialisation. There are a wide range of policy measures available for government intervention in industry. These include the licensing and regulation of production and marketing, controls over labour and capital markets, legislation and incentives in relation to foreign investment and support for technological innovation and trade policies (Table 5.1); and the table does not include related items such as the provision of infrastructure! In this section we will examine some of the major policy options available to Third World governments and

Table 5.1   Industrial policy measures used in developing countries

Area of intervention	Examples of policy measures used
Production and marketing	Industrial licensing, regulation of restrictive business practices, tax incentives to particular industries, creation of industrial estates, price controls, national planning, development and regulation of public enterprises and joint ventures
Employment and factor markets	Minimum wage legislation, labour training schemes, factor restrictions on use of foreign labour, interest rate and credit controls, capital subsidies, tax benefits for business income
Foreign investment	Prohibition of private foreign investment, requirement for domestic majority ownership, constraints on profit remittances abroad and capital repatriation, exclusion of foreign investment from key industries, direct subsidies and tax incentives for foreign investment
Technology	Patent laws, research and development support, regulation of TNCs and technology agreements
Imports	Import licensing, quotas and prohibitions, import tariffs, multiple exchange rates
Exports	Export licensing, taxes and customs duties on exports, income tax concessions for export earnings, export credit, export processing zones, marketing assistance schemes

Source: Donges (1976) as presented in Kirkpatrick *et al.* (1984)

assess how they have fared in their chosen strategies. Before commencing the discussion, it should be appreciated that the post-war years have witnessed considerable industrialisation activity in the Third World. Since the 1960s, output and export of manufactures from developing countries have grown more rapidly than in the industrial countries (see Tables 5.2 and 5.3). There are, however, great differences between the experiences of individual countries. For example, China, Indonesia and South Korea have experienced quite rapid rates of growth in their manufacturing sectors during

Table 5.2 Shares of production and exports of manufactures by country group, 1965, 1973 and 1985

Country group	Share in production (%)			Share in exports (%)		
	1965	1973	1985	1965	1973	1985
Industrial market economies	85.4	83.9	81.6	92.5	90.0	82.3
Developing countries	14.5	16.0	18.1	7.3	9.9	17.4
Low-income	7.5	7.0	6.9	2.3	1.8	2.1
Middle-income	7.0	9.0	11.2	5.0	8.1	15.3
High-income oil exporters	0.1	0.1	0.3	0.2	0.1	0.3
Total	100.0	100.0	100.0	100.0	100.0	100.0

Source: The World Bank (1987) *World Development Report*

Table 5.3 Growth in production and exports of manufactures by country group, 1965–73, 1973–85 and 1965–85

Country group	Growth in production (%)			Growth in exports (%)		
	1965–73	1973–85	1965–85	1965–73	1973–85	1965–85
Industrial market economies	5.3	3.0	3.8	10.6	4.4	6.8
Developing countries	9.0	6.0	7.2	11.6	12.3	12.2
Low-income	8.9	7.9	7.5	2.4	8.7	6.0
Middle-income	9.1	5.0	6.6	14.9	12.9	13.8
High-income oil exporters	10.6	7.5	8.4	16.2	11.5	16.0
Total	5.8	3.5	4.5	10.7	5.3	7.4

Source: The World Bank (1987) *World Development Report*

1965–86, while Somalia and Sudan have seen their manufacturing sectors stagnate and even contract (Table 5.4).

In the 1950s and 1960s, import-substituting industrialisation (ISI) was the dominant industrialisation strategy, especially in the larger economies of Latin America and south and south-east Asia (e.g. Brazil, Argentina, Pakistan and the Philippines). The ISI strategy sought to increase the production of manufactured goods for domestic consumption, usually through a mix of the policy measures listed in Table 5.1. This would promote self-sufficiency, absorb surplus

Table 5.4   Growth of manufacturing in developing countries, 1965–80

Country	Value added in manufacturing (millions of current dollars)		Share of manufacturing in GDP (%)		Annual growth of manufacturing (%)		Share of manufacturing in exports (%)	
	1970	1985	1965	1986	1965–80	1980–6	1965	1986
Low-income countries (excluding China and India)	5,140	15,050	10	11	4.8	4.8	12	29
China	28,794	95,103	30	34	9.5	12.6	46	64
India	6,960	35,597	15	19	4.3	8.2	49	62
Somalia	26	138	3	6	–	–3.4	14	1
Sudan	140	498	4	7	–	0.0	1	7
Middle-income countries	64,310	358,300	19	22	8.2	2.5	8	27
Indonesia	994	11,447	8	14	12.0	7.7	4	22
Tunisia	121	981	9	15	9.9	6.5	19	60
Brazil	10,433	50,089	26	28	9.6	1.2	9	41
South Korea	1,880	24,466	18	30	18.7	9.8	59	91
Industrial market countries	598,270	2,012,650	29	23	3.7	3.0	69	79

Source: The World Bank (1987, 1988) *World Development Report*
Note: In a few cases figures in the table are not for the specified year but for the nearest available year

labour, solve balance of payments problems and encourage further industrialisation. At first, growth rates were high as entrepreneurs found openings in food, drink, tobacco, textile and clothing industries. Ready markets were available for the products of these technologically simple and relatively cheap industries. However, once the easy gains had been achieved ISI ran into severe difficulty. Orthodox development economists (e.g. Little *et al.*, 1970) criticised the high level of tariff-style protection required to shield ISI industries from foreign competition. These barriers were intended to provide protection while industries had infant industry status, but they were usually not repealed and fostered the growth of high-cost, inefficient production techniques, which meant that they hampered the growth of employment and severely limited their contribution to welfare objectives. Biases against exports and agriculture were also alleged. The political theorist O'Donnell (1975), utilising a bureaucratic–authoritarian model, argued that the exhaustion of readily available opportunities for ISI was inexorably linked to increasingly authoritarian rule and political repression by South American regimes. From the dependency school came fierce criticisms (e.g. Cardoso and Faletto, 1979). ISI could not bring development as it failed to alter consumption patterns or change the structure of the ownership of the means of production. Foreign penetration of the economy was encouraged, inappropriate technologies were imported and capital flowed in the direction of the metropolitan countries. Disillusionment with ISI was evident across a range of ideological and analytical perspectives.

In retrospect, branding ISI a total failure was probably an overreaction. Many countries did register dramatic increases in industrial production and established substantial industrial sectors. For policymakers (as distinct from neo-classical economists), the matter of efficiency may have been of secondary concern. Also, for industrialisation to proceed to higher stages it is vital that some base already exists so that there is an appropriate technological infrastructure. Industrial sectors are not created overnight but require a period of learning. Schmitz (1984, p.7) sees the more successful learners as developing countries with relatively long industrialisation experiences stretching back to the 1920s.

The current policy-makers have a number of choices regarding ISI. If they follow the neo-classical economists (and the World Bank and IMF), they will relax trade restrictions thus forcing ISI industries to become efficient or perish in the face of cheap imports. If they heed the dependency theorists, they will opt for significant changes in the economic structure of the country (e.g. land reform, income redistribution) and will demand strong government planning and control of industry. Both paths challenge the domestic status quo and encounter strong opposition from classes and elites which feel their interests threatened.

The perceived failure of ISI led to the favouring of a new strategy – the promotion of export-oriented industrialisation (EOI). The aim of this strategy is to produce manufactured goods for export, primarily for the large markets of the advanced nations. Industrial exports from the Third World have undergone massive expansion since the mid-1960s and the growth records of EOI countries are impressive. However, the success has been confined to a small number of countries known as the newly industrialised countries (NICs). They are comprised of South Korea, Taiwan, Hong Kong, Singapore,

Brazil and, sometimes, Mexico. By 1975 they accounted for 62 per cent of manufactured exports from the developing countries. Excluding Mexico, their manufactured exports went up by 20–40 per cent each year between 1965 and 1978, while manufacturing employment rose by an annual 4–8 per cent with labour shortages and real wage increases sometimes evident (Schmitz, 1984, pp. 8–9). While the impressive performance of the NICs is celebrated by the counter-revolutionaries and others as a vindication of economic liberalisation and the power of the market to bring development, there are doubts about whether the model can be transferred to other countries and whether the counter-revolutionary interpretation of events is correct. First, the vital period of NIC export expansion occurred when world trade was growing rapidly and before the era of new protectionism in industrial countries. Complementing this was the development of a buoyant transnational banking market supplying plentiful loans to the Third World. The contemporary trade and financial scene is very different, and the continued exporting success of the NICs leaves little or no room for competition by newcomers (Cline, 1982, p. 88). Second, most NICs seem to have had significant industrialisation prior to export expansion. Such items as infrastructure, experience, technical skills and entrepreneurial ability were already in place. Previous ISI may have greatly facilitated later EOI. Third, there appears to have been considerable state intervention and much less free play of market forces than the champions of EOI would have us believe. We shall return to this matter shortly. Finally, we should not treat ISI and EOI as mutually exclusive alternatives. Kirkpatrick *et al.* (1984, p. 200) recommend that elements of both 'trade-related' strategies should be employed, the appropriate balance being determined by such things as 'an economy's level of industrialisation, its size and resource endowments, and its overall development objectives'.

As noted above, one of the critical policy decisions is the degree of government involvement in the industrialisation process. Experience suggests that successful industrialisation requires considerable but carefully-selected government intervention. Recent interpretations of the rise of the Asian NICs place considerable emphasis on the role of the state. Deyo (1987) points to 'state-led strategies' characterised by 'continuing, selective intervention by state agencies in private sector decision making and market transactions to achieve strategic goals'. The data on South Korea points to extensive restrictions on direct foreign investment, strict import and foreign exchange controls, and a high degree of centralised planning. It has been suggested that the government directly or indirectly controlled more than two-thirds of the resources available for investment (Schmitz, 1984, p. 12).

However, in other capitalist-oriented countries it can be argued that state intervention, and particularly the establishment of state-owned enterprises (SOEs), has been detrimental to industrial development. SOEs are to be found in many nations manufacturing steel, fertiliser, cement, motor vehicles, electronic items and other products. Their creation has been justified on the grounds of their spearheading industrialisation in countries where there is little or no heavy industry; promoting strategic industries; creating jobs; and limiting foreign control of the economy. Although the World Bank (1987, pp. 66–7) acknowledges wide variation in the performance of state-owned manufacturing enterprises, the general pattern is said to be one of poor results. They have failed to play the strategic facilitating role in the wider process of industrialisation, have produced financial returns inferior to the private sector and have poor social profitability, putting large burdens on public budgets and the external debt. The World Bank is pleased to see governments in the Third World attempting to divest themselves of state-owned enterprises. But the process is far from simple. Not only are businessmen unwilling to take equity in unprofitable ventures, but the powerful groups who derive benefits from SOEs, particularly those employed by SOEs or able to use them as a form of patronage, make the rationalisation and divestiture of state manufacturing assets very difficult.

Socialist industrialisation has obviously been a matter of state control. The Soviet model for rapid industrialisation has proved attractive to a number of countries, notably North Korea and China, despite the appalling human cost of the Soviet experience. Among the major features of the model are a heavily authoritarian state, industry managed directly through state administrative bureaux and public enterprises, a reliance on domestic resources, a preference for heavy industry over light and the promotion of industry over agriculture (White, 1984, pp. 105–6). By the early 1970s, industry accounted for over 60 per cent of North Korean GDP and 33 per cent of the workforce. For China, the figures were 47 per cent for GDP and 19 per cent for workforce. These remarkable industrialisation records had been achieved by following the basic principles of the Soviet model although neither country attempted to make an exact replica of the Soviet experience. Since the 1970s considerable problems have been evident (White, 1984, pp. 108–10). The reliance on political mobilisation and directive planning has resulted in the misallocation of resources, waste, inflexibility and policy errors. Shortage of educated manpower and poor communications raise questions about how effective are central planning systems, especially when it comes to redirecting industrialisation strategy. Political authoritarianism refuses to make way for democratisation while the stress on self-reliance becomes an end in itself. These problems come to the fore as easy growth opportunities diminish, a more complex economy generates pressure for foreign trade and technology, and the population asks when it is going to cease making sacrifices and receive the benefits of industrialisation. The changes in contemporary China represent a liberalising reaction to these problems and forces. Decentralisation and democratisation of policy-making and planning, the promotion of efficiency, greater attention to the market, the search for export opportunities, joint ventures with foreign enterprises and the import of more advanced technology are all elements of China's reformulated industrial strategy. However, recent events in China make the future of these policies unclear. The Soviet model has been of little relevance to the second wave of would-be socialist industrialisers, such as Angola, Mozambique and South Yemen, as these regimes were established in 'relatively small, trade-dependent agriculture-dominated territories which are unsuitable contexts for the classic model of socialist industrialisation' (White, 1984, p. 111). The revolutionary elites in these countries have failed to come up with effective alternative paths to socialist industrialisation and face almost insurmountable problems.

Given the problems of promoting urban industrialisation, the idea of rural industrialisation might prove a favoured policy option in many circumstances if only because no others suggest themselves. It has found considerable support among neo-populist theorists and political leaders. In many Third World countries substantial rural industries in such fields as textiles, pottery and metalworking have been decimated by the import of mass-produced manufactures of Western industry. Whether policy-makers can bring a renaissance in rural industrialisation remains to be seen. The great attraction of rural industrialisation is that it can provide employment and hence additional income in rural areas where unemployment, under-employment, poverty and outmigration are characteristic. According to its proponents its use of simple, labour-intensive, small-scale, cheap technology makes rural industrialisation a realistic and viable alternative to its orthodox urban counterpart. However, there are few success stories and a multitude of problems. For example, the conditions of poverty which rural industrialisation should help to alleviate serve to impede its progress. People often want the products of urban industry rather than rurally-produced substitutes. Assembling the factors of production and distributing the product are fraught with difficulty where infrastructure is poorly developed. How and at what cost would a myriad of small enterprises be organised? And are planners and politicians really committed to rural industrialisation?

To many, it is still seen as a second-rate strategy and one which is considerably more difficult to implement than its large-scale urban counterpart. Where these conditions prevail a passive policy of neglect and indifference is found. Protective policies are occasionally employed to safeguard handicraft industries. But it is generally agreed that the developmental approach is required for success – that is, 'the creation of economically viable enterprises which can stand on their own feet without perpetual subsidy and can make a positive contribution to the growth of real income and therefore to better living levels' (Staley and Morse, 1965, p. 318). In this perception of rural industry, efficiency is essential and new methods and products are encouraged, as is expansion to larger-size productive units.

Perhaps the most controversial policy consideration for Third World industrialisation concerns the role of foreign capital, generally in the form of the transnational corporation (TNC). These large companies based in the industrial countries rank high in many observers' demonology of underdevelopment and are mistrusted (at the very least) by Third World governments. The TNCs are, in various degrees, seen to be the contemporary embodiment of rich-country exploitation of the Third World. Nevertheless the TNCs operate *via* subsidiaries in most developing countries manufacturing items such as pharmaceuticals, food, vehicles and electrical goods. The basic problem for Third World countries is 'to regulate DFI [direct foreign investment] inflows or TNC activities so as to maximise the benefits and minimise the costs associated with them, assessed from the standpoint of the regulator' (Kirkpatrick *et al.*,

1984, p. 211). Three major areas of conflict between TNCs and the developmental objectives of Third World countries can be identified (Kirkpatrick *et al.*, 1984, p. 209). Firstly, developing countries often wish to maximise earnings and minimise foreign exchange expenditures. TNCs may not wish to export but may well desire to repatriate as large a proportion of earnings as possible, using any available method. The pharmaceutical industry is notorious in this connection, employing transfer pricing to secure massive profits, i.e. overcharging the subsidiary, and hence the Third World consumer, for inputs bought from the parent company. Second, developing country governments are often concerned about job creation. TNCs may well employ capital-intensive technology which provides relatively few employment opportunities. Furthermore, TNC operations generally have few backward or forward linkages with other domestic industries and so generate little indirect employment. It may even be that the viability of handicraft industries can be undermined, thus creating unemployment. Finally, developing countries want the transfer of technology which is both useful and appropriate for national needs. They also wish to develop an indigenous technological capacity. TNC interests are rarely in line with these national objectives.

The unintentional generosity of Third World governments to TNCs is becoming less frequent. Led by the United Nations, the developing countries have been working towards the more effective regulation of TNCs. The primary objective of this exercise in international co-operation is 'to create an international framework that will maximise the positive contributions of TNCs to development and minimise their negative effects and at the same time contribute to the security of foreign investment through the establishment of clear and stable rules of the game' (Kirkpatrick *et al.*, 1984, p. 211). It should be noted that TNCs are no longer the exclusive property of the metropolitan capitalist countries. There are now Third World TNCs from such countries as India, Brazil, Hong Kong and Taiwan (Lall, 1983; Wells, 1983).

The pursuit of industrialisation seems likely to remain a leading objective of national development strategies, since in the minds of many policy-makers development is industrialisation. But old obstacles remain and new ones appear. The prospects are not bright, and the likelihood of meeting the Lima target of the Third World producing 25 per cent of world manufacturing, value added, by the

year 2000 are decidedly dim. Despite the appeal of East Asian EOI
because of its undoubted success in a few countries, the EOI path is
unlikely to be replicated. Greater protectionism in advanced countries, in the form of non-tariff barriers, is already in evidence to stem
the enormous flow of manufactures from the existing NICs and
other developing countries. New technologies involving greater
computerisation and automation are rendering developing countries
less competitive as sites for manufacturing for advanced country
markets (Kaplinsky, 1984). Blue collar wages are becoming relatively insignificant as a competitive factor while costs of distance to
market are becoming more important. A more inward-looking
industrialisation strategy may well be the most promising option.
However, governments must be careful not to repeat the errors of the
ISI policies of the 1950s and 1960s. A recent review of African efforts
to industrialise warns against misguided policies which can lead to
the establishment of 'inefficient, inward-looking technologically
slothful industries [that] can seriously retard long-term progress'
(Lall *et al.*, 1987, p. 1223). Policy-makers must also avoid the
potentially stultifying effect of the state on industrialisation. Finally,
Third World countries must contend with the World Bank and IMF
liberalisation policies which seek to generate efficiency by removing
impediments to freer trade in developing countries. Third World
governments worry about their vulnerability to manufactured imports from the advanced industrial countries and the NICs. De-
industrialisation rather than industrialisation could be the lot of
some developing countries.

AGRICULTURE

Alongside industry, agriculture is the other major productive sector
of the economies of poorer nations. Although the share of agricultural output in terms of GDP has steadily declined in most
countries (Table 5.5), agricultural policies continue to have enormous economic, social and political significance. Employment in
agricultural activities still provides livelihoods for the majority of
Third World families. In low-income countries in the early 1980s
around 70 to 75 per cent of jobs were in the agricultural sector (Table
5.5), while in lower-middle-income nations the figure was around 55

Development policies

Table 5.5   Agriculture in the economies of developing countries

Country	Share of agriculture in GDP (%)		Proportion of labour force in agriculture (%)	
	1965	*1986*	*1965*	*1980*
Low-income countries (excluding China and India)	43	38	79	71
China	39	31	81	74
India	47	32	73	70
Somalia	71	58	81	76
Sudan	54	35	82	71
Middle-income countries	22	15	56	43
Indonesia	56	26	71	57
Tunisia	22	16	49	35
Brazil	19	11	49	31
South Korea	38	12	55	36
Industrial market countries	5	3	14	7

Source: The World Bank (1988) *World Development Report*

per cent. Because of this, agricultural policies not only have a large impact on the economy but also on levels of social welfare. This is most immediately evident in terms of the role of agriculture in feeding a nation's population. Although many developing countries, especially in South Asia, have seen food production expand in recent decades, there is great concern about the decline of the average index of food production per capita in many African states. This drop in food production has been dramatically highlighted by the plight of the starving in Ethiopia, Sudan and Mozambique. Between 1975 and 1983, per capita food production in sub-Saharan Africa dropped by around 8 per cent on average, and by almost 30 per cent in Ghana, Somalia and Mozambique.

Before examining agricultural issues in detail it is useful to distinguish between policies seeking to improve the contribution that the agricultural sector makes to the achievement of developmental goals (i.e. agricultural development) and policies of rural development. In many countries, politicians and policy-makers use the terms agricultural development and rural development interchangeably, but the latter is best used to refer to multisectoral (agriculture, small-scale industry, education, health, infrastructure, etc.) approaches aimed at eradicating rural poverty. Here the focus is on agriculture, although much of the discussion is of direct relevance to questions of rural development.

Thorbecke (1979) proposes that there are four basic forms of agricultural development strategy. These are as follows:

1. An industrialisation-first strategy which adopts policies that favour industry and discriminate against agriculture.
2. A 'unimodal' strategy which progressively modernises the entire agricultural sector, which is comprised of relatively uniform, small-scale farm units.
3. A 'bimodal' strategy in which agricultural policies concentrate on increasing the productivity and output of a set of large-scale production units, while technical change in the small-farm sector is allowed to evolve gradually.
4. A strategy for the socialisation of agriculture.

These four categories are not mutually exclusive, for example, 1 and 3, or 1 and 4, can overlap, but they provide a useful framework for the analysis of a number of key agricultural policy issues.

The first approach, industrialisation first, is a strategy that has operated in many developing countries in the post-war period. The classic examples are in Latin America where protectionist, import-substitution industrialisation policies (see previous section) led to agriculture being allocated only a small share of public and private investment, overvalued exchange rates, underpriced capital and low agricultural prices. All of these factors served as disincentives to agricultural production. This situation is not confined to Latin America. Peterson (1979) argues that similar disincentives to farmers in a sample of twenty-seven developing countries have led to levels of agricultural production being depressed by 30 to 40 per cent. Lipton's (1977) urban bias thesis, largely based on empirical evidence from India, argues that an urban–industrial bias is the root cause of pervasive rural poverty and that a subsidised industrial sector and cheap food policies are an indirect means of taxing the farm population and the agricultural sector. According to Lipton, even when the proponents of 'industrialisation first' strategies perceive that there are problems in the agricultural sector they are most likely to adopt a bimodal strategy, favouring larger and more influential farmers. Ultimately, this strategy is self-negating as it dampens down rates of industrial development as rural demand for manufactured inputs and goods grows at a very slow rate.

The unimodal and bimodal strategies afford agriculture a much greater developmental role. Extreme forms of these strategies can be regarded as the pole positions on a continuum of policy options. The unimodal strategy is typified by Taiwan, South Korea and Japan, which have pursued increases in agricultural productivity and farm incomes within the framework of their existing small-scale agricultural production units. The contrasting bimodal strategy is exemplified by Mexico and Colombia where agricultural development has focused on increasing output on a subsector of large farms through the adoption of relatively capital-intensive technologies. The bimodal strategy is also associated with a policy emphasis that favours cash crop and export production over food crop production. (For a discussion of the cash crop versus food crop issue see Johnston and Clark, 1982, pp. 254–8.) The majority of African and Asian countries can be viewed as having intermediate positions but the policies that they adopt will, over a period of time, take them towards one of the modal positions. For example, the Green Revolution of the 1960s and 1970s could be interpreted as moving India's and Pakistan's agricultural sectors into a more bimodal pattern. Furthermore, Johnston and Clark (1982, p. 72) argue that 'to a large extent the two options [unimodal and bimodal] are mutually exclusive; promoting the emergence of a large, highly commercial subsector tends to preclude the possibility of successfully pursuing a unimodal strategy'.

Over the 1970s a growing body of academic and multilateral agency opinion argued that a unimodal strategy is more appropriate for developing countries than a bimodal strategy (Johnston and Kilby, 1975; Asian Development Bank, 1978, 1979; World Bank, 1975, 1978). 'The experience of Taiwan, Japan, South Korea and a few other countries is especially significant in demonstrating both the feasibility and desirability of pursuing a unimodal pattern of agricultural development' (Johnston and Clark, 1982, p.75). This strategy is more likely to create a situation in which the demand for labour exceeds the rate of growth of the working age population, there are increasing returns on labour and, ultimately, there is increased rural demand for industrial products. By contrast, it is argued, a bimodal strategy can achieve dramatic production expansion in the short term, but in the longer term the neglect of the small farm sub-sector means that potential output opportunities are lost and rural poverty remains. The Mexican experience, regarded as an agricultural development success story in the 1960s but encountering declining rates of growth of agricultural output more recently, provides support for this thesis. Despite the weight of theoretical argument and empirical evidence mustered by proponents of the unimodal approach, considerable obstacles often obstruct the adoption of such a strategy. Johnston and Clark (1982) identify seven main obstacles, but most of these have a common root – the existing pattern of the distribution of power in developing countries. In the vast majority of cases a move towards a unimodal strategy would necessitate a weakening of the power base of rural and urban elites who have a key influence on policy-making.

The fourth strategy in Thorbecke's (1979) typology, the 'collectivization, or socialization, of rural areas' is associated with radical, often revolutionary, social change. This category must be treated with caution as there are a variety of differing forms of agrarian socialism and not all are collectivist in nature. China, for example, has pursued a relatively unimodal stance, while Tanzania and Ethiopia have taken a bimodal approach. The central feature of agrarian socialist strategies is that they emphasise the role of the state in planning the agricultural sector, and afford only a minor role, or no role at all, to market forces in allocating resources and distributing production. Arguably, the great experiment with agricultural collectivisation in China contributed significantly to the country's relatively rapid rate of economic growth (4.5 per cent per annum over 1965–84) and the reduction of the incidence of poverty. Data on Cuba indicates that the socialisation of agriculture has been associated with increased productivity (Rodriguez, 1987). However, in other countries – Ethiopia, Mozambique, Tanzania and Vietnam – agrarian socialism has been associated with poor economic performance, declining agricultural productivity, relatively low rates of agricultural job creation and falling per capita incomes (Cohen and Isaksson, 1988). Evidence of the severity of the problems that have been encountered is provided by the recent decisions in China, Tanzania, Vietnam and Mozambique to give individual smallholders a greater role in production and to permit prices for some agricultural products to be set by market forces. With the notable exception of Ethiopia, most states practising agrarian socialist policies are redefining the nature of their agricultural policies into more mixed economic prescriptions.

Many of the points raised so far about the choice of agricultural development strategy are allied to the question of land reform. This term refers to direct state intervention to modify patterns of land ownership and tenancy by introducing new legislation, establishing agencies to implement the new laws, providing for the payment of compensation to those who lose land (sometimes), and organising agricultural support services for the beneficiaries of reform. For many commentators on development in the 1960s and 1970s land reform was a *sine qua non* for agricultural improvement and the subject received considerable analysis (Dorner, 1972; Lehmann, 1974; Myrdal, 1968; and Warriner, 1969). Economic reasoning about the higher productivity of small farm units allied to arguments about the social justice of modifying skewed patterns of land ownership made a strong rational case for reform. There were also sound political reasons in many countries where it was expedient for those controlling the state to deal with a rural populace that was land hungry and threatening to seize land. Given these circumstances, many governments attempted to introduce land reform policies. These ranged from socialist Cuba to one party states such as Mexico and Tanzania, from military regimes (of varying political complexions) such as Brazil and Peru to mixed economy democracies such as India, through to authoritarian capitalist states such as Taiwan and South Korea (Atkins, 1988). As a consequence of this variety, land reform measures have taken a number of configurations ranging from the seizure of estates, their breaking up for small farmers and the 'liquidation' of estate owners; to the setting of land ceilings on how much land an individual may hold; through to milder measures such as permitting existing ownership patterns to continue but introducing tenancy reforms that limit the rents, or shares, that landlords can levy.

Detailed accounts of land reform in different countries can be found in the specialist literature (see Atkins, 1988, for a recent bibliography). Here, our discussion focuses on the example of Taiwan, long regarded as an example of a successful land reform. The Taiwanese reforms of the 1940s and 1950s have been characterised as a gradualist approach with three main stages that created an economically more productive and equitable agricultural system (Dorner, 1972). The first stage comprised legislation that limited the levels of farm rents to 37.5 per cent of the value of the harvest; the second stage involved the sale of state-owned lands resulting in 176,000 hectares, or 21 per cent of the total arable area, being distributed to peasants; the final stage was the implementation of a policy of compulsory purchase of private tenanted lands and their resale to tenants, who purchased by instalments. The success of the Taiwanese land reform has not gone unchallenged, however (Apthorpe, 1979). Even if it is accepted that the reform was effective then the commonly-held notion that the lessons of success could be utilised elsewhere needs to be treated with caution. The feasibility of the Taiwanese reforms was not grounded in an economic analysis, but in the specific socio-political situation of the country in the years following the Chinese civil war. The political pressures on the Kuomintang government to legitimise its control of the country, the existence of an accurate set of land records and the availability of a pool of state-held arable land, were all essential ingredients for the programme that are unlikely to be replicated elsewhere.

In most other countries the results achieved by reform programmes have fallen short of their targets. This, along with the new orthodoxy of development policy that frowns on state intervention, has led to the subject receiving little attention in the 1980s (Atkins, 1988). In retrospect it seems evident that the measures introduced by many governments in the 1950s, 1960s and 1970s were intended to create an illusion of reform, rather than actual reform. For example, Bardhan (1974) argues that India's impressive land reform legislation incorporated deliberate loopholes and exemptions that reduced its impact. Furthermore, it was poorly implemented by a corrupt administrative system and was dependent on a legal process that was slow and inaccessible to prospective beneficiaries of reform. Perhaps, as Worsley (1984) suggests, the propensity of land reform programmes to achieve limited results can be best understood by class analysis.

For land reform, properly managed, did not have to threaten the future of the propertied classes prepared to alter their mode of production. To governments, it offered the prospect of political reprieve: damping down peasant discontent which might induce them to listen to leftists, . . . landowners could unload their marginal lands, and use the compensation they received to modernize their operations on the best lands, or invest it in industry and business, in consumption or retire to Florida (Worsley, 1984, p. 149).

Agricultural policies are not only concerned with the structure of agricultural production units but also with the establishment and operation of an institutional framework that can supply farmers with necessary inputs and services. At the very least an efficient agricultural sector requires the following services:

1. Reliable information on the means by which it can increase productivity (research and extension services).
2. Access to agricultural inputs (fertilizer, pesticide, seed, stock-feed, equipment).
3. Provision of infrastructure (feeder roads, irrigation, storage facilities).
4. Access to sources of credit to finance production.
5. A marketing system paying prices that serve as an incentive to production.

There are vast and complex literatures on each of these topics and on the ways in which they interrelate. However, the institutional options available to agricultural policy-makers can be summarised into the following three main types:

1. Provision by state agencies, e.g. ministries and public enterprises.
2. Provision by member-controlled farmer organisations, e.g. marketing and supply co-operatives and irrigation-user associations (see Chapter 7 for an extended discussion of these organisations).
3. Provision by the private sector, e.g. private traders, commercial banks and manufacturing companies.

In both mixed economy and socialist countries the main institutional form promoted from the 1950s through to the mid-1970s was the state agency. The agricultural sector was perceived as being poorly organised, while it was believed that the private sector could not operate efficiently because of profound market failure in rural areas. In consequence, agricultural research and extension were viewed as natural functions for ministries of agriculture; the manufacture, import and distribution of agricultural inputs were allocated, sometimes with monopoly powers, to parastatal fertilizer corporations and seed companies; responsibility for delivering credit to farmers was given to parastatal agricultural development banks and small farmer credit agencies; and agricultural produce marketing was placed in the hands of state marketing boards. These organisations were usually linked into state-sponsored agricultural co-operatives as the local-level agency for distributing credit and inputs and for bulking farm produce. In many situations these co-operatives were not voluntary organisations, in the sense of the co-operative movement in Europe and North America, but were government-controlled agencies with boards selected by political leaders and appointed managers (for an analysis of the operations of agricultural co-operatives in Africa see Hyden, 1983). The performance of state agencies in the agricultural sector has varied from agency to agency and country to country, but a consensus has emerged in recent years that overall performance has been poor, especially in sub-Saharan Africa (Berg, 1981; Cook and Kirkpatrick, 1988). State-run agricultural finance agencies have high rates of default and can often only be kept operating by continuous subsidy (von Pischke, 1983; World Bank, 1984). Government research and extension services have a very mixed record. Even where output has been increased, as in the case of India's Green Revolution, this has been associated with the strengthening of the position of rich peasants at the expense of poor peasants and share-croppers (Byres and Crow, 1983). State marketing corporations have exploited the monopoly powers granted to them, depressed producer prices and served as a discouragement to farmers (Bates, 1981).

Disillusionment with the services provided by costly public sector and parastatal agencies has led to a recent emphasis on the use of alternative institutional forms. In particular, the major multilateral agencies have argued that the private sector should play a much greater role in the provision of farm services and inputs. Private traders and companies could distribute inputs in rural areas. Commercial banks could be offered incentives to establish rural branches, or the informal private sector, i.e. money lenders, could be used as bank agents (this possibility is under review in Sri Lanka). Profit-making agricultural management agencies could offer and charge for agricultural advice (Hulme, 1983). For other analysts, particularly sociologists, anthropologists and political scientists, the role of the third sector, of private voluntary (PVOs) or non-governmental organisations (NGOs) is highlighted (Korten, 1980; Esman and Uphoff, 1984; Gorman, 1984). They argue that the most pressing institutional need in the agricultural sector is for the establishment of a network of diverse member-controlled voluntary organisations that can identify member needs and interests and take the necessary steps to service these needs and promote these interests (see Chapter 7).

In reality, in all except the most authoritarian of regimes, agricultural services and inputs will be provided by a mix of the three options that have been identified. It seems likely, however, that the common solution to perceived institutional problems of the 1950s and 1960s – establishing a new state agency – will be abandoned and that alternatives emphasising the roles of the private sector and the voluntary sector in agriculture will be afforded more attention.

POPULATION

It took all history until 1850 for the world's population to climb to 1000 million (1 billion). By 1930, some eighty years later, another billion had been added. Growth rates accelerated still further so that by 1960 the world's population had surpassed the 3 billion mark. Only fifteen years later, 4 billion was reached. The growth rate has slackened slightly since then but the current world population still exceeds 5 billion. Almost three-quarters of this total is to be found in the developing countries of the world where growth continues at around 2 per cent per annum.

From the beginning of the nineteenth century, improvements in public health and medicine in the industrial countries led to a gradual decline in mortality (death rates). This was eventually complemented by falling fertility (birth rates). The new pattern of low mortality and low fertility resulted in a low rate of natural increase – and the small nuclear family household we encountered in the last chapter. In the Third World, the promotion of better public health and the import of medicine has facilitated a twentieth century decline in death rates. Lowering of infant mortality rates has been particularly marked, although they have generally stayed far above industrial country figures. Birth rates have remained high in most developing countries thus making the rate of natural increase soar and the populations extremely youthful, 40 per cent generally being fifteen years or under.

While colonial governments were obviously aware of rapid population growth they generally maintained a policy indifference. This attitude quickly evaporated in the post-war era when there was a widespread acknowledgement in official circles that rapid population growth was not only prevalent but was also a problem.

Examination of the relationship between population growth and development proceeded apace. Population policies were formulated on the advice of population experts and by the end of the 1960s the population problem had been pushed to the forefront of development concern. U Thant, the Secretary-General of the United Nations, stressed the urgent need 'to defuse the population explosion' while the Pearson report (1969, p. 55) declared that 'no other phenomenon casts a darker shadow over the prospects for international development than the staggering growth of population.'

Why were the alarm bells ringing so loudly on the matter of Third World population? Why were effective and acceptable population policies being anxiously sought? A number of persuasive reasons were widely canvassed. First, sharp increases in population require even sharper increases in public expenditure on such things as roads, health, education and housing if people are to receive the benefits of development. Such increases in expenditure are frequently impossible for poor countries to afford. Second, each year increasing numbers of job-seekers enter the labour market. Economies cannot sustain high enough rates of growth to accommodate these young people. Furthermore, the vast labour surplus allegedly results in a depression of wage levels as many aspirants fight for few openings. Third, considerable pressure may be placed on the natural environment. The cultivated acreage may extend into marginal land. Erosion could occur. Deforestation may destroy watersheds and lead to uncontrolled run-off and hence flooding. Farmers simply may not be able to produce enough food to feed national populations. Rising land values and rents may be encouraged by population growth and may force people off the land and into the city slums. Fourth, strong inverse correlations were found between child health and family size. Large family size has entailed higher dependency ratios (i.e. the number of persons dependent on one income earner). In situations of low income and poverty it becomes almost impossible to raise one's living standards. Finally, there was concern that a rapidly rising, and increasingly urban, population which was not receiving the benefits of development could lead to political instability. Visions of rebellion, revolution and social chaos abounded. Radical commentators, drawing from Marxist ideas, rejected such analysis and suggested that capitalist underdevelopment was the real culprit. Overthrow of the world capitalist order or increased and improved efforts for genuine development would in fact solve the so-called population problem. But even Marxist governments have eventually found it expedient to adopt some form of population policy in order to arrest swelling numbers and/or to redistribute them.

The main goal of population policies has been to reduce fertility rates. During the 1950s, 1960s and 1970s governments adopting an anti-natalist approach have pursued this largely by public information programmes and the establishment of networks of family planning clinics providing contraceptive technologies to the public at low cost or free of charge. However, more recent sociological research has pointed out that the machine model on which these programmes were based has meant that they have often been inappropriate for the social categories they were attempting to influence and that impacts have been limited (Warwick, 1982). A transactional approach that recognises local cultural conditions and political contexts and that places client welfare, rather than national targets, at the centre of its activities is more likely to achieve high adoption rates and is more justifiable in moral terms (Warwick, 1982). Mamdani's (1972) pioneering study, based on an interpretation of the views of intended recipients of a family planning programme, had earlier demonstrated that while smaller family size might be desirable from a calculus of the public good, from the calculus of individual poor Indian households, having a large family was a rational strategy for survival.

For many poor rural families an additional child is not only an inherent source of satisfaction and pleasure but also has economic value. The costs of raising an additional child are relatively low, as mothers command poor wage rates and can commonly combine child-rearing with traditional economic activities such as agriculture, crafts and petty trading. Within a few years the child can contribute to family welfare by fetching water and firewood, watching over grazing animals, scaring birds off crops and many other simple tasks. In the longer term, for the parents, having a large family provides them with a greater likelihood of support in their old age and makes the household less vulnerable to theft or attack.

A consequence of these findings has been that in the 1980s the population policies promoted by international agencies have become more broadly based and they no longer exclusively emphasise family planning techniques. The high rates of fertility occurring in many countries are now not simply viewed as a cause of poverty but also as a consequence of poverty. Birdsall's (1980) analysis indicated that

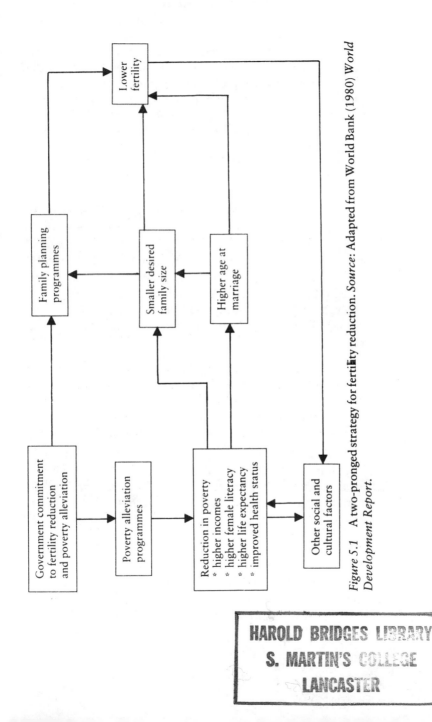

Figure 5.1 A two-pronged strategy for fertility reduction. *Source:* Adapted from World Bank (1980) *World Development Report.*

only 15 per cent of the variation in fertility rates between countries could be explained by family planning programmes, while around 60 per cent could be explained by social and economic factors, such as levels of income, literacy, health status and life expectancy. Fertility and poverty are seen as being mutually reinforcing so that efforts to lower fertility through family planning programmes must be complemented by attempts to alleviate poverty, improve health and increase literacy rates (especially for women). If fertility rates are to be lowered then programmes must not only make contraceptive knowledge and materials available but must also create a socio-economic situation in which the target households desire a smaller family (Figure 5.1). To differing degrees, the governments of developing countries are currently responding to the implications of these findings for their population policies. In the remainder of this section we examine the ways in which a few selected countries have tackled the population problem.

It is appropriate to start with China, the country with the world's largest population. In 1949, leaders of the newly-established People's Republic of China rejected any suggestion that the size of the growth rate of its population might be a problem. Even though the 1953 census figure of 582.6 million came as something of a shock to observers, being 82.6 million more than the highest estimate, a policy to limit population was not forthcoming. Mao believed that a large and impoverished population was ideal for the Great Leap Forward and essential for building socialism. Although a family planning programme was introduced in 1956 it faced technical problems and lacked strong political support. Reductions in fertility for the period 1959–61 were thus less to do with official initiatives than with the devastation and dislocation caused by a drought-induced famine. In 1962, a new birth control campaign was launched focusing on the popularisation of late marriage and the dissemination of intra-uterine devices. The 1964 census gave no cause for celebration, placing the Chinese population at some 691 million, while the commencement of the Cultural Revolution in 1966 ensured the disruption of any implementation of a population programme. Policies to 'bring population growth under control by planning' resurfaced tentatively in 1968 and by 1972 had been 'greatly intensified' (Johnson, 1987, p. 156). Controlling population growth was deemed essential to 'modernisation' and the raising of living standards. From that time considerable decline in the national birth rate has been reported. According to official estimates, the birth rate was 37 per 1000 population in 1952 and the death rate was 17, giving a rate of natural increase of 2 per cent per annum. By 1979 the birth rate had been more than halved to 17.9 per cent per 1000 and even though the death rate had been cut to 6.2 per 1000 the annual rate of natural increase had fallen to around 1 per cent (Johnson, 1987, p. 155).

In a relatively short time China has succeeded in producing a spectacular decline in its population growth. Its policies for reducing fertility have been based on a system of incentives, disincentives and the 'voluntariness of the masses'. There has been vigorous encouragement of the one-child family, *via* both propaganda and economic allowances. Social security provisions for the elderly have been introduced to allay the worries of parents with only one child. Technical guidance on birth control has been made readily available through an army of family planning workers. All types of contraceptives are manufactured in China and provided free, as are abortion and sterilisation. It has been estimated that 70 per cent of married couples of reproductive age have adopted contraceptive measures. Late marriage and late childbirth have been advocated and to some extent enforced by the raising of the minimum age of marriage for both men (from 20 to 22 years) and women (from 18 to 20 years).

Critics have argued that the system is coercive. They say that it is characterised less by voluntariness and more by penalties, force and arm-twisting. Even the US government has withheld money from the United Nations Fund for Population Activities since 1985 on the grounds that the implementation of the one-child-per-family policy has resulted in abuses such as forced abortion and sterilisation. The Chinese deny such allegations and are pressing on with unrelenting vigour with their plan to limit population growth. In the early 1980s planners set a target of 1.2 billion people by the end of the century and spoke of reaching zero growth between 2020 and 2030.

Such ambitious objectives have, however, proved too optimistic. Fertility levels have been rising in China so much that the rigid application of the one-child family was officially abandoned in 1984. Realising opposition at the grass roots level and an inability to enforce the one-child model on every married couple, the authorities introduced flexibility into the system. The pursuit of economic modernisation has involved a policy of liberalisation. Market forces now partially influence the allocation of and access to resources such as housing, jobs, land and food. The power of local officials has been eroded and their capacity to enforce government regulations such as those on family planning has been greatly undermined. It appears that the traditional desire to have sons remains strong despite the official adherence to the adage that women hold up half the sky. Recent evidence points to an under-reporting of female births and that the Chinese population will reach the 1.3 billion mark by the year 2000 (*Far Eastern Economic Review*, 2 March 1989). It has been argued that the grass roots abandonment of the one-child family was due to the demand for labour following economic liberalisation. This view seems overly simplistic as it assumes Chinese families engage in unusually long-range labour planning. It also overlooks the fact that children are actually being displaced from employment opportunities and that young people typically move to townships and take wage-paying jobs in the expanding enterprises there. The socio–economic environment in which family planning policy and experience is located is extremely complex (Yang and Hull, 1987). The future is therefore difficult to predict but in January 1989 a new birth control drive was launched. Perhaps more important to fertility levels than the new reliance on legal means of enforcement is the way in which economic development progresses. However, the tragic events of June 1989 mean that it is again unclear as to what form of development policies will be pursued and make the forecasting of demographic trends in China an increasingly speculative exercise.

Sub-Saharan Africa stands in stark contrast to the Chinese experience. The rate of population growth in sub-Saharan Africa is extremely rapid and it is the only region in the world which has not recorded a decline in population growth rates. In 1960, the population growth rate was 2.5 per cent per year but had risen to 3 per cent by 1983. Such a rate entails a doubling of the population every twenty-two years. A steady fall in death rates has been accompanied by hardly any change in the high birth rates. As death rates are not particularly low they could be expected to fall still further. This could give population growth yet another boost. And developmental problems abound. Poverty is widespread and is accompanied by illiteracy and malnutrition. Food production has suffered frequent setbacks because of such factors as drought and the invisibility of the women food producers to the planners. Economies have often stagnated. Countries have failed to move beyond excessive reliance on a few primary products whose prices fluctuate considerably.

Despite the region's relatively low level of urbanisation, there has been a substantial movement of population to towns and cities which cannot cope with employing, housing and providing services for this human influx.

While outsiders may have regarded Africa's rapidly increasing population as a ticking time-bomb for a number of decades the view has not necessarily been shared by domestic observers. African leaders have in the past resented Western efforts to interfere in determining the size of their major asset – population. It was noted that in a subcontinent where thirty-four countries out of forty-seven have populations of less than 5 million occupying huge territories, it is not surprising that rapid demographic growth has not been considered a problem by the countries concerned. The prevailing attitude 'has tended to be to watch the annual increase with some degree of quiet satisfaction' (Mabogunje, as quoted in Miro and Potter, 1980, p. 12). Few governments felt it necessary to introduce any policy to curtail population growth. By 1974, only two countries (Kenya and Ghana) had adopted such policies (Johnson, 1987, p. 219). The fact that birth rates in these countries have remained high indicates that despite adopting formal measures to curb population growth there have either been no significant changes in the services provided to the population or that people are simply not interested in availing themselves of these services. Miro and Potter (1980, p. 15) refer to nine governments which had institutions responsible for populations' policy formulation in the late 1970s but which probably 'remain more as formal legislative or administrative units than as operative mechanisms'.

In the past few years much of the African indifference or hostility to moderating population growth has evaporated. Obvious degradation of the environment, the ravages of prolonged drought and the popular desire to have access to educational and health services have persuaded governments to place population planning on the policy-making agenda. The international agencies have poured resources into Africa and the latest reports from the field indicate that rates of contraceptive acceptance have been rising and it is hoped that East Africa will show substantial fertility decline in the near future. For West Africa it is tentatively forecast that substantial fertility decline could now come in the medium term. But there is a long way to go as in the mid-1980s only 5 per cent of couples were using contraceptives in sub-Saharan Africa (Johnson, 1987, p. 218).

As a final case we will look at the third most populous country in the developing world, Indonesia. In 1950, the first official estimate of population by the new republic placed Java at 50.5 million and Indonesia at 77.2 million. By 1971, the figures were 119 million for Indonesia and 76 million for Java. Not only was Indonesia's population growing at a rate in excess of 2 per cent per year but 65 per cent of the population was located on Java, an island roughly the size of England and Wales but which accounted for under 7 per cent of Indonesia's land area. Thus, Indonesia faced the dual problem of rapid growth and extremely high population densities on the over-crowded island of Java.

After two independent decades of pro-natalist policy the Indonesian government declared its intention to introduce policies to reduce fertility. The first Five-Year Development Plan (1969–74) identified a target of 3 million family planning acceptors and sought to keep population growth at levels below the increase in national income so as to raise per capita income. This would also be of benefit to the health of the mother in particular and the family in general. In the early 1970s an ambitious goal was set to reduce the birth rate by half to 22 per thousand population by 1991. In the period 1967–70 to 1980 a 25 per cent decline in total fertility rates had been recorded for Indonesia although there were substantial interprovincial variations (Hugo *et al.*, 1987, p. 153). It was contended that more than 30 per cent of eligible couples were practising family planning. The outer islands which were originally excluded from the family planning programme generally have higher fertility rates than the inner islands of Java and Bali. The outer islands were progressively incorporated into the family planning programme from 1974 onwards.

The successful Indonesian strategy which, like China, demonstrates that low-income countries can substantially reduce population growth, was based on 'placing the family-planning programme in villages, not clinics and de-centralizing it to give responsibility to village officials and volunteers' (Johnson, 1987, p. 170). Field workers were trained for duties in their home communities. This avoided reliance on unknown and possibly untrusted field workers from outside. Traditional institutions, such as the *banjar* or village council in Bali, were employed to promote awareness and acceptance of family planning. The virtue of a small, happy, healthy family was championed widely, loudly and repeatedly. The sustained official campaign to reduce family size has also coincided with a wider societal desire to do just that while a rising age of marriage has been judged to be less to do with legal changes setting trends but rather following them. Despite the success of the programme so far, it should be kept in mind that in the early 1980s nearly half of Indonesia's married women of reproductive age were not using contraceptives. In its 1988 report on Indonesia, the World Bank issued stern warnings about 'a social time-bomb' – the necessity of finding work for the 1.7 million people that population growth will add to the workforce each year in the 1990s.

Transmigration, Indonesia's other strategy for tackling over-population, has persistently failed to achieve its targets for resettling people from Java and Bali to the sparsely-populated outer islands such as Sumatra, Kalimantan, Sulawesi and Irian Jaya (Hardjono, 1977, p. 7). Disappointment with the results achieved by sponsoring migrants led transmigration officials to examine the possibility of stimulating spontaneous migration, i.e. people organising resettlement for themselves. However, since 1986 the entire programme has been cut back because of the poor results achieved, the difficulties of financing the transmigration programme and concern from aid donors about the impacts of transmigration on indigenous outer island tribal groups and the environment (Hugo et al., 1987).

In conclusion to this section, the diverse results of population planning must be highlighted. While a number of Asian countries have achieved significant reductions in birth rates, other countries, particularly in sub-Saharan Africa, are actually experiencing in-creased fertility. The alarmist image of a population time-bomb, prevalent in the 1970s, is now discounted by many commentators but there is a broad consensus that high rates of population growth are both a cause and a consequence of the colossal levels of poverty evident in the Third World.

EDUCATION

In the 1950s and 1960s the major policy objective in the education sector was to expand enrolment. Other policy measures (e.g. build-ing more schools, training more teachers) tended to feed into this overriding aim of getting increasing numbers of children into school

Table 5.6 Expansion of the education system in developing countries, 1960–85

Country	Percentage of age group enrolled in education					
	Primary (6–11 years)		Secondary (12–17 years)		Tertiary (20–24 years)	
	1960	1985	1960	1985	1960	1985
Low-income countries (excluding China and India)	46	67	6	22	1	5
China	102	124	24	39	0	2
India	61	92	20	35	3	9
Somalia	9	25	1	17	0	1
Sudan	25	49	3	19	1	2
Middle-income countries	81	104	17	49	4	14
Indonesia	71	118	6	39	1	7
Guatemala	45	76	7	17	2	8
Brazil	95	104	11	35	2	11
South Korea	94	96	27	94	5	32
Industrial market countries	114	102	68	93	17	39

Source: The World Bank (1980, 1981, 1987, 1988) *World Development Report*
Notes: In a few cases figures in the table are not for the specified year but for the nearest available
years.
Figures in excess of 100 per cent indicate the enrolment of younger and older children from
outside the specified age groups into that particular level of education

as fast as possible. Rarely has a policy been so universally popular. The modernising economists deemed it a component of the necessary investment in human resource development. Economic growth could only proceed as planned if there were sufficient people with the required technical, managerial and industrial skills. The modernising sociologists saw mass education as an excellent way of inculcating people with the attitudes and values appropriate for modernisation. Politicians of all persuasions saw education as an ideal vehicle for the propagation of their own particular brand of ideology: this would facilitate nation-building in fragmented polities. Among the population at large, increasing the availability of education was wildly popular. It opened up opportunities for formal sector employment. This meant social mobility, higher income, guaranteed income and improvement in the standard of living. Finally, there was a widespread belief, probably deriving from the Western welfare state, that people were entitled to education and should not be condemned to a life of illiteracy.

The outcome of this convergence of interests was a massive increase in school enrolments. While governments routinely failed to meet most of their ambitious planning targets, this was certainly not the case in the education sector. Enrolments everywhere swelled. In 1950 there were approximately 70 million children and young people in the educational systems of the developing countries (Hardiman and Midgley, 1982). By 1965 the number had almost trebled to 200 million while by 1975 the figure stood at 315 million. Although there are substantial differences between enrolment levels in the selected countries, in all cases and at all levels the enrolments have been going up (Table 5.6). With this expanded provision of education, adult literacy has made impressive gains from approximately 40 per cent in 1960 to nearly 60 per cent in 1977. What makes these achievements even more remarkable is that they have been made in the context of rapidly-expanding populations. Each year there are more children entering the school-age group yet enrolments have risen both in absolute terms and as a percentage of the age group.

The rising numbers in the classrooms should not blind us to the fact that there are considerable problems facing the policy-makers. The enormous growth in enrolments tells us nothing about the quality of education being provided. There have been frequent criticisms ranging from accusations of poorly-trained teachers to inappropriate curricula and ill-equipped schools. Increased numbers of students may put an intolerable strain on the existing staff and infrastructural resources. Extremes can be reached such as one rural school which we once visited where there was nothing to write with or write on. Enrolment statistics are not necessarily attendance statistics. There is widespread evidence that many children who are enrolled do not attend school regularly or do not attend at all. Drop-out rates can be very high. Such behaviour is especially associated with poverty. Children may be required to perform domestic tasks such as looking after younger children. Their income-earning capacity may sometimes be needed. They may be frequently ill. The family may not have the financial resources to enable them to attend. There is also spatial inequality in the provision of education. Remoter and poorer areas are less likely to have schools and those that do exist are generally worse-equipped than those in richer and urban areas. Unless some form of quota or state subsidy system is in operation then progression beyond primary level for children from the remote and poor areas and settlements is extremely difficult.

Table 5.7   Gender and access to education in developing countries, 1965–85

Country	Percentage of age group enrolled in education							
	Primary				Secondary			
	Male		Female		Male		Female	
	1965	1985	1965	1985	1965	1985	1965	1985
Low-income countries (excluding China and India)	58	75	31	56	13	28	4	16
China	–	132	–	114	–	45	–	32
India	89	107	57	76	41	45	13	24
Somalia	16	32	4	18	4	23	1	12
Sudan	37	58	21	41	6	22	2	17
Middle-income countries	92	109	79	101	26	57	19	51
Indonesia	79	121	65	116	18	45	7	34
Guatemala	55	80	45	69	10	17	7	16
Brazil	109	108	108	99	16	–	16	–
South Korea	103	96	99	96	44	97	25	91
Industrial market countries	107	101	106	101	65	91	61	92

Source: The World Bank (1987, 1988) *World Development Report*
Notes: In a few cases figures in the table are not for the specific year but for the nearest year available.
Figures in excess of 100 per cent indicate the enrolment of younger and older children from outside the specified age groups into that particular level of education

Regimes espousing some form of Marxism-Leninism as the state ideology seem to have performed better than other Third World countries in educational provision. Not only have they supplied more education but also it appears to be more equitably distributed (Groth, 1987). This also applies to the sphere of female participation in education. As we saw in our earlier discussion of gender, while disparities between male and female enrolments have been lessening, full parity for women is a long way off in many Third World countries (see Table 5.7). With questions of educational efficiency and productivity moving to centre stage, policy-makers, who are anxious to contain the spiralling costs of education, may even show a decreasing concern with the education of women. In order to ensure that women get a fair deal! It will be necessary to design specific policies on women's education. This does not mean inventing yet more courses on sewing, cooking, nutrition and anything else in the domestic sphere. Kelly (1987) has suggested a three-pronged attack involving schools being made more available and accessible to women (e.g. experiments in scheduling and pacing the school day), enabling women actually to attend school (e.g. by introducing appropriate technologies designed to lighten women's and girls' household tasks) and linking education to workforce opportunities for women (e.g. programmes to remove discriminatory practices in employment and wages).

The large increases in education enrolments have not been without costs – large financial ones. More classrooms are required each year, more teachers must be trained, more teachers must then be paid, more equipment is necessary and becomes more expensive the higher the rung on the educational ladder, and more administrators are recruited to organise it all. All this requires more money. Mounting costs of education have claimed progressively larger shares of government expenditure. Education is frequently the single biggest item in the budgets of the Third World countries, accounting for up to 20 per cent of total public expenditure. These percentages are often more than double those found in the industrial market economies. The cost problem is intensified as countries attempt to expand secondary and later tertiary institutions. The cost of educating a student increases dramatically as one moves up the educational ladder from primary to tertiary. For example, in Papua New Guinea it was calculated that 3000 university students were consuming the same amount of public money as 160,000 primary school students.

In the present era of fiscal restraint policy-makers are faced with difficult choices. Cutting back educational expenditure is unpopular with the public. Higher levels of education in increasing amounts is often equated with development. If teachers are well organised, their large numbers and strategic locations as opinion-makers can make them a formidable political force. Equally formidable might be the claims of other ministries and departments who wish to increase their share of the expenditure cake and see the huge appropriations for education as a possible area for cost-saving. A recent report claims that cost-cutting in education has been underway for some time with expenditure per head on education declining in 33 per cent of African countries and 66 per cent of Latin American countries since the end of the 1970s (*New Internationalist*, February 1988).

One final item of cost concerns the international brain-drain which has seen many highly-educated personnel from Third World societies migrate to industrial countries where they secure better remuneration. Medical personnel are the obvious example. In such cases, there is the allegation that Third World countries not only lose valuable skills but actually subsidise the developed countries by paying for the training of the skilled personnel who migrate. But some countries actively encourage temporary labour migration in an effort to earn much-needed foreign currency via remittances and to avoid the political discontent which domestic oversupply of skilled workers might create. The Philippines is the leading example, sending hundreds of thousands of technically-skilled workers (from doctors to bulldozer repairers) to the Middle East or anywhere else that will pay for such skills. Annual remittances for the Philippines from this source are believed to be in excess of US$1 billion.

While most seem to agree that education and economic development are linked there is considerable confusion about the precise nature of this relationship. Developed countries have universal primary and secondary education and large tertiary sectors. Educational enrolment patterns in the NICs are increasingly mirroring these. But does pouring money into education necessarily produce development? Historical evidence indicates that high educational levels have not been a prerequisite for the onset of rapid economic growth. Universal primary education came to Great Britain only in 1870, a century after the beginning of the industrial revolution. But conditions facing Great Britain were much different then than those confronting the developing nations now. The World Bank (1987, p. 63) maintains that 'lack of education is a greater obstacle to industrialization and development than lack of physical assets', although cautions that investment in education must be complemented by investment in appropriate physical assets and technological knowledge. Others have expressed concern that investment in education has created the phenomenon of educated unemployment. Such investment only creates jobs in education but does little if anything to solve the problems of unemployment and underemployment which beset Third World countries. It leads to the serious ailment described as the 'diploma disease' (Dore, 1976). Education becomes obtaining qualifications in order to get a job rather than learning to do a job. That the content of curricula might be inappropriate for development may escape the policy-makers. But popular pressure creates greater demand for more of the same. Qualifications are needed to secure the highly desirable formal sector positions. With educational institutions producing an excess of graduates a process of educational inflation is encouraged. Employers demand certificates of higher and higher levels as job entry requirements – instead of grade 6 for bus conductors, grade 12 and perhaps even university degrees become necessary! Marginal improvements in productivity are inadequate compensation for the extra financial investment in the education needed to obtain the higher qualifications.

The effects of education on rural communities have been hotly debated for some time. One school of thought argues that education encourages the migration of the brightest and most able from rural to urban areas. The education they receive is often irrelevant for rural life and rural development and encourages them to seek employment opportunities in urban areas. This thesis finds support in the consistently strong correlations between educational attainment and migration from rural areas; i.e. the higher a person's level of education the more likely he or she is to migrate. Whether this represents a loss of the brightest and best is somewhat contentious. There is some data which points to circularity in migration, i.e. migrants returning home with new skills and even capital after a period in urban employment. Hill (1986, p. 134) believes that the haphazard selection methods of higher education means that the educated villagers are the lucky rather than the cleverer ones. Thus, she contends that there is no validity in the argument that the brightest migrate leaving the unenterprising so that everybody suffers more than before.

The evidence on whether formal education can or does contribute towards rural development is inconclusive. Thompson (1981, pp. 118–23) cites African case studies which show little or no relationship between farm productivity and schooling. By contrast, Orivel (1983, pp. 26–7) claims solid evidence for the positive effects of formal education on production, productivity and farmers' income. He notes that 'better-educated farmers make a better choice of inputs, combine them more effectively and judge the appropriate quantity better.' Their education facilitates communication, gives them a better vocabulary, enables them to establish superior contacts and allows access to written information. A Kenyan case study by Moock (1981) came up with a positive correlation between a farmer's output and a farmer having received four or more years of formal education. This coincided with the findings of a World Bank study of twenty low-income countries, which claimed that four or more years of schooling produced an average 6.9 per cent increase in productivity. Whether such productivity increases are directly at-tributable to formal schooling is a matter of conjecture.

Radical educational theorists have argued that formal schooling is in fact a mode of oppression, an activity which prevents development from taking place (Illich, 1972; Freire, 1972). It is an ideological device used by the dominant classes to justify and maintain inequi-table social orders. Students are receptacles which the teacher fills with the required knowledge. Invention, inquiry and creativity are discouraged. According to Illich the answer (for both rich and poor countries) is to deschool. These dehumanising institutions (schools) should be abolished. Any institutional part of the education system should be facilitative and not directive. One should choose what one wishes to learn and not be told what one has to learn. Freire believed that the prime goal of education was to raise critical consciousness so that people could 'perceive social, political, and economic contradic-tions, and take action against the oppressive elements of reality' (Freire, 1972, p. 15). While agreeing with the basic observations of the radical critique, Dore (1976, p. 136) has noted that education has to be more than just raising critical awareness. People need to acquire knowledge and learn skills in order to escape from poverty. Mere recognition of an iniquitous state of affairs through conscien-tisation will not provide those skills and knowledge. Dore also pointed to certain countries (e.g. China) where schools taught conformity to the existing order, the value of hard work and practical agricultural techniques. In those countries, such educa-tional activity was contributing to measurable improvements in material livelihood for the majority of rural dwellers. Later writers who draw on the ideas of the radical critique of Third World education have certainly acted on some of Dore's suggestions and have produced books which combine the political action of raising critical awareness with practical applications. For example, there are excellent books on health education (Werner, 1978; Werner and Bower, 1982). They provide a wealth of clearly and imaginatively-expressed advice and instructions on diagnosing illnesses and treat-ing them, teaching methods and teaching aids all aimed at the villager and village-level health worker. They stress that implement-ing measures to improve the health of the poor constitutes a political challenge to local elites, dominant classes, government institutions and big business.

The approach of the radical educationalists is one which champions the use of non-formal education, i.e. organised instruction which takes place outside the normal curricula and workings of conventional schools, colleges and universities. But this extension approach to education and training need not be one which comes into conflict with government authority. Indeed, most non-formal/ extension activity is conducted by government agencies. Village health workers, business development officers, agricultural extension personnel (see also Chapter 6) and adult literacy teachers are among the thousands of non-formal educators operating in the Third World. Governments view non-formal activities as complementary to the formal education system. In some national development strategies, non-formal education can be awarded an extremely important role on the grounds that it is both a cheap and effective method of education for development, especially in rural areas. However, there is much criticism from rural people, politicians, academics and extension workers themselves (e.g. Benor and Harrison, 1977, pp. 6–9; Coombs and Ahmed, 1974). The training of extension workers can often be inadequate and outdated. The lack of knowledge of extension teaching skills (as distinct from specialist technical knowledge) is common among extension workers. Specialists (e.g. agriculturalists) may be assigned multi-purpose roles (e.g. agriculture, health, statistical surveys, legal advice, etc.) which they may be ill-equipped to handle and which dilute their efforts for rural development. There are often poor ties between extension workers and research activities. Conversely, specialist bias can obliterate awareness of 'the mutually reinforcing nature of the linkages of poverty' (Chambers, 1981, p. 9). Communication of recommendations from research findings to the field is badly-developed while the flow of information on field problems in the other direction is usually as bad. Extension agents are often asked to look after large numbers of people spread over large areas while they are given poor housing, low pay and little incentive to perform well. The co-ordination of extension work between different government organisations can be poor, leading to duplication and wasteful resource utilisation. The directive approach can produce a lack of villager co-operation. The formal educational training of the extension worker may lead to biases against the informally-acquired skills and knowledge of rural people. The poor are not sought out by many extension workers, who prefer to deal with better-educated and better-off members of the community. Thus, poverty remains unperceived and out of sight.

Agricultural extension workers are invariably male and have failed
to provide advice to the females, who are the major agricultural
producers in many African and Pacific countries. While there are
many individual non-formal education success stories where people
have improved their living standards by the adoption of new or
modified practices, there are vast areas and poor populations in the
Third World which have yet to experience the beneficial impact of
effective non-formal education. Improvements in organisational and
technical efficiency, coupled with better conditions of service and
teaching methods, could considerably increase non-formal education's contribution to development. But there is always the problem
stressed in the radical critique – that actions taken to liberate people
from poverty will clash with the interests of dominant classes, elites
and institutions. As the latter groups are well-represented in government they may take steps to ensure that non-formal education is
depoliticised or remains in bad shape. Thus, the potential threat of
non-formal education to the status quo is negated.

THE ENVIRONMENT

In Chapter 3 we encountered ecodevelopment amongst the neo-
populist approaches to development. A central concern of this
approach was to ensure that the process of development did not
result in environmental degradation and destruction. Initially, Third
World leaders were not impressed, suspecting that the West's new-
found concern with the environment was another neo-colonial plot
designed to hold back developmental initiatives. Unfortunately, the
ecodevelopers were correct in their assertions that the environment
in the Third World was under sustained attack and was not holding
out. Governments, often at the prompting of international agencies
such as the United Nations Environment Programme (UNEP), have
gradually come to accept that environmental problems abound and
that more attention and resources should be devoted to their solution. They have begun to appreciate that the environment and
development are intimately and irrevocably interrelated, 'since any
impact on man's environment also influences his state of wellbeing
or welfare' (Bartelmus, 1986, p. 19). But one should not run away
with the idea that an all-powerful environmental movement is

Table 5.8 Major environmental problems in developing countries

Environment	Problem	Example
Natural environment		
Air	Air pollution in major cities	Of the world's largest cities, Mexico City has highest lead content in its petrol and its people
Land	Soil erosion and degradation	One third of cropland in China and India suffers excessive soil loss
	Desertification	60,000 sq. km. affected annually
Water	Freshwater shortage and pollution	Per capita availability of water for human consumption to decline by 50 per cent by the year 2000
	Pollution of ocean and coastal waters	Washing of tanker tanks puts 1million tons of oil into the sea each year
Fauna and Flora	Deforestation	Each year a tropical forest area the size of Great Britain is destroyed
	Species endangered or lost	10–12 per cent of the world's wild plants and animal life to disappear by the year 2000
Ecosystems	Pollution of coastal ecosystem	Discharge of sewage, industrial effluents and chemicals from agriculture into coastal waters
Natural disasters	Floods, droughts, storms, earthquakes, volcanic eruptions	In 1984–5, 30 million people in Africa affected by drought
Man-made environment		
Bioproductive	Loss and degradation of arable land	Irrigation can cause salinisation and waterlogging thus reducing soil productivity
	Pesticides	2 million people poisoned annually
	Overfishing	World fishing catches per person have declined by 15 per cent between 1970–85
Human settlement	Squatter and slum settlements	One third of the urban population live in overcrowded makeshift shelters lacking basic sanitation and clean water
Health	Malnutrition and disease	One child in four is seriously undernourished
	Work-induced illness	Backaches, eye problems, headaches, skin disorders in electronics industries of Asia

Source: Adapted from Bartelmus (1986) with additional information from various sources

sweeping the Third World. There are many actors who by design or the sheer necessity of survival continue to inflict injury on the environment. For example, transnational corporations remove vast quantities of resources with little or no thought for the environmental consequences, while at the other end of the scale poor rural dwellers accelerate the diminution of forest resources in an increasingly desperate search for necessary cooking fuel. A few examples of environmental degradation will demonstrate the magnitude of the issues facing policy-makers (for a summary see Table 5.8).

Forests are vitally important as 'they provide lumber, fuel and habitat for a multitude of species; they also protect soils and regulate water balances and climates' (Bartelmus, 1986, p. 25). Unfortunately, they are being destroyed at an alarming rate. Each year an area of tropical forest the size of Great Britain is removed from the face of the earth. Rapidly expanding populations make an extremely heavy demand on wood for cooking and heating. It is reported that over 100 million people are experiencing 'acute firewood shortage' (Lanly, 1982) while the UNDP maintains that twenty-three countries have already run out of firewood. Multinational and domestic logging companies continue to remove enormous quantities of lumber for industrial uses, e.g. furniture, coffins, paper. There have been frequent examples of logging in banned areas, overlogging and failure to meet replanting schedules. Transfer pricing is common, so that Third World countries can actually end up subsidising the destruction of their own environment. People living in the logging areas receive scant payment, if any. For example, in the Trans-Gogol area of Papua New Guinea the Jant Company of Japan have clear-felled (i.e. removed all trees) for processing in their woodchip mill. The local people have been disappointed by meagre financial returns, the failure of the company to replant as promised and the destruction of an environment which provided them with many of their vital subsistence needs (De'Ath, 1980). The accelerated shrinkage of forests can also be attributed to the financial and legal environments created by politicians to promote development. Hecht (1985) has shown how the promotion of the livestock sector in Amazonia has taken place in an investment climate which positively encourages environmental destruction. In effect, the Brazilian government is subsidising the destruction of the Amazon and, if Binswanger (1989) is correct, what is required to save the rain forest is not more government intervention but a removal of the tax and credit subsidies that distort market forces in ways that make deforestation a profitable enterprise.

Sometimes the accusing finger can be pointed at nature itself. Thus, the great fire of Borneo, regarded by some as the twentieth century's biggest ecological disaster, devastated 3.6 million hectares of rainforest in Kalimantan in 1982–3. The cyclical El Niño phenomenon, which brings exceptionally dry weather, was blamed along with nomadic shifting cultivators practising slash and burn techniques. The same culprits have been officially identified in the latest (1987–8) round of forest fires reportedly raging around Indonesia (*Inside Indonesia*, April 1988). But if the culprits have been around for centuries why are they creating such devastation only now? The El Niño may be intensifying while logging may be forcing shifting agriculturalists on to less land and making them use it more frequently. Furthermore, research has found that while fires in primary tropical forest may allow up to 50 per cent of trees to survive, logged-over forest, where there is much litter on the ground, burns hotter and longer setting off long-lasting peat and coal fires under the surface. The miniscule resources devoted to controlling these devastating fires in Indonesia demonstrate both a paucity of government resources and officialdom's reluctance to take concerted action on environmental problems which may have limited short-term political and economic impact.

A second major problem concerns the degradation of land and its loss in productivity through soil erosion, salinisation, alkalinisation, waterlogging and chemical degradation. Commenting on Ethiopia, the UNDP notes that 'uninterrupted cultivation, primitive farming practices, uncontrolled clearing of natural vegetation and heavy overgrazing have transformed much of the country's highlands into bare landscapes, all but destroyed by erosion' (UNDP, 1987, p. 5). Some 2,000 tonnes of fertile topsoil per square kilometre are being washed away by rain and lost each year in Ethiopia. When land is degraded in semi-arid or arid areas desertification is likely. UNDP estimates that almost a quarter of the earth's land area is subject to some form of desertification. In parts of the southern Sahara the desert is overrunning farms, villages and towns at the alarming rate of 16 km a year. Irrigation tends to boost the salt content of water returning to streams and rivers. Chemicals, in the form of insecticides, pesticides and fertilisers, appear to be wreaking considerable havoc. While DDT was initially hailed as a life-saver for the Third

World, especially for its undoubted success in decimating *Anopheles* mosquito populations in places where malaria was endemic (e.g. Sri Lanka), it has come under closer scrutiny for its harmful effects in recent years. Resistant strains of *Anopheles* are multiplying in many malarial areas while there is concern about toxic build-ups affecting man and the rest of the natural environment. It has been estimated by the UN that approximately 2 million people are poisoned by pesticides each year and that 400,000 die. New studies indicate that these figures may be underestimated. Poor farmers are especially prone to buying cheap and highly toxic chemicals and rarely wear protective clothing. Thus, in the Philippines it has been estimated that 80 per cent of rice growers have been 'poisoned' in the last five years while a '27 per cent increase in death' in Luzon has been held to correlate with the use of insecticides (*South*, May 1988).

Such pollution is not confined to rural areas, as any visitor to the Third World knows. The vast urban metropolises face increasing problems of pollution. Millions of inhabitants of squatter settlements and slums live in overcrowded, insanitary conditions, in poor housing with inadequate access to clean water supplies. Even in the NICs the environmental problems refuse to go away. For example, in Hong Kong, which translates as fragrant harbour, there is a nasty smell coming from the water these days (*South*, April 1988). Hydrogen sulphide is being emitted from an excess of sewage produced by 6 million residents, 2 million tourists, several million chickens and half a million pigs. Coral is dying, beaches have been closed, red-tides and fishkills have become more frequent, and heavy-metal contamination has been found in oysters. Action is, however, being taken and co-ordinated by an environmental protection department which aims to drastically reduce this serious pollution problem. In addition to public works currently in process, a twenty-year disposal strategy is being formulated. The latest pollution scandal to emerge is the dumping in developing countries of toxic and radioactive waste from industrial countries. The media seems only recently to have latched on to this trade which exploits the lack of environmental legislation and operates at the fringes of legality, yet it appears to have been going on for 'decades' (*South*, August 1988).

A final concern is that environmental destruction reduces the species of flora and fauna. For example, it is estimated that between 10 and 20 per cent of the world's wild plants and animal life will have disappeared by the end of the century. The rapidly shrinking tropical rainforests will account for most of the disappearances. Man's pursuit of profit will greatly help. There is a thriving trade in endangered and banned species from Third World countries. An ornamental panda skin fetches US$50,000 in Taiwan while powdered rhino horn (allegedly an aphrodisiac) is literally worth its weight in gold. Governments are either powerless to do anything about this US$4–6 billion annual trade or find more urgent priorities for their scarce resources. The elimination of different species goes beyond important ethical and aesthetic considerations. It represents a loss of potentially valuable genetic resources. Many writers have noted the usefulness of wild plants and animals in such fields as medicine, food, pest control and the restoration of ecosystems.

Our brief survey clearly demonstrates that while environmental degradation and destruction can be caused by natural disasters (e.g. drought, earthquakes, tropical storms) man has proved far more effective in inflicting damage on the environment. The effects of natural disasters have been intensified by human works. For example, widespread felling of trees on Himalayan watersheds means that soil is exposed and in times of heavy rains, severe erosion of topsoil occurs. The lack of forest cover makes for rapid, highly erosive run-off, which then causes siltation and flooding downstream. We should thus be examining the productive systems which seem to foster such destructive practices. Redclift (1984) has argued from a radical political economy perspective that environmental breakdown proceeds because of development. The breakdown is rooted in prevailing social and economic institutions (especially those of capitalism) which militate against the poor. The 'mindless commitment to economic growth' is identified as a major contributor to the environmental degradation. While some might disagree with Redclift's Marxist methods he is none the less correct in offering explanation of environmental degradation in terms of the political, social and economic organisation of society. The environment should not be depoliticised.

Many of the technological solutions to environmental problems are either already available or could be found through further research. Simple, centuries-old indigenous techniques can be employed. For example, in poverty-stricken Burkina Faso, rows of heavy stones placed across slopes along contour lines slow down run-off and so reduce erosion. Crop yields have been increased by up to 50 per cent. Modern science and traditional knowledge can be combined in Integrated Pest Management (IPM) which seeks to minimise the use of chemical pesticides and maximise the use of natural controls (e.g. altering planting or harvesting times, crop rotation, mixed cropping). In China's Jiangsu province, cotton farmers have adopted a complex IPM system and so reduced pesticide usage by 90 per cent. Mexican farmers have utilised a species of wasp (23 billion of them in 1983) to control pests on 500,000 hectares of sugar cane, fruit and vegetables. Scientists are now taking a close interest in the neem tree in India as it appears to bristle with chemical weapons which might be employed to help other plants fight against their enemies.

So what are international organisations and Third World governments doing to combat environmental problems? The UNDP claims that its involvement in environmental issues has been 'serious, substantial and sustained', involving US$1 billion spread over 1800 projects between 1972–86. This is not, however, a large amount considering the magnitude of the problem. The World Bank's increasing interest in conserving natural resources was reflected in the creation of an environmental department in 1987. At the time of writing, the World Bank is considering concessional financing to offset environmental protection costs in projects that it funds. It is also negotiating with UN agencies and other interested parties on the formulation of a Tropical Forests Action Plan. This proposal aims to achieve a balance between the harvesting and planting of trees by the year 2000 and could involve an expenditure of US$150 billion. At present, for every ten trees that are cut down only one is planted. But critics are suspicious of the World Bank's role in forestry projects and wonder whether it will be commercial forestry which reaps the benefits. Could it all go the way of a government-sponsored project in Karnataka state in India? In this project, local people were to acquire both fuel and fodder from the planting of eucalyptus, but most of the trees harvested ended up as raw material for a company manufacturing rayon and pulp. To compound the problems of the poor farmers, the new trees drew an excess of moisture from the land leading to lower food crop yields. As we shall see in the next chapter, it takes more than good intentions to formulate a policy and transform it into a coherent plan of action.

All Third World governments now declare their commitment to environmentally-sound development, but Bartelmus (1986, p. 65) believes that for most this is only lip-service to the 'integrated approach to environment and development'. Environmental objectives are simply added to the list of national development plan objectives and subsequently relegated to a lowly status or even forgotten. The medium-term horizon of such plans works against long-term environmental planning. Institutions set up to formulate and implement environmental policy are often hamstrung by limited resources and powers. Inter-sectoral co-ordination of environmental matters is particularly undeveloped 'because data gaps and institutional barriers and jealousies prevent interdepartmental cooperation' (Bartelmus, 1986, p. 67). At the project level, matters have been improving as 'environmental impact assessment' (EIA) becomes more widespread and in some cases mandatory. The EIA predicts the effect of a project on man's health and wellbeing, both of which depend on the wellbeing of the ecosystem. For a project to be given the go-ahead it must be seen to be environmentally acceptable. Previous neglect of such considerations has led to the creation of new environmental problems which can carry an enormous economic cost. For example, if a mine is allowed to discharge waste into a river this may kill fish in the river and along the coast. Siltation may cause flooding, destroying crops and infrastructure and the economy of thousands of people living near the mine may be severely disrupted.

While policy-makers are obviously paying more attention to environmental matters as they come to appreciate the interelationship between the environment and development, much remains to be done. Finding the imagination and political will to formulate and implement environmentally-oriented policies will continue to prove difficult despite the new-found concern with the environment in the Third World. Financial resources are fiercely contested and the environment still has too few spokesmen of power and status. There are always more pressing problems for governments to deal with. Resource conservation may also clash with the desire to maximise resource exploitation – and there are many persons and institutions willing to accept short-term gains and forget about long-term consequences. This leads us back to the central problem of policy-making and the environment, that it is not simply a technical and legal matter of saving the environment from man. The political economy which man has constructed appears to lead to environmental destruction and degradation. The present challenge is perhaps as Redclift (1984, p. 130) alleges, 'to alter the global economy in which our appetites press on the "outer limits" of resources'.

CONCLUSION: DEVELOPMENT POLICIES AND POVERTY

The materials presented in this chapter have reviewed development policies in five particular areas and commented on the results achieved. Although different goals have been set for these different policy areas, the discussion has shown that, at least in theory, if successful these policies should have contributed to the alleviation of poverty – a central objective of development. Industrial and agricultural policies should have increased output, raised incomes and created new employment opportunities; slower rates of population growth should lower dependency ratios, permit governments to improve the levels of services they provide and reduce unemployment and underemployment; education policies should produce a more productive labour force, better able to care for its families' interests; and environmental policies should help to ensure that the achievements of development are sustainable and that adverse consequences are mitigated. In our conclusion we examine the available evidence about the impact that development policies have had on the welfare of the poor and comment on the major issues facing those responsible for formulating policies to eradicate poverty in the 1990s.

Ahluwalia (1974), using 1969 data, estimated the incidence of poverty at the end of the first two 'development decades'. He calculated that 578 million people, 48 per cent of the total population he studied, fell below an 'arbitrary' poverty line of US$75 annual per capita income. In a different study the International Labour Office (ILO) proposed that in 1972 some 1200 million people in the non-communist developing world, 71 per cent of the population, were 'seriously poor', while 706 million, 39 per cent of the total, were 'destitute' (ILO, 1977, p. 22).

Clearly the early development decades had not managed to make significant inroads into the alleviation of poverty and the 1970s were characterised by calls for policies that sought to tackle poverty directly (Bhagwati, 1988) by placing a greater emphasis on 'basic needs' and targeting domestic and international resources on the poor. While the World Bank (1980, p. 35) was involved in financing many of these targeted initiatives, it maintained its ultimate faith in economic growth and declared that poverty and GNP per capita were strongly correlated. It was, however, admitted that some low-income countries had good basic needs records (e.g. China and Sri

Lanka) while some middle-income countries had poor indicators for certain basic needs (e.g. Morocco and Ivory Coast had literacy rates below those of many low-income countries).

As the 1980s dawned the international agencies were a little more optimistic about achievements in the war against poverty. Although a colossal 780 million people in developing countries (excluding China and other centrally-planned economies) lived in absolute poverty available evidence indicated that the proportion of people in absolute poverty had actually declined (World Bank, 1980). There had been striking advances in life expectancy and literacy rates and evidence that in a number of countries population growth rates were slowing down. Although monumental problems remained and the eradication of poverty was nowhere in sight, the policy-makers did seem to be on the right track. Eight years later in 1988 the World Bank has no good news to report from the poverty front. Poverty is on the rise. Between 1970 and 1980 the number of people with inadequate diets in developing countries (excluding China) increased from 650 million to 730 million. In twenty-one out of thirty-five low-income developing countries the daily calorie supply per capita was less in 1985 than in 1965. 'Scattered information from individual developing countries confirms the general impression of deteriorating social conditions in many developing countries' (World Bank, 1988, p. 4). Increases in the numbers of people below the poverty line were reported for countries such as the Philippines, Brazil, Jamaica and Ghana. Between 1979 and 1983 life expectancy declined in nine sub-Saharan African countries. Real wages have dropped and growth in employment has faltered. The scenario is grim. Unserviceable levels of national debt, mounting external and internal expenditure imbalances, rising inflation and a host of other macroeconomic ills confront developing countries and make the living conditions of the poor even more difficult.

Many developing country governments are currently implementing or negotiating stabilisation and structural adjustment programmes under the auspices of international financial institutions. Such programmes almost inevitably mean that there is less public money available for investment in satisfying the basic needs of the poorest. There has been a renewed stress in international policy circles on the wisdom of following an indirect route (i.e. stabilising the economy and then pursuing rapid economic growth in a liberalised economic framework) to poverty alleviation. The proponents of this view point to the East Asian miracle economies as proof that rapid and sustained economic growth can beat poverty. However, whether this experience can be replicated in other countries is highly doubtful (see p. 111, earlier in this chapter). Concern about the short and medium term human consequences of adjustment are now being widely voiced and UNICEF has spearheaded an alternative approach to assist governments to stabilise their economies (Cornia, Jolly and Stewart, 1988). This calls for structural adjustment with a human face. It recognises that the macroeconomic problems facing developing countries must be overcome by adjustment but argues that accompanying policy measures – such as policies to support the productivity of small scale producers, further investment in low cost primary health care, rural works programmes and nutritional interventions – should also be pursued so that the poor and vulnerable do not have to bear the bulk of the costs of adjustment. Internal IMF publications (Heller, 1988) have begun to argue this case and point out that adjustment policy may need to be balanced by 'compensatory policies' to help the poor to maintain their already low levels of living during adjustment policy implementation. Perhaps these well-substantiated cases will influence the major financial institutions, although it could be argued that they may modify their approaches for other reasons. In a fascinating paper Nelson (1984) examines the political economy of stabilisation and points out that when the power relationships that permit the leaders and elites of developing countries to maintain their positions are analysed the groups that dominate policy-making are often unwilling to adopt orthodox stabilisation programmes because of the domestic political risks that this engenders.

The extent to which political leaders depend on patron–client networks thus bears directly on their ability to implement stabilisation [and adjustment] measures . . . if a politician's main means of building and maintaining political support is the direction of the jobs, contracts, licences, foreign exchange, subsidized goods and services, and other benefits to his political friends, and away from his political enemies, he cannot lightly relinquish such control to price mechanisms that do not distinguish supporter from opponent (Nelson, 1984, p. 994).

There is some evidence that the World Bank and IMF are paying greater attention to the political ramifications of their policy prescriptions. Adjustment in the 1990s may take on a more human face, not because the key actors in setting conditions believe that this is the best policy, but because they believe it is required if adjustment is to be politically feasible.

Whatever the outcome of the present macro-level policy debate – whether to emphasise outright liberalisation or whether to adopt a more cautious approach of liberalisation, accompanied by limited compensatory policies that require continued government intervention to support the poor – decisions are likely to result in proposals for development projects, the cutting edge of development. It is these, and the role that sociologists can play in their formulation, that are the subject of the next chapter.

6

APPLIED SOCIOLOGY AND
DEVELOPMENT PLANNING

This chapter examines the case that sociologists concerned with social change in developing countries should adopt a more applied stance and involve themselves directly in development policy-making and planning. It incorporates the work of social anthropologists, human geographers and other non-economic social scientists. They have much in common with applied development sociologists and at times their activities are indistinguishable from those of sociologists. A particular focus for this chapter is the role that sociologists can play in the design of development projects.

The argument that sociology should take a more applied role in development interventions has been forcefully made by Cernea, a rural sociologist who works for the World Bank.

Sociologists have to face the nuts and bolts of development activities, to roll up their sleeves and deal with the mundane, pragmatic questions of translating plans into realities in a sociologically sound manner. They need to link data generation, action-oriented research, social analysis, design for social action, and evaluation into a continuum, and thus stretch sociology's contributions far beyond simple pronouncements (Cernea, 1985, p. 10).

The case for the consideration of the social and cultural aspects of development interventions is not a recent concern. Indeed, the colonial administrations of the early part of this century employed anthropologists and ethnologists to generate data and provide advice on native institutions and land tenure, though it must be pointed out that their goals were essentially imperialist and not developmental (Lackner, 1973). Over a quarter of a century ago the distinguished economist Hoselitz (1960, p. 26), discussing the nature of development planning, argued that 'the plan embrace not only prescriptions for economic adjustments but also for the channeling of associated cultural and social change'. In the late 1960s, as the initial disappointing experiences with development planning began to be catalogued, the failure to take account of the 'human factor' was constantly cited (Apthorpe, 1970, p. 7). The need for sociological involvement in the planning process has continued with the 'recognition that repeated failures have plagued development programmes which were sociologically ill-informed and ill-conceived'. This reluctant recognition leads to increased interest in identifying and addressing the socio-cultural variables of projects (Cernea, 1985, p. 3).

Perversely, the recognition that social and cultural factors merit serious consideration in development planning has not as yet led to the evolution of a praxis for applied development sociology, nor to the institutionalisation of sociologists or social anthropologists in the planning process of governments and development agencies. Some non-government development organisations and North European official aid agencies are exceptions to this situation. Although some have interpreted this state of affairs as being due to the exclusion of sociologists from the practice of development, it is necessary to recognise that a variety of factors, both external and internal to the discipline, are related to the slow growth of applied development sociology.

Externally, one can point to such factors as the general ignorance about what sociologists could contribute, allied to a tendency of technical project personnel, including many economists, to assume that social and cultural features are ephemeral, intangible and of little importance in comparison to the physical, economic and logistical elements of a project. For example, recent research on a project in Papua New Guinea (Hulme, 1989) has documented the way in which planners thought in great detail about the selection of the most appropriate rubber clone to plant (a technical matter), but very little about the people who were to be selected to grow the rubber (a socio-political matter). Yet they were fully aware that no rubber clone could reach maturity without human assistance. A second obstacle is the erroneous impression, held by many, that sociologists are, *ipso facto*, purveyors of left-wing ideologies (Hall and Midgley, 1988, p. 3) or, as an agricultural expert once told us, 'a bunch of pinkos'. While the earlier chapters have shown the interest that sociologists have had in Marxist and neo-Marxist ideas they have also shown the fierce criticism that surrounds these theories and point to the fact that a personal belief in such perspectives is no more likely for a sociologist than for any other social scientist.

More grounded in reality are the fears of policy-makers and administrators that sociological and anthropological interventions are often likely to reach conclusions indicating that conventional project approaches need to be dramatically modified or, alternatively, implemented on longer time scales than domestic political considerations and the budgetary schedules of aid agencies regard as convenient. As Hall (1988, p. 40) expresses it, 'the fear of dissent' is greater from sociologists and anthropologists than it is from technical specialists. This is a problem, but this very fear of dissent provides a concrete illustration of the need for new professional inputs in the development planning field.

Within the discipline there are also factors that militate against practical involvement in decision-making, not least the fact that most sociologists have little to contribute to planning and policy-making agencies. In general, there is a lack of relevant training in sociology (Hall, 1988, p. 39). The concepts and theories which effective involvement requires have been given scant attention and are poorly developed. Many sociology courses give the student very limited preparation in basic social science skills (data collection methodologies, data analysis, results presentation) and produce graduate students who are economically illiterate and consequently unable to take part in multi-disciplinary development planning teams. Undergraduate and postgraduate students may be proficient in providing general explanations of poverty in developing countries, but how many would be able rapidly to identify 'the poor' in the context of a specific development proposal? Sociology and anthropology are caught in a catch-22 situation in which the present lack of involvement of the disciplines in development planning ensures that the training of the next generation of social scientists is inappropriate for practical tasks. As Sutherland (1987, p. 7) expresses it, there has been 'a lack of commitment from a sufficient number of anthropologists and sociologists to become actively involved themselves, or even to encourage their students to become involved, in applied social research'.

Equally problematical is the resolution of ethical questions. It can be argued that it is only by non-involvement in policy-making and planning that a social scientist can maintain intellectual integrity and be 'free of the normative constraints imposed by his [/her] clients' (Horesh, 1981, p. 617). This is fine if one defines the role of the social sciences purely in terms of analysing and explaining social phenomena, but surely the discipline's callings are also to change existing situations? If they are not, then decision-makers will not be far off the mark to view social scientists as being prone to 'idle academicism' (Hunter, 1969, p. 27) and perhaps to treat them as idle academics!

A third factor, related to the previous paragraph, concerns the debate about whether the findings of sociological enquiry should be applied to society through an 'enlightenment model', that is, through passive dissemination to policy-makers, planners and the general public via formal and non-formal education and the media, or by an 'engineering model', that is, by the direct application of research findings in specific practical contexts (Janowitz, 1970). In contemporary sociology, the discussion of the appropriateness of these different models has centred on the differences between them and has generally come down in favour of the enlightenment model. This has been unfortunate as it has meant that those involved in practical development activities (sociologists among others) are seen as 'negative academics' (Chambers, 1983, pp. 30–3) who 'look for what has gone wrong' rather than what might go right and have a preoccupation with historical events rather than contemporary or projected events. It has also tended to lead to the concealment of a possible third model – that is, a dual approach in which the application of findings is through both 'enlightenment' and 'engineering' and in which complementarities between the two models are built upon. Effective social engineering can only occur in the presence of conceptual and theoretical supports that are the products of an enlightenment model. Conversely, the products of an enlightenment approach are sharpened, tested and refined by the actions and discoveries of those involved in the direct application of sociological findings to development interventions. While there are numerous reasons for the present dominance of economists in the professional sphere of public (and private) sector decision-making processes, surely one of the most apparent is the way in which economists have vastly expanded their theoretical frameworks and practical methodologies by the persistent interaction of pure and applied approaches to economic analysis? Practice requires the generation of theory and theory is nourished by the findings of practice. An applied stance does not entail sociologists becoming naively positive about development interventions, nor does it mean that the discipline has to generate standardised planning packages that can be utilised in any culture, or mix of cultures, at any time (the sorts of products that economists have generated). It does mean, however, that the variables that sociologists recognise as being fundamental to the understanding of society – the values of different groups and how these influence behaviour, social organisation, family structure, differentiation, legitimation, cultural constructs, status, participation in society – would have a greater opportunity for inclusion in development decision-making agenda, rather than being avoided or ignored because of their apparent intangibility and the failure of any discipline to make an effective case for the systematic consideration of such factors in development decision-making.

One response to the need for a sociological contribution to development planning has centred on the concept of 'social planning' (Apthorpe, 1970). Social planning gradually evolved in the 1970s, although it must be noted that this is a sub-discipline which is only partially established and faces many problems. Firstly, there is the question of whether it has disciplinary status at all. As the social planners Hardiman and Midgley (1982, pp. 5–6) note, 'there is still some confusion about the academic content of social planning . . . [and] it may be argued that without theory and armed only with an eclectic collection of ideas, social planners are likely to end up being confused'. Allied to this is the question of who social planners are and where they are located in decision-making structures. Conyers (1982, p. 197) acknowledges in a textbook on the subject that 'many countries do not as yet have a fully developed social planning structure . . . consequently we shall find ourselves considering what sort of organisational structure should exist, rather than what actually does exist'. This sounds a little unconvincing, particularly as in recent years some of the countries that had developed social planning structures, such as Papua New Guinea, have subsequently downgraded the function. The failure of this sub-discipline to establish itself, both theoretically and practically, indicates its immaturity and points to the need for an applied development sociology to develop theory and define an approach which is not totally eclectic.

Cernea's (1985, p. 7) recent review of the contexts in which sociological analysis has been used in the practice of development finds that ex-post evaluation and social impact assessment are the most common activities. He points out that while sociology has been able to make contributions in both of these areas this may have had adverse consequences on the evolution of applied development sociology. Firstly, in both ex-post evaluation and social impact assessment the sociological input comes after the project identification and design stages, so there is no influence over the actual design nor over the design process, and no experience in these areas accrues to the sociologist. Secondly, the use of sociologists in this way has tended to discourage interdisciplinary linkages, partly because the sociologist may be working in isolation from the design team and partly because the role of evaluation/impact assessor is likely to yield critical findings that can be interpreted by designers (technical specialists and economists) and managers as questioning their competence and expertise. 'Wise after the fact, they are defined as the ones who simply complain about what others have actually done' (Cernea, 1985, p. 7).

In the future, applied sociology must strive to expand its involvement throughout the decision-making cycle of development intervention. This will entail applied research into project identification, project design, the monitoring of implementation and the feeding back of this research into redesign activities. A consequence of this will be the need for sociologists to become more prescriptive. Prescription, however, will not be based on scientific laws that permit the sociologist to solve problems through intellectual cogitation alone, but by taking part in and promoting a social learning process that links thought and action (Johnston and Clark, 1982; Korten and Klauss, 1984). The practice of development planning, especially rural development, is already moving in this direction. Sociologists could play a major role in pointing out to professionals from more reductionist disciplines something that has always been obvious to those who conduct detailed social research at a grass roots level. No amount of intellectual activity can provide blueprints for the achievement of development goals. Prescriptions and plans must not be final and must incorporate a constant iterative process that can incorporate the lessons generated by action.

Opportunities for involvement in development planning are becoming increasingly available (see, for example, the reports on land settlement, farming systems research and evaluation in this chapter), but sociologists and anthropologists must be prepared to sell themselves by expounding the case for their involvement and developing new products that have practical utility. Despite the established analytical capacity of these social sciences to understand and interpret development situations, the disciplines have, to date, evolved few conceptual tools that are of prescriptive value. Inroads are being made with regard to methodologies for social action (Cernea, 1983, 1987a) and the design of community organisations (Uphoff, 1986; Paul, 1986). However, the discipline of applied development sociology remains in its infancy and an intensive period of involvement in development interventions and reflection on experience is required. The pages that follow provide examples of three specific contexts in which sociologists and anthropologists have applied their skills and insights in development planning. They indicate the directions in which theories and methodologies are advancing and convincingly demonstrate that applied social research is of practical utility in achieving development goals. The role of social scientists in the design of community organisations, an area in which both theory and methodologies have advanced rapidly in recent years, is examined in the following chapter.

THE PLANNING AND MANAGEMENT OF NEW LANDS SETTLEMENT SCHEMES

The study of schemes to settle people on new lands has been a major research focus for social scientists in the post-war years. An enormous amount of data and hypotheses have been generated but there have been few attempts to treat the topic in a systematic fashion and knowledge has, until recently, remained fragmented. The need for some form of applied social theory to guide settlement practice has, however, long been evident. Socially, new lands settlement schemes are one of the most complex of all development interventions, entailing not only the creation of new agricultural systems, homes, infrastructure and services but also new sets of social relationships and the rapid modification of existing cultural values and norms. Long (1977) classifies such activities as a 'transformation approach' to development, seeking to create new social and economic institutions, rather than gradually build on what already exists.

Although the term 'land settlement scheme' is widely used this is not a natural category and schemes have taken a wide variety of forms. The term refers to projects in which a group of people moves to occupy unused or under-utilised (in a market economic sense) rural land, under the guidance of an agency external to the settler community. The focus, here, is on voluntary settlement, where the settler is perceived as having some control over the relocation decision, rather than involuntary or forced resettlement in which the settler has no choice but to migrate, e.g. when lands are flooded for large hydro-electric schemes. Land settlement schemes have been a persistent and popular development strategy for governments of all political persuasions and for international development agencies since colonial times. Notwithstanding this popularity, the work of a large number of social scientists has indicated that such schemes are commonly 'failure-prone', in economic terms, and are often associated with adverse social consequences (Hulme, 1987).

The bulk of social science research on land settlement has taken an applied stance by evaluating project or programme performance, detailing the major obstacles that have hampered scheme development and framing recommendations about how specific obstacles could be avoided and how performance could be improved in the future. Depending on their personal interests and disciplinary backgrounds, researchers have made recommendations about site selection, site preparation, scheme layout, linkages to the urban hierarchy, settler capital and credit, land tenure, administration, settler selection and social organisation. A particular focus for sociologists and social anthropologists has been a 'social consequences' approach, based on the examination of the impact of schemes at the individual, family and community level and often concluding that schemes are responsible for a range of social problems for both settler and host communities (Hulme, 1988, pp. 48–51). Many useful points have been made by such studies but they have rarely treated issues in a systematic fashion nor have they attempted to frame generalisations. One exception to this state of affairs is the work of the rural sociologist Raanan Weitz and his colleagues at the Settlement Studies Centre in Israel. Weitz's (1971) concern originated with regard to the problems encountered in the operation of settlements for recent immigrants to Israel in the 1950s. He believed that many of these problems were rooted in the failure of planners to consider 'human factors' and he elaborated the case for the comprehensive design of settlement schemes and developed theoretical models from which individual farm plans, settlement layouts, regional plans and sectoral plans could be formulated. These theories were initially tested in Israel and were later extended to developing countries. It must be noted, however, that the use of Israeli models, such as the *moshav* in Nigeria, encountered severe problems and that despite Weitz's attempts to generate flexible models, the products of his research were modelled on assumptions best suited to the Israeli context.

In the 1970s the interest in neo-Marxist conceptual frameworks spilled over into the study of land settlement schemes with attempts by Palmer (1974) and Barnett (1977) to explain the operations of schemes in terms of core-periphery relationships. But even Barnett's work, which is the best along these lines, finds itself stalled in the impasse of neo-Marxist sociology (see Chapter 3). Along with Dunham's (1982) and Hulme's (1987) arguments for a more political approach to the analysis of decision-making about the sanctioning of land settlement schemes, these frameworks are severely limited in terms of their prescriptive ability and the guidelines that they offer for action.

Recently, however, thanks to the efforts of Thayer Scudder, a veteran researcher on settlement issues, there has been what promises to be a major breakthrough in the task of creating a conceptual framework 'for the systematic social analysis of settlements and . . . for their planning, implementation, management and evaluation' (Scudder, 1985, p. 130). This framework is the result of a massive review of the available information on settlement schemes along with extensive personal research. The middle-range theory that has been postulated is an inductive product grounded in decades of field research and experience.

The main thrust of Scudder's argument is that settlement schemes commonly under-perform because of 'inadequate attention to settler families and the communities in which they live' (Scudder, 1985, p. 127). Applied sociological analysis shows, however, that 'people and the sociocultural systems in which they are imbedded and inter-related (including settlement agencies) respond to new land settlement in predictable ways' (Scudder, 1985, p. 131) and it is thus possible partially to predict social behaviour. Settlement plans based on an analysis of anticipated settler behaviour, rather than the usual set of arbitrary or prejudiced assumptions, can yield improved results. Scudder then presents a four-stage conceptual framework, partly based on the earlier work of Chambers (1969), which can be used as an instrument for predicting settler behaviour and planning schemes.

These four stages are as follows:

1. Planning, initial infrastructural development and settler recruitment.
2. Transition.
3. Economic and social development.
4. Handing over and incorporation.

The progression through these stages is generally in the specified sequence, although at times stages three and four may be reversed and, in settlement schemes that have been poorly planned and managed, the scheme may be stalled at stage two indefinitely. The time-frame for this sequence is variable but Scudder recognises that even on a reasonably successful project it is likely to take a generation.

The first stage can be sub-divided into two sub-stages. The first concerns the examination of alternative project types, the identification of the intended farming system, the specification of linkages with the regional economy and the planning of relationships between the host community and settlers. The second sub-stage is the development of the initial infrastructure, settler recruitment and settler arrival on the scheme.

The transition stage (stage two) occurs from the period of initial settlement until settler families are established; that is, they are able to produce sufficient food or income to meet their subsistence needs safely without subsidies or governmental handouts, and feel at home in their new location. This stage usually takes at least two years for most families and more often it is five to ten years. During this stage settlers are risk-averse and are unlikely to be willing to adopt technical, agricultural or socio-political innovations. This risk aversion is a rational (from a settler perspective) coping response to the stress of relocation and should not be mistaken as a permanent condition, as it often is by scheme managers. Settlers can be expected to wish to concentrate on social relations with their family and co-ethnics and to prefer area-of-origin housing types, farming practices, labour patterns and social practices despite the fact that these may be inappropriate for their new environment. At the end of the transition stage a dramatic shift occurs with most settler families adopting a dynamic, open-ended stance.

Consequently, stage three is characterised by less concern with the domestic mode of production and a willingness to experiment with a wide range of investment strategies in the search for higher levels of labour productivity and income. Commonly, settler families will acquire or rent additional land, diversify their cropping patterns, introduce livestock and invest in a range of off-farm activities – craft production, baking, tailoring, retail stores and providing transport services.

Stage four is characterised by two main processes. The first is the handing over of scheme management functions to line departments, local government, settler organisations or the private sector along with the creation of a mechanism by which first generation settlers can transfer control of their land to second generation settlers. The second process is the loss of the scheme's enclave identity and its incorporation into the region's administrative and political structures.

This is a brief summary of a detailed framework and the reader wishing for a more comprehensive exposition should consult the original source (Scudder, 1981). The contention is that this framework can be applied by scheme designers and managers not to give them automatic answers to issues, but to provide a conceptual structure to guide decision-making. This framework does not fill a vacuum, but instead seeks to replace a rule of thumb theory about settler behaviour that has not been thought through, although it has its roots in modernisation theory, and which underlies many settlement decisions. As Scudder (1985, p. 149) puts it, 'the conventional wisdom, still strong among settlement planners and administrators, is that settlers are drawn primarily from traditional societies that are both static and conservative and that they must therefore be carefully supervised and led. This view is simply wrong'. What types of guidance does Scudder's framework provide?

First stage

The framework highlights the need for careful and lengthy planning and alerts scheme planners and managers to the fact that most settler families will experience a period of severe stress after relocation. At the time of settler arrival there should already be a minimum level of infrastructural provision. This will vary with specific national contexts and settler expectations, but feeder roads to the settlement blocks should be ready and a primary health care facility and primary school should be accessible on foot. At the recruitment stage greater recognition needs to be given to the consideration of settler family attributes, rather than just the attributes of the male head-of-household, and attempts should be made to ensure that the selected community possesses a variety of skills (on-farm and off-farm) and that a range of age groups are represented. To keep costs down and hasten progress through to the transition stage the possibility of mixing spontaneous and sponsored settlers should be explored. If possible, settlers should build their own houses but, if housing is provided, it should be planned so that it does not limit the settler's future options in terms of house style, providing separate living areas for sons and relatives and having a household vegetable and fruit plot. To help hasten the settling-in period settlers should be close to co-ethnics. Long-term settlement stability will be fostered by having clustered settlements, rather than the dispersed layouts that agriculturalists often prefer, and by having a precise land tenure policy which is explained to settlers on several occasions during the early years.

Second stage

The framework strives to assist planners and managers to keep down the drop out rates that are often high during the first few years of scheme initiation and to complete the transition stage as quickly as possible. This is the stage at which scheme personnel are likely to believe that they must organise and coerce settlers on almost all matters and at which long-term settler dependency on government agencies may be induced. Scudder's ideas point to the need for planners and managers to recognise the risk-aversion of transition phase settlers as a temporary situation. This stage can be completed more quickly if co-ethnics are allocated house and farming plots adjacent to each other, self-help groups are encouraged for house building and land clearance, research-backed extension services are available, farmer training courses are mounted and efforts are made to ensure that primary schools and health posts are adequately staffed and stocked so that wives and children are less likely to return to home regions and create labour bottlenecks. Managers should be aware of the possible advantages of encouraging private sector involvement in marketing, credit, input provision and transportation, rather than asserting a settlement agency right to monopolise all of these functions. In order to reduce dependency, scheme administrators should plan to recoup all the recurrent costs of land development and water provision from settlers and to explain this policy carefully to settlers from the outset. The allocation of a small amount of funding for hardship credit to help individual families overcome unexpected problems can make a significant contribution to lowering abandonment rates.

Third stage

The framework guides planners and managers to recognise that once the majority of families have passed through the transition stage there are sound reasons for reducing government intervention in the scheme. Rather than attempting to maintain the project as an enclave, efforts should be made to allow individual settlers, settler organisations and co-operatives and private sector agencies to take on more economic and social functions. The management may have to make profound internal adjustments in terms of recognising the importance of non-agricultural and off-farm activities, in contrast to the agricultural emphasis of stage two, and ensuring that more flexible credit and support services are available. It is not uncommon at this stage to find scheme managements actively discouraging non-farm activities because they believe that their schemes are meant to be purely agricultural and because the majority of staff are professional agriculturalists. Managers should anticipate that subsistence activities and agricultural activities will become less crucial than at earlier stages. Efforts should be made to ensure that lines of credit are available for small-scale industrial projects.

Fourth stage

Scudder's model has limited applicability at this stage, largely because settler social behaviour is often of less significance now than formal politics and bureaucratic politics. The framework points out that the eventual withdrawal of the settlement agency (in reality a rare occurrence!) should be planned from the start and that a mechanism for transferring land to the second generation should be clearly established.

Scudder's sociological framework for the analysis of new land settlements needs to be further refined, especially stages three and four, but it provides an excellent example of the way in which applied sociological research can contribute to development planning in a cross-cultural context. The framework has been utilised for the preparation of World Bank and USAID policy guidelines and by a number of sociologists and anthropologists involved in planning for aid agencies. In particular, it is influencing the planning of the resettlement programmes associated with the Namada Dam in India and the 'Three Gorges' project in China. It provides a tool for the systematic application of sociological knowledge to settlement schemes and makes it more difficult for technical specialists to plead ignorance of this knowledge. One cannot expect the framework to be wholeheartedly received by all involved in such activities as it points to the need for longer planning and slower initial implementation, which may be contrary to the personal preferences of some individuals and groups. National governments and aid agencies find it hard to accept that some projects may take a generation before their objectives are achieved. Applied sociology can help them confront this situation, rather than ignore it.

AGRICULTURAL KNOWLEDGE SYSTEMS

Rural sociologists and social anthropologists have devoted considerable attention to changing agricultural practices. They have been particularly interested in examining formal and informal agricultural research, which seeks to generate new or improved crop varieties, livestock strains, husbandry methods and agrotechnologies, and the processes by which research findings are disseminated.

Insights and interpretations have been many and varied but it is possible to identify general trends which are related to the dominant theoretical frameworks of their eras. In the 1950s and 1960s, modernisation theory provided a conceptual structure for the analysis and explanation of the way in which new and improved agrotechnologies would be adopted by particular farming populations. Modernisation theory did not much concern itself with the study of the generation of new technologies, largely because of its stance towards technology. Modern technology was a technical, not a social, issue. It did not have a value dimension, and the adoption of modern technologies was usually assumed to be beneficial in terms of their impacts on production and levels of living and the cumulative changes which adoption induced in social attitudes and behaviour. Modernisation theory suggested that the main problems in modifying agricultural practices would not be in the research process which was largely controlled by people with modern values. The great difficulties lay in the dissemination process, in which social and cultural obstacles to the adoption of new techniques and products could be anticipated in rural populations with traditional attitudes and conservative values.

It was along these lines that Foster (1962, 1965) produced fascinating accounts of what he interpreted as the social and cultural obstacles to innovation and change in Mexican peasant groups. While the possibility of farming groups totally blocking change to an agricultural system could not be ruled out, social scientists steeped in modernisation theory postulated that a diffusion process, not unlike the economists' trickle down mechanism, would occur and that a small proportion of the traditional farming society which had more entrepreneurial tendencies (usually termed innovators) would adopt the new technologies. The successful application of these modified practices and the innovations would diffuse through society over time following a normal curve distribution (Figure 6.1). At the end of the process even the most conservative farmers, the laggards, would abandon tradition and embrace agricultural innovation. This was a comforting construct as it provided a rationale for agricultural researchers to stay behind the fences of their experimental stations and provided a framework for extension workers to understand slow or varying rates of adoption. Its prescriptive implications were that extension workers should concentrate their efforts on that stratum of society that they believed to be innovators. Hence, it

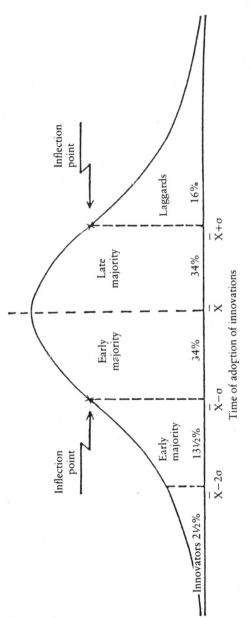

Figure 6.1 Adopter categorisation on the basis of relative time of adoption of innovations. *Source:* Rogers (1962).

supported the popular progressive farmers' policies of the 1960s. Eventually, the fruits of technology would trickle down from progressive farmers to their laggardly neighbours.

In retrospect, the naivety of this school of thought, when applied to developing countries, is striking. It failed to consider the ways in which structural features of rural society would influence adoption patterns; it treated indigenous agricultural systems as static (despite enormous evidence to the contrary); and it made the Eurocentric and elitist assumption that the products of agricultural research (essentially field stations staffed by American and European agriculturalists) would be automatically relevant to economically and socially diverse populations operating in a multitude of ecosystems.

Dependency theorists pointed out these weaknesses with a vengeance. They also changed the analytical focus by presenting interpretations which took a more conspiratorial view of agricultural research and extension, treating them as mechanisms by which precapitalist economies were penetrated by the core economies so that surplus could be extracted from the periphery. When these concepts were applied to specific cases they led to the conclusion that induced agricultural change (i.e. research and extension) had served to promote the adoption of cash crops, from which surplus could be most easily appropriated, and had consciously underdeveloped food production in Third World countries. These findings led some social scientists into the counterproductive activity of 'cash crop bashing', or as Johnston and Clark (1982) put it more elegantly, 'the condemnation of cash crops'. For many sociologists and social anthropologists in the 1970s, coffee, cocoa, coconuts (for copra), tea, rubber and oil palm were crops that were to be absolutely condemned and had no place in Third World agricultural systems. The cosy compact of the diffusion days was lost and the relations between social scientists and agriculturalists, never particularly strong, have remained decidedly cool ever since.

The 1980s have been characterised by a more pragmatic approach in which social scientists have not sought to fit agricultural research and extension into grand theories, but rather to study their nature, processes and methodologies. Agricultural research, rather than extension, has become a particular focus for applied study, following the rapid agricultural changes and dramatic production increases associated with the Green Revolution. The staggering agricultural and environmental problems that Sub-Saharan Africa faces, along with increased competition for research funding, have done much to make social scientists with rural interests consider the relevance of their work.

Before pursuing these recent contributions, some thought should be given to the question of whether social scientists have a role to play in agricultural research. Perhaps such research is best left entirely in the hands of agricultural specialists? Certainly many agricultural scientists see no role for applied social research in this field (Simmonds, 1985, p. 86). Our contention is emphatically that agricultural research is too important a subject to be left to agricultural scientists and agricultural economists. There are three main arguments to support this contention. Firstly, as the distinguished agricultural economist Collinson (1985, p. 74) notes, socio-cultural factors are fundamental to the understanding of farmer responses to the products of agricultural research and so applied social analysis is necessary to provide feedback to agricultural researchers about the ways in which existing research products have been received. Secondly, as has been well documented (Chambers, 1983), agricultural scientists have demonstrated a tendency to identify research priorities which, while inherently interesting to the scientist, are not a priority for the client group they are meant to be serving. The inclusion of one of the more consultative social sciences – social anthropology, human geography, rural sociology – in agricultural research activities can be of utility in introducing a greater client-orientation to programmes and for developing methodologies for client inputs to the research process. Finally, applied social research can contribute to the improvement of agricultural research processes by analysing the social behaviour of the actors and organisations involved in agricultural technology generation, helping them to identify the values inherent in their research stances and making them consider the appropriateness of their position *vis à vis* developmental goals. As Paul Richards (1985, p. 156), paraphrasing Maxwell (1984), points out, for too long the bulk of agricultural research in developing countries has pursued knowledge rather than wisdom. The knowledge created may have been useful for career development and institutional prestige, but it has not contributed to human welfare in proportion to the resources that have been expended. Therefore, a strong case can be made for the inclusion of applied social research as a constituent element of agricultural research. There are considerable differences of opinion, however, about the way in which the inclusion of applied social research should take place. Should it be as a major participant in agricultural research teams (i.e. the fielding of a sociologist/social anthropologist in all research projects); as a short-term consultant to full-time research teams; or as an indirect contributor developing research methods and training materials for full-time agricultural scientists? The evolution of farming systems research (FSR) in the 1970s has helped to foster a more focused debate on the contribution of applied social research to the generation and dissemination of new agricultural technologies.

Farming systems research (FSR) refers to the application of a systems approach to the identification and development of technologies appropriate for location-specific farming situations (Collinson, 1985, p. 71). It has its origins in farm management economics and seeks 'to achieve a holistic understanding of the farm, the farm family and its strategy. It requires that a multi-disciplinary team, rather than a group of agricultural scientists, be the unit for research'. Collinson (1985) recognises four main concepts underpinning the FSR approach, as follows:

1. Small farmers behave rationally and purposefully. They have varying levels of motivation and ability, but they work towards the achievements of self-defined goals. The farmers' priorities are the engine of the farming system, but they vary in relation to a complex of factors and change over time.
2. Small farmers operate their farms as systems. They do not seek technical or economical optima from a single activity, but compromise the quality of management of individual activities in the interests of the performance of the system as a whole.
3. All small farms differ but research must focus on a set of farms that are sufficiently similar to be regarded as parts of the same system. The sources of variation – natural, economic, socio-cultural and levels of resource endowment – must be carefully examined to distinguish between different systems.
4. Small farmers change their practices in a gradual, step-by-step pattern, often after small-scale experiments with new practices. They do not usually transform their practices dramatically in a short time period.

The collection and analysis of socio-cultural data is an integral part of such an approach (Figure 6.2). However, the relative importance

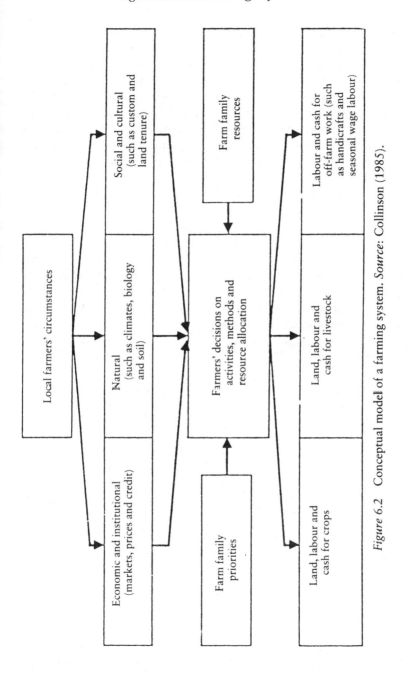

Figure 6.2 Conceptual model of a farming system. *Source:* Collinson (1985).

attached to this socio-cultural input and its content and methodologies are a contentious subject with different disciplines and individuals holding dramatically different views. At one extreme are agricultural scientists, such as Simmonds (1985, p. 51) who recognises a need for economists, perhaps 'with well-developed social perceptions', but see no role for other social scientists. At the opposite extreme stand Cernea and Guggenheim (1985), who directly challenge Simmonds's viewpoint and argue strongly for the inclusion of a sociologist or anthropologist in all FSR teams. Sutherland (1987) has examined the contribution that sociologists and social anthropologists can make to FSR in Africa, and although he acknowledges the need to formulate a more systematic role, and not rely solely on the intuitive skills of the social scientist, his job specification for a FSR sociologist remains imprecise, and the additional skills that such an individual would contribute to a team are not clearly identified. He furnishes examples of situations in which sociologists and social anthropologists have been of proven use (IRRI, 1982; Rhoades, 1984), along with a listing of activities in which a sociologist's involvement is beneficial. These include the identification of target groups, ensuring that disadvantaged groups and women are included in the analysis, checking that population samples are socially representative, preparing socio-cultural profiles, defining the basic units of research, encouraging the collection of indigenous technical knowledge, using rapid rural appraisal field methodologies, fostering farmer involvement in the research process and creating opportunities for farmer participation in trials and the examination of research findings. The case for a sociological input is well made, but if comprehensive institutionalisation of this input is to occur then a more precise role for the social engineer must be defined and the additional skills that are to be contributed must be clearly identified.

Robert Chambers, a distinguished scholar of development whose wide-ranging writings (see, especially, Chambers, 1983) incorporate elements of political science, political economy, sociology, social anthropology, management and public administration, believes that arguments about the role of social scientists in FSR teams remain largely academic, as they fail to take account of the resource situation of most Third World agricultural research institutions. While the centres which constitute the Consultative Group on International Agricultural Research (CGIAR) may be able to field multi-disciplinary teams, the bulk of agricultural research is conducted at poorly-funded national institutions. 'Most research stations will be without social scientists . . . [and] in practice, a single scientist, or a pair, may manage to get out [of the research station] using a small vehicle if they are lucky; or motorcycle, bicycle or public transport . . . (Chambers and Jiggins, 1987b, p. 112). Furthermore, FSR has not lived up to its holistic ideals and 'farming systems research is rarely taught and . . . is tending to turn itself into a variant of the TOT [transfer of tehnology] model' (Chambers and Jiggins, 1987a, p. 39). FSR, it is argued, has not facilitated researcher-farmer interactions in terms of identifying priorities, exchanging information and designing experiments. It is merely the orthodox, scientist-controlled approach to crop research seeking to generate new technologies on experimental plots for subsequent transfer to farmers, but utilising more field knowledge than has usually been the case. The experiments and research remain the property of the scientists.

Chambers and Jiggins view the failure of agricultural research and FSR to become more client-oriented, and particularly poor farmer-oriented, as the result of 'normal professionalism' with an 'output orientation'. Normal professionalism has several elements but is characterised by the perception that its methodologies are value-free, a bias toward the better off and better-educated, and a belief that the knowledge of the scientist/extensionist is superior to that of their clients. These findings lead to the conclusion that more appropriate agricultural research does not require the addition of social engineers in research programmes, but the gathering together by agricultural and social scientists of 'well established experience, to test new techniques and disseminate a systematic methodology' (Chambers and Jiggins, 1987b, p. 116) that is termed the 'farmer-first-and-last model'. This suggests that sociologists should adopt what might be called an engineered-enlightenment approach, not being directly involved in agricultural research but being actively involved, and arguing the case for their involvement, in the training of agriculturalists and the generation of research methodologies. Four methods for this task are elaborated: 'training scientists in reversals of attitudes . . . identifying and working with RPF [resource poor farmers] families . . . consulting farmer groups and panels . . . organising innovation workshops' (Chambers and Jiggins, 1987b). These are tools in the search for a new professionalism. There is a strong thrust to this argument and it has already managed to identify a clearer role for social scientists in agricultural research than the social engineering approaches, as well as being more specific about methods.

A stimulating analysis of induced agricultural change in West Africa, which has parallels with much of Chambers and Jiggins's work, has been presented by the agricultural geographer Richards (1985). By reference to specific case studies he demonstrates the disappointing results achieved by the transfer of technology model in the food crop sector in West Africa. He finds that there is a wide gap between what agricultural science has to offer and the needs of typical West African small-scale farmers. This gap is accentuated by the unsuitability of centralised agricultural research activities in low population density regions with diverse ecosystems. Scientists remain largely ignorant of the evidence that 'smallholder farmers in Africa are active experimenters' (Richards, 1985, p. 156) and indigenous agricultural knowledge remains 'the single largest knowledge resource not yet mobilised in the development enterprise' (Richards, 1985, p. 140). These findings are used to argue that agricultural research and extension must be reoriented along populist lines to focus on stimulating and utilising research in the informal sector. Although the political and bureaucratic implications of this argument are not subjected to any detailed analysis this remains a forceful case for even more radical policy changes and reversals than Chambers and Jiggins propose. Box (1988), adopting a framework close to Richards, has proposed that biographical analysis, adaptive trials and network articulation are mechanisms by which interfaces for knowledge exchange can be created between researchers and farmers. This is another promising line of enquiry.

To conclude this section it must be noted that applied social research into agricultural research and extension has amassed a substantial body of knowledge about the influences of sociocultural factors, both of farmers and of development professionals, on changes in agricultural practices. A clear sociological framework for analysis has not emerged however, as it has for new land settlement, and there are a wide variety of opinions on the role of applied social research both within the social sciences and in other disciplines. Long's (1988) work on 'knowledge interfaces' provides possible bases for the creation of a comprehensive applied sociological framework for the analysis of agricultural knowledge systems and the building of methodologies that rely less on an individual's intuitive ability and more on sociological concepts. Social research has done much to reorientate the research priorities of agricultural scientists and to act as a broker for the interests of disadvantaged groups. However, substantial and influential involvement in this field will only be achieved on the basis of well-elaborated applied theory.

PARTICIPANT–OBSERVER EVALUATION OF DEVELOPMENT PROJECTS

Projects have long been regarded by many as the cutting edge of development and during the 1960s and 1970s enormous efforts were devoted to creating methodologies for project appraisal and implementation (e.g. Gittinger, 1982). In the late 1970s and early 1980s attention focused in particular on the monitoring and evaluation of development projects. It was argued that timely studies of what was happening on projects could help managers make more effective decisions (i.e. project monitoring), while studies of completed or near-completed projects could provide useful feedback to planners and policy makers (i.e. ex post evaluation). The monitoring and evaluation methodologies that subsequently evolved emphasised the use of large-scale sample surveys of project impacts on beneficiaries and statistical manipulation on the data gathered (Casley and Lury, 1982). Monitoring and evaluation was institutionalised in government and multilateral bureaucracies by the establishment of specialist monitoring and evaluation (M and E) units and the training of full-time professional evaluators. Such activities have contributed to the improvement of decision-making in some situations but there are many cases in which the personnel involved in monitoring and evaluation believe that their findings have had little influence on decision-makers (French and Walter, 1984). Of the many factors that lie behind such disappointing experiences a few are particularly notable. These are that the complexity of the data collection and analysis methodologies utilised has led to results arriving too late to be of use to project managers; that specialist monitoring and evaluation units appeared to be judging, rather than supporting, management actions; and that the issues tackled by M and E studies were often not those on which managers placed a high priority. Project managers have often been disdainful towards M and E activities and have viewed them as academic exercises. For monitoring purposes they have relied on the reports of field officers and short field trips.

Other criticisms of the orthodox M and E approaches arose from social scientists who were concerned that methodologies had outstripped organisational capacities. Chambers (1983) provides examples of the 'survey slavery' to which many monitoring and evaluation exercises became wedded. This is the determination to produce detailed results from lengthy questionnaires in situations where it is apparent that responses to these questionnaires are highly unreliable and samples are unrepresentative. The reaction of a poorly-educated villager to the arrival of an unknown government official on his doorstep who is of a different socio-economic class, perhaps a different ethnic group, may not speak his language well, and who is in a hurry to ask a lot of questions (many of which are very personal) is at best suspicion and is likely to produce answers prone to evasion or fabrication. The poor quality of the data collected from beneficiaries can be seen as inherent in evaluations based on 'studying specimens' approaches (Feuerstein, 1986).

The problem of creating methodologies that could provide timely feedback to project managers and give them information on beneficiary responses to project interventions has concerned the anthropologist Lawrence Salmen. He has been especially interested in making urban upgrading projects more effective and his personal experiences and disciplinary background led him to view monitoring and evaluation from an unusual perspective. Conventional approaches treated the reality of a project as a single construct for all involved. Salmen, in contrast, believed that there were widely differing perceptions of what a development project was doing and how it functioned, and that these perceptions could be conceptualised as 'two worlds that meet, not always smoothly . . . the world of project beneficiaries and that of the professionals . . . whose job is to design and execute development projects' (Salmen, 1987, p. 2). This led him to the premise that project managers generally do not have an adequate understanding of the world they are trying to change, that is, the beneficiaries' constructs of reality. Evaluation (Salmen uses this term to refer to activities that are more commonly called monitoring) must therefore seek to relate these worlds by providing

managers with rapid, cost-effective feedback on beneficiary perceptions of project interventions and of their needs and preferences. The
obvious discipline providing tools relevant to such a situation was
ethnography which attempts to be 'interpretive, mediating two
worlds through a third' (Agar, 1982, p. 783). The mediator between
these two worlds is what Salmen calls a 'participant–observer evalu-
ator', who operates as a broker between project management and
project beneficiaries.

The methodology that Salmen has developed is based upon well-
established principles of ethnographic and anthropological research,
although the observation periods that he utilises are shorter than are
usual in these disciplines. Participant evaluation has been described
as follows:

> [it] involves some amount of genuinely social intervention in the field with
> the subjects of the study [or evaluation], some direct observation of relevant
> events, some formal and a great deal of informal interviewing, some
> systematic counting, some collection of documents . . . and open-endedness
> in the direction the study takes (McCall and Simmons, 1969, p. 1).

Salmen's methodology uses this approach to provide project
managers with feedback on the social contexts of the interventions
they manage and details of the interpretations that project beneficiaries place on events. He first experimented with the techniques in
Rio de Janeiro, but the formal testing of his methodology was
conducted from 1982 to 1984 on urban upgrading projects funded
by the World Bank in Guayaquil (Ecuador) and La Paz (Bolivia).
Both of these cities had experienced rapid expansion of their populations in recent decades and had large numbers of low-income
migrants living in poor housing without access to potable water,
sewerage or community facilities. The two projects were intended to
provide 42,000 low income families with improved houses and
access to basic services.

Salmen used his participant-observer evaluation approach while
living for five months in the 8 de Diciembre settlement in La Paz and
for five months in the Floresta settlement in Guayaquil. In each city
he lived in rented accommodation within areas that were subject to
the upgrading plans. He introduced himself to residents and gradually got to know people, using conversational interview techniques
and personal observation to gather information. Once established
and accepted he also ran a number of small-scale surveys based on

more formal structured interview techniques and enlisted the assistance of two or three local field assistants. His book (Salmen, 1987) provides a detailed account of the methods used, of the findings and insights that these offered and of their influence on project decision-makers. In both cities he found that beneficiary behaviour was not as project planners and managers had anticipated. In Guayaquil, communities that exhibited a strong desire for urban improvements had rejected the project. How could this contradiction be understood? The implementing agency, which was the municipal authority, interpreted the rejection as being partly due to a lack of confidence in the authority itself.

Salmen's research revealed, however, that the key factor related to the flow of communications between project staff and potential beneficiaries. The project management had channelled information, and received feedback, through the leaders of *cooperativas* (these are not cooperatives, but refer to the organisational units in which people originally settled in the area) in the settlements. Where people had refused to take part in the upgrading scheme the *cooperativa* leaders were active members of a political party that was critical of the existing government which supported the upgrading project. In consequence, much of the information that they relayed to the people was misleading or incorrect. For example, they did not advise their constituents that the project management had agreed to change the project designs so that domestic water connections would replace the unpopular standpipes that had originally been proposed. The leaders managed to foster concern among their followers about the high rates they would have to pay for improved services, when in fact the costs were equivalent to what most families were paying to buy contaminated water that was trucked in to the settlement. Project staff, by focusing on technical aspects of the plan and ignoring the socio-political dynamics of the communities involved, had missed simple opportunities, such as holding meetings in the settlement and distributing a news-sheet, that could have assisted in the uptake of project outputs. Salmen's work also assisted project management in understanding why some families in settlements that had taken part in the upgrading were reluctant to have domestic water connections, and in designing a programme to tackle this problem.

In La Paz, he monitored what the World Bank believed to be one of its most successful urban projects. He found that despite considerable achievements many beneficiaries were dissatisfied with the project. This was largely due to the project management failing to communicate clearly what were and were not project and beneficiary responsibilities. The project staff had assumed that the settlement communities were sufficiently cohesive to organise ground levelling and pavement laying, when in fact the communities needed external assistance with group formation before these tasks could be tackled. Most interestingly, Salmen found that despite the project's focus on housing and infrastructure, the majority of residents in the 8 de Diciembre settlement were not homeowners, as the plan assumed, but renters. The benefits of the programme had gone to homeowners and absentee landlords while the renters, many of whom had lived in the area for five to ten years, were in some cases worse off. For example, absentee landlords had not connected water to their rental units but public standpipes had been removed following upgrading, so that renters now had to go a greater distance to fetch water. Some landlords had raised rents as the project led to increased house prices in the settlement, but they had not improved their properties. Salmen's findings led to the redesign of aspects of the project so that absentee landlords were required to connect their properties to water and sewerage systems, and a line of credit was established to encourage resident homeowners to build rental units. He also helped staff to reformulate the *piso-techo* (floor-roof) housing scheme of providing partially built houses to homebuyers. This had until then achieved very low rates of residency.

Having proved the utility of participant-observer evaluation Salmen then sought to demonstrate that this was a relatively easily transferable technique, and not a method that relied entirely on the expertise of gifted individuals. Transferring the methodology to different countries, different contexts and to the nationals of the countries concerned presented a range of problems, but the second generation participant-observer evaluations, run in Brazil, Bolivia and Thailand, in relation to a range of different project activities, produced favourable results (Table 6.1). 'The consensus of operational management staff, both at the Bank and in the three countries . . . was that participant–observer evaluation increased the ability of management to improve project performance' (Salmen, 1987, p. 97). The influences of these evaluations on project decisions are noted in Salmen's volume. The national personnel who conducted these exercises received training from Salmen, were recruited as a third force (i.e. as short-term consultants, not project staff nor benefici-

Table 6.1 Second generation participant–observer evaluations

Country	City	Project component	Evaluation methodology
Brazil	Natal	Artisan co-operative	Participant observation (PO)
		Fishing co-operative	PO
	Recife	Slum relocation	Qualitative interviewing (QI)
		Slum upgrading	PO, QI
	Florianopolis	Milk co-operative	QI, Institutional assessment
		Fishing co-operative	PO
		Washerwomen's association	QI, PO
Bolivia	Villa Ulla	Wool production	QI, PO
	Ingavi	Agriculture	QI, PO
	Los Andes	Agriculture	QI, PO
Thailand	Bangkok	Low-cost housing	QI, PO
		Slum relocation	QI
	Chiang Mai	Low-cost housing	PO, QI

Source: Salmen (1987), p. 85

aries) and monitored projects for four to six month periods. The local costs worked out at about US$7000 per project evaluated, which was a small amount in relation to project costs. The loan components alone averaged out at US$9 million and proved that the method was not only desirable but also affordable. The technique is now being used in a range of World Bank projects, and is being considered by other agencies.

The demands placed on participant–observer evaluators are considerable. They must rapidly acquire a thorough knowledge of a project, be able to adapt participant–observer methods to the specific setting, be able to blend qualitative and quantitative approaches, have an understanding of organisational behaviour and be able to relate to concerns identified by project management, consider project goals but not let their findings be constrained by these goals, establish trust with technical specialists and poor beneficiaries, serve as a bridge between management and beneficiaries and strive for reliability of the data they collect through the quality of their work and frequent triangulation exercises. Suitable evaluators were found for all the second generation evaluations conducted according to Salmen's methodology. While there is no specific set of qualifications appropriate for participant–observer evaluators, numerate people with experience in qualitative, open-ended social research are at an advantage. The wider use of this technique is thus likely to create a demand for social scientists to act as evaluators and also to train evaluators.

The methodology itself is a concrete example of the type of products that anthropologists and sociologists can develop to make the practice of development more effective. This is not the only suggestion that has been made by social scientists to modify the orthodoxy of monitoring and evaluation. Feuerstein (1986), a nurse who subsequently became involved in community development work, has produced a handbook that makes an excellent case, and describes detailed methodologies, for the reorientation of evaluation so that project beneficiaries become active partners in evaluation, rather than passive specimens. Her approach is now used extensively in developing countries by professional and para-professional staff. It further illustrates the useful contribution that non-economic social scientists have begun to make in relation to educating the professionals who dominate much development decision-making into the consequences of adopting normal professional stances in situations in which their understanding of the socio political situation of the target group is partial.

CONCLUSION

Despite the considerable attention that sociologists have devoted to the study of change in developing countries, the concern that many sociologists have expressed about the impact of development interventions, and the evidence that contemporary planning methodologies ignore the human factor, the involvement of sociologists in development planning remains very limited. A host of factors internal and external to the discipline contributes to this marginality, but uppermost is the lack of interest and commitment of academic sociologists to practical involvement in development activities. The vast majority of sociologists and social anthropologists with interests in development have adopted an enlightenment approach to influencing development policies and projects and have been relatively scornful of the few who have pushed for more direct involvement in decision-making. This has meant that applied theoretical frameworks have advanced relatively little, especially in comparison to disciplines such as economics, and that the training of most sociology students equips them with few skills or insights that would be of use to development agencies or beneficiaries. At present the claims of many sociologists for a more influential role for their discipline in development will be of little value unless they also adopt a more applied stance in their own empirical research and in their efforts to construct conceptual apparatus. Such a stance does not mean that sociologists need to become naively prescriptive, nor does it mean that they should engage in a charade of producing standardised planning methodologies that are cross-culturally transferable.

This chapter has examined three functional areas in which applied social analysis has made a practical contribution to development activities. These were Scudder's grounded theory on the behavioural responses of settlement scheme migrants to their changing circumstances; the design and operation of agricultural research and extension systems; and the use of participant–observer techniques in project monitoring and evaluation. To differing degrees, sociological analysis has contributed to improved developmental results in each of these activities. However, if sociologists and social anthropologists are to become more than odd jobbers then comprehensive, applied theoretical frameworks must be created. Then the arguments for the routine inclusion of applied social researchers in development decision-making cannot be ignored.

Although theoretical frameworks for the application of sociological knowledge to development interventions are in their infancy, it is possible to identify a number of specific topics around which sociological contributions are emerging, as follows:

1. Data collection methodologies: the research efforts of sociologists and social anthropologists have pointed to the way in which conventional survey methodologies are likely to exclude the knowledge and perceptions of those whom development programmes are meant to assist. In response, a set of supplementary techniques have evolved that create opportunities for beneficiaries to relay their needs and priorities to development

planners and which give technical staff access to indigenous technical knowledge. These include rapid rural appraisal (Chambers, 1983, pp. 199–201), participant–observer evaluation (Salmen, 1987) and biographical analysis (Box, 1988). These techniques have already proved useful, but their elaboration and codification into formally presented methodologies remain urgent tasks.

2. Modelling beneficiary behaviour: frameworks for explaining social behaviour have been extended into attempts to model beneficiary responses to development interventions. The most detailed exercise has been conducted by Scudder (1981, 1985) in relation to beneficiary behaviour on new land settlements. This has demonstrated that while behaviour cannot be precisely predicted, grounded theory can replace the wildly inaccurate rule of thumb assumptions that most development plans make about beneficiaries. Additionally, it can point to existing institutions, such as informal extension systems and labour pooling schemes, that could be utilised to achieve project goals. Opportunities for similar normative frameworks await development in such areas as beneficiary behaviour to new technologies in artisanal fisheries, the problems of refugees (Mazur, 1988), the utilisation of common resources and changes in pastoral production systems.

3. The time scale and nature of development projects: empirical studies reveal that development project planners consistently underestimate the time required for project implementation. While part of this underestimation is a result of over-optimistic assumptions about project management capacities, a major part is due to erroneous assumptions about the rate at which project beneficiaries will respond to modified incentive systems. Related to this are the findings of applied social researchers that the same development intervention will have different impacts in different contexts. In consequence, project planning must be seen less as a set of best option decisions and more as an experimental and iterative process that needs continuous monitoring and redesign. This finding has greatly influenced the integrated rural development projects initiated by agencies such as NORAD (Norway) and SIDA (Sweden), but does not appear to have been recognised by the World Bank or Asian Development Bank.

4. Sensitising technical specialists: applied sociological research has identified the value premises that underpin the professional behaviour of technical specialists and the biases that this leads to in the research agenda that they define and the recommendations they feed into project-planning exercises. A strong case can be made for the involvement of social scientists in the design of training programmes and research methodologies that make technical specialists aware of the consequences of their normal professionalism on development activities. There is still much to be done in the elaboration of these techniques, that will ensure that the expertise and professionalism of technical specialists do not become obstacles to development.

5. Community participation and social organisation: a major concern for sociologists and social anthropologists has been the design of planning methodologies that foster community participation in decision-making and assist in the formation of local level organisations for disadvantaged publics, so that they have increased influence over decisions that affect them (Leonard and Marshall, 1982; Korten, 1980, 1987). Those activities have been only briefly referred to in this chapter. As they are such a vast topic the following chapter is devoted to their analysis.

7

SOCIAL ORGANISATION AND DEVELOPMENT

The development policies and projects that have been examined in the previous chapters not only impact (in beneficial and negative ways) on the lives of individuals, but they also involve changes in the nature of social and economic organisations and institutions. This may entail the modification of existing organisations or the creation of new ones. Whichever change takes place, the design of organisations for development is an important issue and demands considerable attention. As Johnston and Clark (1982, p. 34) remark:

One of the greatest challenges for policy analysis is the design of organisational structures which can mobilise local experience and integrate it with improved expertise. In seeking to promote this design function, we therefore emphasise the importance of local organisations for articulating needs and delivering services. We recognise, however, that organisational resources are at least as scarce and valuable as capital, land, and technical knowledge.

Traditionally, sociologists have adopted an enlightenment approach to such analysis and have studied and criticised the organisations entrusted with the implementation of development policies and programmes, but have rarely become involved in the direct application of their findings. More recently the applied orientation adopted by some social researchers (and described in Chapter 6) has led to a growing involvement with the design of social and economic organisations in an attempt to improve the effectiveness of development interventions (Cernea, 1987b).

This topic is the focus of the present chapter. In it we review the historical experience of induced local organisations in developing countries and examine the contributions that sociologists have made to the understanding of the severe problems that beset these organisational experiments. It is apparent that these early interventions underestimated the complexity of the existing social institutions and oversimplified the changes in individual attitudes and behaviour and group relationships that organisational innovation necessitated. At the time these programmes were implemented there was much potentially relevant sociological and anthropological knowledge available, but this was not utilised. The chapter then examines contemporary work on popular participation, local organisations and the role of non-governmental organisations in development. From this it proceeds to analyse the experiences of two recent experiments in organisational innovation which, arguably, have achieved great success. These are irrigator organisations in the Philippines and the Grameen Bank in Bangladesh.

Throughout the chapter it should be borne in mind that, depending on the perspective, there are differing aims for promoting new or modified organisational forms. The first, exemplified by Paul (1987), sees such changes as an instrument for achieving improved project or policy outcomes. The second, typified by Gandhi and Nyerere, sees the creation of new organisations as an end in itself, because the successful establishment of an organisation is seen as empowering those who have previously been unable to exert an influence on society. In this interpretation, induced organisations take on a more ideological role and are seen as a stage on the way to a more socially just society.

THE HISTORICAL EXPERIENCE: CO-OPERATIVES AND COMMUNITY DEVELOPMENT

The obvious starting point for an examination of the process of induced organisational change in developing countries is a review of the experience of co-operatives and of community development initiatives. During the early development decades of the 1950s and 1960s planners and policy-makers assumed that these initiatives would restructure social and economic interactions in ways that would permit the achievement of higher standards of living for the mass of the population. However, experience revealed that the optimistic assumptions underpinning these moves were inappropriate for the socio-economic environments in which they were operating.

Co-operatives

The establishment of co-operatives has been an element of development strategies in both socialist and capitalist societies. For the former it was seen as a step on the way to the socialisation of the economy. For the latter it was a method of stimulating entrepreneurship and boosting productivity. The International Labour Organisation (ILO) defines a co-operative as:

an association of persons . . . who have voluntarily joined together to achieve a common economic end through the formation of a democratically controlled business organisation, making equitable contributions to the capital required and accepting a fair share of the risks and benefits of the undertaking.

Typically co-operative principles emphasise open membership, democratic decision-making procedures (one member, one vote), distributing any surplus on a basis proportional to the members' business transactions through the society and promoting co-operation (or necessitating co-operation) as a social movement (Youngjohns, 1977).

In the majority of developing countries co-operatives have colonial origins. The British authorities enacted co-operative legislation in India in 1904 and subsequently these statutes, sometimes with minimal modification, were transferred to other Asian, African, Caribbean and Pacific colonies. Co-operatives were particularly promoted in the agricultural sector for credit, input supply, storage and marketing (single or multi-purpose). In this sector they were seen as filling an organisational vacuum or as replacing the undesirable existing institutions of the moneylender and trader. These latter were viewed as exploitative because they were thought to charge usurious interest rates (for a critique of this view, see Wilmington, 1983 and Singh, 1983) and to be inherently dishonest. In addition, the colonial authorities believed that co-operative organisation would serve to educate the population in civics by demonstrating the superiority of modern, democratic institutions over the traditional institutions of the tribe, clan or caste. Somewhat paradoxically, they were seen as a means of building modern economic organisations out of the social co-operation that was believed to be a central characteristic of village life. The reader should note that while co-operatives and community development approaches in Europe and the United States have usually been non-governmental, in developing countries they have been government policies.

The notion of the co-operative as a desirable organisational innovation continued after independence with many new leaders arguing that co-operatives were the foundation for rural development (for an example, see the 1969 speech of President Nyerere of Tanzania, reprinted in Nyerere, 1973). Ideologically, co-operatives were compatible with socialist, capitalist or mixed economy strategies. Pragmatically, they could encourage the accumulation of capital among poor sections of the population and could enlist producers into the administration of government agricultural programmes (Howell, 1982, p. 106). In addition they could help to attract international aid.

This rosy image of the role of co-operatives came to grief in the late 1960s and early 1970s as a series of evaluations (Apthorpe, 1970; Fals Borda, 1969; Inayatullah, 1970; UNRISD, 1975) found that all was not well. Co-operatives were inefficient in terms of their ability to provide members with goods and services at the right time and at a reasonable price. They were also dominated by wealthier farmers, landowners and traders so that poorer rural people received few, if any, benefits.

The studies revealed that state-promoted co-operatives created numerous opportunities for malpractice by public servants and co-operative officials, because of the confused accountability and political manipulation of such organisations. Even where malpractice did not occur, the complexity of co-operative financial procedures, for memberships with low levels of literacy and numeracy, often led to collapse because of mismanagement. In areas where there was pronounced socio-economic inequality, the newly-established co-operatives were captured by local elites and served to reinforce their dominance over other groups. Even the highly acclaimed co-operatives at Comilla in Bangladesh were eventually captured (Blair, 1978). Hyden (1983) interprets the failure of co-operatives in East Africa partly as a rejection of these institutions by the rural populace which, correctly, perceived them as an attempt by the state to control production at the local level. Experience in a number of other countries such as Ghana, Papua New Guinea and Tanzania, where governments withdrew from co-operative sponsorship, adds further support to Hyden's thesis.

Not all co-operatives have produced poor results, however, and some, such as the AMUL Dairy Co-operative in India (Paul, 1982) and the Portland-Blue Mountain Coffee Co-operative in Jamaica (Gow *et al.*, 1979) have performed well. Nevertheless, the critical studies led to a profound change of attitudes about the wisdom of promoting co-operative organisational forms. How much poor results are attributable to poor organisational design, however, and how much they are due to factors based in the broader political and economic environments in which co-operatives were based remains a matter of debate. Often, co-operatives were associated with community development programmes and it is these which we examine next.

Community development

The origins of the community development approach can be traced back to the United States in the early part of this century. In developing countries, the movement is usually seen as emanating from a pilot project in the Etawah District of Uttar Pradesh, India. This commenced in late 1948 and was supported by funding from the Ford Foundation. The Etawah project involved the mobilisation of villagers by a multi-purpose village-level worker to increase agricultural output and improve rural infrastructure, largely through self-help efforts. The project's initial results were so impressive that in 1952 the Indian government decided to incorporate the approach as a Community Development Programme (CDP) to upgrade agriculture, health, education and infrastructure in rural areas with the help of a large amount of US aid. In addition, the CDP was 'to initiate and direct a process of integrated culture change aimed at transforming the social and economic life of the villages' (Dube, 1958, p. 8).

The Second Five Year Plan extended CDP to cover all of rural India. Conceptually, community development was seen as a participatory strategy in which a village-level worker (VLW) acted as a catalyst to stimulate community organisation and foster community awareness and education, resulting in social action to meet the village's felt needs. The VLW, trained in community organisation and basic rural skills, mobilised villagers, administered governmental matching grants and linked the village to necessary external technical advice. The need to manage tens of thousands of VLWs across India led to the creation of a vast bureaucracy operating at the national, state, district and block level. This had major impacts on the programme, reducing its participatory focus and leading to VLWs adopting conventional patterns of bureaucratic behaviour.

While the Indian government was attempting to spread the CDP across the entire country, aid agencies were promoting community development internationally. This led to a massive wave of community development programmes across Asia, Africa and Latin America and ultimately more than sixty countries initiated such programmes and established ministries, departments or offices of community development.

However, the popularity of community development was relatively short-lived as by the late 1950s disconcerting reports of the results of the CDP in India were being published, and soon these were mirrored in other countries. Dube (1958) conducted a study of CDP in two villages in Uttar Pradesh and provides vivid detail of the local level impact and the problems that arose. Many of the agricultural changes promoted were of little relevance to smaller farmers, while *shramadan* (unpaid voluntary labour) improved road networks, which assisted the local elite in trading but did little for the poorer groups which were coerced into providing the bulk of the labour. These reports were confirmed from other parts of the country, and two particular criticisms developed against CDP. Firstly, the CDP was inefficient in economic terms and vast resources were producing relatively little evidence of stimulating agricultural production. Secondly, those benefits that did accrue from the CDP fell largely into the hands of more affluent farmers. Long (1977, p. 155) suggests that around 70 per cent of the agricultural benefits went to such farmers. Artisans and agricultural labourers were largely bypassed by the CDP. Commonly, the VLWs aligned themselves with the traditional local elites and this entrenched the position of these groups. Subsidised inputs and technical advice were channelled to them. By the mid-1960s it was evident that the CDP had done little to alleviate poverty and food scarcity in India, but there was considerable evidence that it had increased disparities between big and small farmers and between regions.

The problems that beset the Indian CDP were replicated across the world. By 1965 community development had fallen as national leaders became disillusioned and aid agencies withdrew their support (Holdcroft, 1978). The bureaucracies created to implement CDP were reoriented towards social work in urban areas or merged with other ministries.

Many of the problems that brought community development programmes into disrepute can be seen as arising out of the inadequacy of the concept of community that underpinned these initiatives. Robertson (1984, p. 143) argues that in the 1950s (and still in the 1980s) development planners have a stereotype of the rural community: as 'simple, homogeneous, harmonious, durable and relatively autonomous'. In reality each of these images is unfounded when the evidence assembled by sociologists and social anthropologists over the years is considered. In particular, the relationships that exist between villagers are multiplex and constantly changing; there are pronounced socio-economic differences in most rural areas so that the felt needs of one group may be irrelevant or in direct opposition to the felt needs of another group; there is constant conflict, both overt and covert, in most rural communities and, at best, village life in many areas might be typified as an uneasy truce; finally, in most situations the autonomy of village life has been subject to constant erosion during the present century as the state and its agencies have become more pervasive and as the village economy has become cash based. Worsley (1984, p. 145), with a mixture of despair and derision, comments that, ideologically, community development 'drew upon a de-politicised version of mid-West populism mixed with a vulgarised North American psychology from which any vestige of conflict theory had been removed'.

The unsatisfactory results of co-operative and community development strategies elicited a variety of responses from those concerned with development policies. For some aid agencies, it led to an emphasis on blueprint approaches to development programming which entrusted the planning and implementation of projects to technical specialists and paid scant attention to local organisational issues. As Esman and Uphoff (1984, p. 50) comment, 'difficulties in starting or sustaining effective local institutions have kept many agencies from making organisation a central part of their development strategy'. For a second group, notably the neo-Marxist scholars of the 1970s, the failure of these improvement approaches provided further evidence that only radical change, sweeping away the existing social structures, could create the conditions under which development could occur. For a third group, on whose work we shall now focus, the experiences of co-operatives and community development provided lessons on which new, and potentially more successful, experiments could be based.

THE LEARNING PROCESS APPROACH: LOCAL ORGANISATIONS AND LOCAL INSTITUTIONAL DEVELOPMENT

What lessons could be drawn from the relatively poor performance of co-operative and community development approaches?

1. Little, or no, attention was afforded to analysing local social structures and considering the ways in which these structures would interact with the organisational forms that were being promoted. As a consequence, mechanisms for reducing the likelihood of programme benefits being monopolised by local elites and for discouraging field level officers from aligning themselves with such groups were not considered.
2. The lack of analysis of existing social and economic structures meant that these programmes assumed that a standard organisational form was appropriate in very different organisational environments. The experience indicated that different types of organisation are required in different contexts and that there is no best model that can simply be transferred.
3. Responsibility for group formation was placed in the hands of a conventional bureaucratic agency and in consequence it was treated as a conventional bureaucratic product. The commitment of the large ministries and departments that implemented co-operative and community development policies to the qualitative aspects of these policies (i.e. popular participation, 'bottom-up' planning, meeting felt needs, voluntary self-help) was lacking. It is unlikely that conventional bureaucratic methods of group formation can mobilise disadvantaged groups, and treat them as partners in development, without dramatic bureaucratic reorientation. The experience suggests that alternative approaches to group formation must be sought.
4. Although the programmes were surrounded by rhetoric about participation, self-help and felt needs they were generally tightly controlled by the state. This led intended beneficiaries to

perceive the programmes as being state-imposed (Dube, 1958). Indeed, if Hyden's (1983) interpretation of co-operative policies in East Africa is correct, then they were used by those holding state power to control production and exchange of agricultural output at the local level. This experience suggests that future programmes must try to distance themselves from the apparatus of state. This finding presents severe problems in many countries where the state is seen as being in control of virtually all development initiatives.

5. The co-operative and community development approaches were based on the premise that there should be only a single channel for providing any specific service or good to a village. To duplicate delivery by having several linkages was seen as being inefficient. The possibility that multiple delivery channels might create competition which would offer choice to the beneficiaries, permit different needs to be met and encourage efficiency, was rarely considered. The belief that a single best option organisational plan should link services to villagers may be desirable from a bureaucratic viewpoint, but not necessarily from the viewpoint of the client.

6. Underlying the co-operative and community development approaches was a concept that saw local institutional development as the selection of a specific organisational technology, followed by the training of public servants about how this organisational technology operates. Subsequently, these public servants diffuse the organisation to local populations. Clearly, this was inadequate and adds support to an alternative premise: that local institutional development is a relatively slow process involving experimentation with different organisational forms, the monitoring of their performance and constant redesign. Additionally, such experimentation should occur in realistic situations, rather than highly-resourced (in financial and manpower terms) pilot projects, such as Etawah and Comilla, which cannot subsequently by replicated.

These findings, and many others, were picked over by academics and planners throughout the 1960s and 1970s. There were many calls for more participation in development programmes, but relatively little critical analysis of what forms such participation might take. In some situations the calls appeared to be largely rhetorical, especially when made by centralised authoritarian regimes. In others, they appeared to be based on the naive belief that the poor had limitless time and energy to devote to participatory activities and that participation could be achieved without conflicts of interests. As Johnston and Clark (1982, p. 170) remark, 'the term "participation" appears with great frequency, emotion and looseness'. Such imprecision added to the rhetorical value of participation but pointed to the lack of thought on the topic. Fortunately, some scholars, especially in the United States, applied themselves to analysing the concept, clarifying and specifying its meaning (e.g. Cohen and Uphoff, 1980) and conducting detailed empirical studies of its use. These efforts have done much to reduce the vagueness surrounding the term.

David Korten's (1980) work, which proposed a 'learning process approach' to community organisation as the basis for rural development, stimulated many social scientists into more focused applied research on the nature and performance of local level organisations that sought to elicit participation. He explicitly contrasted the negative experience of co-operatives and community development with 'five Asian success stories'. These were the National Dairy Development Board in India, Sarvodaya Sharamadana in Sri Lanka (this is the agency that provided the family in case study 5 of Chapter 2 with kindergarten services), the Bangladesh Rural Advancement Committee, Thailand's Community Based Family Planning Services, and the Philippine National Irrigation Administration's communal irrigation programme. On the basis of this comparison it is argued that a learning process approach, rather than a blueprint approach which emphasises the role of technical specialists, is more appropriate for the achievement of developmental goals. The successful development interventions that Korten (1980, p. 497) describes:

> . . . emerged out of a learning process in which villagers and program personnel shared their knowledge and resources to create a program which achieved a fit between needs and capacities of the beneficiaries and those of the outsiders who were providing the assistance. Leadership and teamwork, rather than blueprints, were the key elements.

To achieve 'fit' between beneficiaries, organisation and programme, three organisational attributes are necessary – the ability to embrace error, plan with the people and link knowledge-building with action. In Korten's idealised learning organisations, learning is enhanced, as those who gain useful knowledge are personally affected by the programme and have a vested interest in feeding new knowledge back into programme redesign. Social scientists can play a key role in the process as 'capacity builders' and as the providers of 'tools' for agency personnel and villagers. These tools are not the orthodox academic survey methods but are specifically-designed methodologies appropriate to the rural context. For example, the use of disciplined observation, guided interviews and informant panels rather than formal questionnaire survey (Korten, 1980, p. 501).

Korten's line of reasoning made a good case of 'the need for action based capacity building', but it provided precious little insight about the precise means by which such an approach could be oper-ationalised. It stimulated awareness on the issues of community organisation, participation and approaches to development pro-gramming, but it provided few guidelines as to what could be done in practical terms and who should do it. The success of the programmes that he analysed appeared, in a large part, to result spontaneously from a fortunate combination of dynamic leadership and target group need. Korten's work enlightened, but by its very nature, did not specify how a 'learning process approach' could be turned into an operational strategy.

Johnston and Clark (1982, pp. 155–224), building on some of Korten's concepts, helped to advance the analysis by examining the practical implications of these ideas. They first pointed out that development planners who believed it was possible to think through developmental problems were deceiving themselves, regardless of how sophisticated and intellectually demanding the analytical tech-niques they employed:

The sad fact is that analysts, planners, and politicians simply do not know what kind of local organisation is actually in the poor's interests. The delusion that sufficient cogitation can overcome this ignorance – that the 'newest direction' will finally be the right direction – may be a greater obstacle than ignorance itself to designing better reorganisation programs (Johnston and Clark, 1982, p. 169).

In consequence, those involved in planning interventions must re-cognise the experimental nature of their plans and the importance of constant monitoring and redesign.

Secondly, those programme planners and managers, who 'treat participation as a free good, desirable in unlimited quantities' (Johnston and Clark, 1982, p. 171) must recognise the falsity of this notion. A more appropriate concept is to think of participation by intended beneficiaries in a programme as an investment of their time, energy and resources to achieve desired benefits. This leads those involved in practical action to recognise the need to concentrate their interventions on benefits that are desirable and tangible to the poor (experience suggests that these will most commonly be income enhancement and capital formation rather than social services); to ensure that, if feasible, some benefits accrue to members relatively early on in a programme; and to look for ways of reducing energy-consuming conflicts by harmonising organisational objectives and carefully considering the criteria for membership. These issues have been recognised before, but too often the perspective has been that of the outsiders (bureaucrat, aid agency consultant, non-government organisation representative) rather than that of the intended beneficiaries.

A third area that Johnston and Clark identify for practical consideration is the linkages between local organisations and government agencies. This cannot be ignored, as some proponents of participation appear to do, because it is almost inevitable that a relationship with government will be established, and such relationships can be of use in providing local organisations with technical advice, resources and supporting services or facilities. Their analysis of this issue points to the desirability of an approach to development administration which emphasises a facilitator role. The examination of possible methods of reorienting bureaucracies to facilitate, rather than control and regulate, provides another entry point for the operationalisation of Korten's learning process. Such examination is in its preliminary stages at present, and there is a clear need for sociologists to allocate more time to the study of organisational behaviour in the public sector in low-income countries. Röling (1988) would caution against this, however. For him local organisations can only be effectively formed through the intervention of a third party or intermediate organisation – that is a national or international level NGO.

The most significant recent contribution to the understanding of participation and local level organisational behaviour and performance has come from the inter-disciplinary Rural Development Committee at Cornell University. Their work has culminated in Esman and Uphoff's (1984) seminal volume on the role of local organisations in rural development. In this study a large number of hypotheses about the relationships between community-based organisations' performance and their environments and structures are examined. By conducting a quantitative analysis of 150 organisations, the authors tested generalisations that had been made earlier on the basis of individual or small numbers of case studies.

With regard to local organisational environments it was found that thirteen variables, out of the eighteen examined, were not significantly related to organisational performance in statistical terms. While this might appear to be no conclusion at all, it does seem to point to the contingent nature of local organisation operations and adds support to the arguments of those (e.g. Korten, Johnston and Clark) who view local institutional development as a process of 'choosing and learning', rather than one of 'discovering and knowing'. It also refutes the notion that there are a set of insurmountable environmental obstacles which will disrupt organisational performance whenever they occur. A number of significant correlations do occur, however. Surprisingly, social heterogeneity and social stratification are found to correlate positively, and at a statistically significant level, with enhanced local organisation performance. This is an important finding as it challenges the commonly-held notion that such organisations function best in socially-homogeneous societies with limited differentiation. Less surprising is the finding that local organisations produce better results in communities which already have relatively participatory norms for decision-making.

While local organisations can do little to modify their physical, socio-economic and political environments, there are a number of potentially autonomous choices that can be made about their structures. Hence, Esman and Uphoff's analysis of the ways in which structural variables relate to performance is of considerable practical significance. In particular, it throws light on the question of whether small, informal, homogeneous-membership, single function structures (Hunter, 1976; Tendler, 1976) or larger, more formal, multi-tier, multiple function structures (Inayatullah, 1972; Uphoff and Esman, 1974) are to be preferred. Their results are numerous and the issue of causality is complex because of the close correlations between several of the structural variables being examined. Here, only a few major points can be made, and the interested reader is recommended to refer to the original volume.

When testing the single function versus multiple function hypothesis a positive correlation is found between the number of functions and performance, but not at a statistically significant level. A qualitative examination of the histories of the case study institutions leads the authors to propose that, when the temporal dimension is considered, many successful local organisations commence with a single function and diversify into further functions as their management capacity improves over time. They argue that this pattern is a feature that organisation designers and managers would do well to consider.

With regard to whether less formal or more formal (i.e. having a number of rules which are recorded in writing) organisations perform better, a negative correlation is found between the degree of formality and performance, and this is statistically significant in relation to indicators of agricultural production and the accessibility of services to the poor. This suggests that designers and managers should be cautious about seeing the formalising of rules as a means of improving performance. However, as there is a close relationship between the degree of formalisation and the strength of linkages with government, causality is not clear.

In terms of decision-making structure, ranked in terms of executive (individual), committee (group of members) or assembly (all members), the associations are not significant, but there is some evidence that organisations emphasising executive decision-making perform less well. No clear relationships emerge in respect of group size, but both vertical linkages (i.e. multi-tiered structures) and horizontal linkages (i.e. with other local organisations) correlate positively with performance and appear to reinforce each other. This suggests that organisational structures that link into unions or federations and which are networked locally should be given serious consideration whenever this is a feasible option. Linkages with government revealed a more complex pattern in which both low linkage and high linkage were associated with reduced performance. Perhaps not surprisingly, Esman and Uphoff find that the degree of participatory orientation (i.e. the extent to which organisations actively promote membership involvement and equity) correlate with good performance and, in particular, correlate significantly with an increased ability to raise the incomes of poorer members and to increase the access of the poor to services.

This exhaustive analysis leads Esman and Uphoff to pose the question, how can local organisations be made more effective? They find that there is no universal prescription as each solution has the potential to create new problems, and approaches that emphasise a set of mutually-reinforcing innovations are to be prefered. Such innovations are numerous and include the use of modified electoral systems for office-bearers, leadership rotation, the use of specific membership criteria, the redesign of benefits, training (of members as well as office-bearers), committee structures and internal and external auditing procedures. There is an infinite set of possible combinations of modified practices, and any innovation, or set of innovations, must be seen as an experiment to be closely monitored and subsequently redesigned. The question of how to improve the leadership of local organisations, without such measures fostering oligarchy and paternalism, remains an issue on which little headway is made.

Those who seek to improve the performance of local organisations also face difficulties in relation to the paradox of assisted self-help. In theory, government can support and promote community organisation, especially by the use of catalysts and community organisers; but the likelihood of the manipulation of government-assisted local organisations, by the bureaucracy or politicians, seems just as likely to lead to poor performance. Aid agencies have the potential to assist local organisations in practical terms (finance, advice and manpower), and also in terms of the opportunity that they have to impose conditions on loans and grants made to national governments. These can be used to discourage government from taking control of non-government organisations. However, the pressure on aid agencies to shift funds quickly serves to undermine such conditionality measures.

The works reviewed above have done much to refine the concept and practice of local institutional development. However, the issue of how local and community organisations relate to broader power structures has remained neglected. It is often unclear as to whether proponents of community organisations see such organisations as an efficient service delivery mechanism, or as a step on the road to redistributing power at local and national levels. For example, Esman and Uphoff (1984) do not attempt to measure organisational performance in terms of ability to exert influence on local elites, to lobby for policy changes or to strengthen the position of political parties that represent the poor's interests (in democratic states). Korten (1980) sidesteps the issue by defining 'popular participation' as being unrelated to 'political participation'. The latter, however, is defined purely in terms of formal political institutions. This stance does little to answer the legitimate questions of those who ask whether community organisations and local organisations (or whatever terminology is used) will remain insignificant in size or will simply reproduce the co-operative and community development experiences when they expand with government assistance. Examining the way in which such organisations may change, or be changed by, class structures has barely been tackled. It may be that choosing and learning is an appropriate strategy, but an essential part of such a strategy is that its proponents monitor its wider impacts. Korten (1987) writes of 'third generation' NGOs, community-based organisations that not only provide relief and development services but also influence public policy. Such a notion identifies a great challenge for NGOs, but its proponents must take on the task of examining how such organisations can adopt such an explicitly political role.

Midgley (1986) has addressed this issue, and has attempted to examine the range of possible interpretations of state involvement in community participation initiatives. He identifies four 'ideal typical modes'. The first is the 'anti participatory mode' in which 'the state acts on behalf of the ruling class, furthering their interests, the accumulation of wealth and the concentration of power. Efforts to mobilise the masses for participation will be seen as a threat and suppressed' (Midgley, 1986, p. 39). Slightly more favourable is the 'manipulative mode . . . [in which] the state supports community participation but does so for ulterior motives. Among these are a desire to use community participation for purposes of political and social control' (Midgley, 1986, p. 40). The third type, the 'incremental mode', is characterised by 'official support for community participation ideas but also by a *laissez-faire* or ambivalent approach to implementation that fails to support local activities properly' (Midgley, 1986, p. 42). The final model is the 'participatory mode' when 'the state approves fully of community participation and responds by creating mechanisms for the effective involvement of local communities in all aspects of development' (Midgley, 1986, pp. 43–4).

While Midgley's four modes form an interesting effort to classify state involvement in community participation his typology is found to be of limited utility when applied to empirical materials. Only a small number of instances of the anti-participatory mode can be identified – Chile, Kampuchea (under the Khmer Rouge), Haiti and

Somozan Nicaragua. The fourth category, the participatory mode, is found to be a pure ideal with no evidence that it reflects a real-world experience. In consequence, almost all cases fall into the second and third categories, but, as it is virtually impossible to define a boundary between the manipulative and incremental modes, and as the information on which to allocate specific country experiences to these categories is often largely subjective, the typology is of little use for analysing empirical evidence. In practice, both the manipulative and incremental modes will manifest themselves through similar actions and require data about state motivation if they are to be separated. As an analytical framework Midgley's approach can also be criticised for treating the state as a monolithic entity rather than an arena for continuous conflict in which different major actors and agencies may be operating in different modes at any specific time.

The analysis of the ways in which those who control state power use their positions to define the nature of the state's relationship to community organisations thus remains an unresolved theoretical issue. Although the issue may appear removed from the immediate concerns of the practitioner it is a matter to which proponents of participation and community organisation must apply some thought. It is of crucial importance to individuals deciding whether to devote their energies to a participatory approach within the existing power structures or whether to put those energies into an organisation that subverts the state and seeks to restructure society by radical means. While the foreign 'do-gooder' can argue for community organisation approaches in almost any situation with limited personal risks, host-country counterparts may be taking on a dangerous role when they openly attempt to promote organisational innovations for the poor. For example, some twenty-one leaders of the Farmer Federation of Thailand which spearheaded demands for land reform were assassinated between March 1974 and August 1975 (Morrell and Samudavanija, cited in Esman and Uphoff, 1984, p. 184).

The case study materials available indicate that while community organisation approaches are not a panacea for development, they can make real contributions to the welfare of poorer people, can provide a possible means by which poor people can gain a greater awareness of the possibility of change (in a Freirian sense) and can exert pressure for social change. In the following pages two specific examples of successful community organisational approaches are presented. These provide a vivid illustration of the potential and problems of such approaches and of the roles that social scientists might play in their evolution.

DEVELOPING IRRIGATOR ASSOCIATIONS: COMMUNAL IRRIGATION SYSTEMS IN THE PHILIPPINES

Effective irrigation requires the application of suitable irrigation technologies alongside appropriate social organisations that can maintain and govern these technological systems. The first of these requirements is recognised to be the domain of engineers, while the latter has been of particular interest to social scientists (for example, see Bacdayan, 1974; Geertz, 1967; Leach, 1961). The task of improving and introducing irrigation systems has often tended to emphasise technological factors and has been seen as the sole responsibility of engineers. The role of the social organisations that are to operate new or improved irrigation facilities have been largely ignored. Indeed, a common assumption of those practically involved in irrigation projects has been that government officials will be responsible for all aspects of the operation of an irrigation system. Only in very recent times have social scientists begun to get involved in the analysis and design of the organisations that commonly have to take responsibility for system maintenance, water allocation, resource mobilisation and conflict management (for a review of the tasks that irrigation institutions must undertake, see Coward, 1985).

In the Philippines, as in many other south and south-east Asian nations, community-based irrigation systems have been in operation for many hundreds of years (Lewis, 1971), as villagers have banded together to control local water resources in ways that would make water supply to agriculture more stable and reliable. Although colonial and subsequently independent governments were most interested in large-scale national irrigation schemes they also intervened in the operation of community irrigation systems through public works programmes and grants. This was the situation in the Philippines until 1974 when a presidential decree authorised the National Irrigation Administration (NIA) to provide support for communal systems. The NIA is a large state agency which (in the mid 1980s) employs 30,000 staff and oversees the operations of 508,000 hectares of national irrigation schemes and 615,000 hectares of community irrigation schemes.

When taking responsibility for communal irrigation schemes the 'NIA viewed its work primarily as the construction of physical facilities and paid minimal attention to forming irrigators' associations' (Bagadion and Korten, 1985, p. 55). As most of its professional staff had engineering backgrounds the NIA decided to contract the social organisations aspects of its community irrigation activities to another government agency with a more broadly based staff, the Farming Systems Development Corporation (FSDC). This was in part because the NIA recognised that it had little capacity to develop irrigator associations, but it also revealed a number of premises underlying NIA operations. These were that construction and organisation were separate tasks; that co-ordination between these tasks was not a major issue; and that social organisation was a task that occurred after engineering work had been completed.

The initial results of this two agency arrangement were unsatisfactory, so in 1976 an alternative approach was launched on a pilot basis. The concept underpinning this new approach was that the NIA should hire its own community organisers who would live in the project area and strengthen irrigator asssociations several months before engineering work commenced. It was believed that involving irrigator associations in the preliminary tasks of system redesign would provide a useful means of developing management skills within the membership and eliciting farmer commitment to the association. Effective involvement in the redesign exercise required that farmers and NIA engineers had to meet regularly to examine proposals and take decisions by a means acceptable to both parties. Structuring the irrigator-engineer interface became the key role for community organisers and gradually a complex process for irrigator-engineer interaction evolved (Table 7.1). This process meant that technical staff acquired detailed local information and learned about local preferences and priorities. At the same time, irrigator associations were strengthened as their members saw that they could influence decisions and acquire additional skills. The pilot project faced numerous problems, but means of overcoming these were found and in 1979 the experiment was extended to two further projects. During this period, social scientists from the Institute of Philippine Culture, management specialists from the Asian Institute of Management and irrigation engineers from the International Rice

Table 7.1 Procedure for rehabilitating communal irrigation schemes, National Irrigation Administration, Philippines

Phase 1
a. Community organisers enter local communities at selected site, and begin working with, and organising, irrigator associations.

b. Community organisers and NIA technical staff hold initial discussions with farmers about the project. Initial engineering studies are conducted.

Phase 2
a. Further studies of topographical and hydrological system are made with farmers (i.e. walking the ground with engineers).

b. Community organisers and technical staff design a planning process and provisional timetable.

c. Farmers take part in surveys and prepare water permit applications.

d. Joint NIA–irrigator association planning sessions.

Phase 3
a. Initial decisions about location and modification of major irrigation canals are made by farmers and NIA staff.

b. Irrigator association is formalised (i.e. laws are documented, disseminated, amended and ratified by members).

c. Irrigator association is registered with Securities and Exchange Commission.

d. Association holds meetings for farmers to discuss plans.

Phase 4
a. NIA staff revise plans in the light of discussions at farmer meetings.

Phase 5
a. Joint NIA–irrigator association meetings to discuss designs with farmers.

b. Farmers apply for and acquire rights of way.

Phase 6
a. NIA staff prepare detailed project estimates and programme of work.

b. Preparations are made for an NIA–irrigator association conference to make the final construction plans.

Phase 7
a. First pre-construction conference is held.

b. Materials and equipment are procured and access road constructed.

c. Committees are established to oversee implementation (procurement committee, cost control committee, equity participation committee, manpower placement committee, quality and control committee).

d. Preparations are made for second pre-construction conference and contract signing.

Source: Adapted from Bryant and White (1984)

Research Institute conducted action research studies. So that the lessons generated from the experiment could be systematically recorded and utilised, monthly 'process documentation reports' were inaugurated and these were reviewed by an NIA-chaired Communal Irrigation Committee which, in effect, guided the experiment. In 1980, twelve new projects started using the participatory approach. This increased to twenty-four new projects in 1981 and 108 new projects in 1982. In 1983, the participatory approach became the standard procedure for all community irrigation schemes. By 1987, some 1135 communal systems, covering 180,000 hectares, had been rehabilitated using the new approach (Bagadion and Korten, 1985).

The capacity-building process that the NIA evolved closely follows David Korten's conceptualisation of a learning process approach. It commenced as a small-scale experiment that was closely monitored by technical staff and social scientists and then modified. It linked a community organisation to a source of technical expertise, and, as the experiment proceeded, knowledge gained during implementation was systematically evaluated, documented and used to redesign future actions. As the pilot project became effective it was gradually expanded to other areas. Personnel involved in the initial experiment became the supervisors and trainers for the new schemes. A powerful and well-informed steering committee identified necessary changes in agency policy that would support the new approach. It was not until five years after start-up that the pilot project was replicated on an appreciable scale, and three more years before it became standard procedure.

Full adoption of the participatory approach has been associated with many changes. Within the NIA a new cadre of community organisers has been established, numbering 395 by 1987 (Bagadion and Korten, 1985). Initially, community organisers were part of an NIA-Ford Foundation project but they are now an integral element of the NIA field-level structure and report to the provincial irrigation engineer in their respective regions. The NIA has introduced new techniques, such as the use of socio-technical profiles, and in turn these have meant that average project lead time has been increased by several months. Mechanisms for co-ordinating the engineering and the organisational tasks in each project have had to be developed (see Bagadion and Korten, 1985, for flow chart details of co-ordination). The involvement of farmers in project design has led to an increasing proportion of works contracts being awarded to irrigator associations themselves and to the introduction of financial recording and reconciliation procedures that meet irrigation association as well as NIA needs. Finally, technical staff now take part in post-construction activities, particularly the planning of operations and maintenance systems for rehabilitated irrigation facilities.

Such changes have required 'fundamental shifts in the norms and attitudes of NIA personnel' (Bagadion and Korten, 1989). Staff have had to adopt a more interactive approach to their relations with farmers, have had to tackle professional propensities to distance themselves from their clients and have to think about the 'software' (i.e. non-physical aspects) of development programmes. These changes have not come easily nor automatically, but they have been fostered by modifying the incentive structure operating within the NIA. Prior to the participatory approach, project performance was measured in terms of physical accomplishments, especially the engineer's estimate of the theoretical irrigated area rehabilitated by the project, and by the attainment of financial disbursement targets. Subsequent to the new approach, physical accomplishment has been measured in terms of the area actually cultivated by farmers after construction. In addition, the achievement of a 10 per cent equity contribution by irrigation associations is now used as a performance indicator. Both of these changes act as an incentive to NIA field staff to ensure that facilities meet farmer needs and that farmers support the design proposals. As an added incentive, provincial irrigation offices are now partially funded by the collection of equity and amortisation payments from communal irrigation systems within the province. This means that the budget level is dependent on client satisfaction and, in consequence, behaviours that facilitate consultation with farmers are encouraged. These measures have led to 'a new organisational culture more compatible with the need to build local social capacity for irrigation' (Bagadion and Korten, 1989).

But does a local capacity-building approach actually generate improved system performance? A major study of the NIA (de los Reyes and Jopillo, 1986) revealed considerable evidence that this was the case. This evaluation compared the achievements of twenty-four participatory projects (i.e. those fielding community organisers and following the experimental approach) with those of twenty-two non-participatory projects (i.e. the original NIA approach) in which engineering and organisational tasks were separated. The study

Table 7.2   Field level effects of the participatory approach to communal irrigation
system by the National Irrigation Administration, Philippines

	Participatory schemes * (*n*=24)	Non participatory schemes * (*n*=22)
Functionality		
% of rehabilitated canals abandoned or erased by farmers	9%	18%
% of structures viewed as defective by irrigator associations	13%	20%
Increase in Irrigated Area		
Wet season	18%	17%
Dry season	35%	18%
Increase in Productivity per Hectare		
Wet season yield	7.3%	2.3%
Dry season yield	21.5%	−1.2%
Leadership Structure		
% of Irrigator association leaders owning no land	47%	35%
Water Management		
Use of water rotation when water is scarce		
Wet season	25%	18%
Dry season	58%	36%
Irrigation System Maintenance		
Voluntary labour (hours per hectare per year)	12	12
Maintenance staff employed by irrigator association (per system)	2.7	1.8
Recovery of Construction Costs		
Farmer equity per hectare	P357†	P54†
Farmer equity per system user	P348†	P44†
% of amortisation payments	82%	50%
Total Rehabilitation Costs		
Costs per hectare	P15648†	P15600†

Source: de los Reyes and Jopillo (1986)
* See text for explanation of these terms
† Costs in 1984 pesos (in 1984, US$1.00=P20, approx.)

(Table 7.2) found that the participatory approach shared a number
of characteristics, detailed here:

1.   It produced infrastructures that were judged to function better.
2.   It was associated with larger increases in the area under irriga-
     tion during the dry season.
3.   It was associated with higher levels of productivity.

4. It had greater levels of participation in management by non land-owning (i.e. poorer) systems users.
5. It was more likely to be associated with water rotation practices that ensure that all members get a share of available water resources at times of scarcity.
6. It had greater contributions of community-provided maintenance efforts.
7. It had higher levels of equity contribution by members and better rates of repayment of amortisation charges.

The cost of the new method was virtually identical to that of the earlier method (P15,648 per irrigated hectare as against P15,600, at 1984 prices). The higher cost recovery rates achieved by the participatory schemes meant that for the government these schemes showed much better rates of financial return. While there is some evidence that the participatory projects produce a better economic return than the non-participatory projects, a comprehensive cost-benefit analysis could not be made because of the lack of data about the additional production costs incurred for the achievement of higher agricultural yields on the participatory schemes.

Overall then, the NIA's decision to opt for an approach to communal irrigation system rehabilitation that linked engineering works with social organisational efforts is borne out by the empirical evidence. However, the very success of the approach may now be generating new problems with which the NIA must grapple. In particular, the open and flexible approach to the structuring of irrigator associations (see Table 7.1) that evolved in the pilot stages, may now be giving way to a more standardised approach. Now that community organisers are a large group integral to the NIA bureaucracy, rather than a small group of committed individuals engaged in an exciting experiment, a tendency to bureaucratise all procedures and promote an NIA-preferred irrigation association structure, rather than let farmers decide what structure they think most appropriate, may be discerned (Tapay *et al.*, 1987). As well, 'recent developments suggest that the NIA is placing greater emphasis on the establishment of the organisation as the end result, rather than the establishment of an organisation which fosters genuine participation of members' (Tapay *et al.*, 1987, p. 139). The challenge of creating a 'learning process approach' is not merely to evolve a successful operational strategy, but also to maintain the quality of the approach when operations are scaled up and personnel are likely to be less committed than those involved in the early stages.

The NIA experience in developing a local capacity-building approach points to a number of potential lessons. These include support for the argument that investment in social organisation building must cover its costs by enhancing economic performance; that such organisations must be given authority over key decisions if they are to gain strength and become effective; that external catalysts can help to develop local organisations; that the members of a local organisation should hold equity in the activity in which they are involved; and that such initiatives should commence as small-scale pilot projects that are subsequently systematically monitored and modified until suitable for gradual expansion. Many of these lessons are being taken up in other irrigation projects in Asia (for example, see Uphoff, 1987, on the Gal Oya Scheme in Sri Lanka).

These are all lessons that are reinforced by the next case study, the Grameen Bank, although it operates in a different functional area. There are, however, two major differences that the reader should note. The first is that the Grameen Bank was initiated by the voluntary sector, not the government. The second is that the Grameen Bank actively seeks to create entirely new organisations, cutting across existing social structures, rather than building on what already exists, as does the NIA.

GROUP CREDIT FOR THE POOR: THE GRAMEEN BANK IN BANGLADESH

A common public policy in many developing countries has been the direction of credit, often at subsidised interest rates, to poorer rural people in an attempt to stimulate economic growth and alleviate poverty. Commercial banks have been seen as unwilling to lend to the poor, while moneylenders and traders have been viewed as charging exploitative rates of interest. However, the massive resources that have been channelled through state and parastatal institutions by such efforts have usually produced disappointing results (von Pischke, 1983; World Bank, 1984). High administrative costs allied to low interest rates and poor recovery rates have meant that most agencies involved in this activity have not been financially viable. There is also much evidence that funds have been diverted to better-off groups and that the poor have not benefited.

In Bangladesh, the Grameen Bank has bucked this trend and has managed to make a profitable business out of lending to hundreds of thousands of low-income borrowers. It has demonstrated that the poor are bankable. Throughout the 1980s the Grameen Bank has served as an inspiration for many development workers. Its success has led to international experimentation and has encouraged a renewed interest in credit strategies.

The Grameen Bank (in English this would be the Village Bank) started out in August 1976 as the Grameen Bank Project in the village of Jobra, Chittagong District. The project was the brainchild of Muhammad Yunus, a Professor of Economics at Chittagong University, who believed that the poor could be reliable borrowers and could be trusted to make wise investment choices. Over a three-year period Yunus experimented with organisational structure and procedures on this action-research project. By trial and error he developed a set of responses to the challenge of lending to the poor. The aim was to provide low-income households (the types of families portrayed in case study 1 of Chapter 2), having no access to formal credit, with small sums of money (US$30 to US$50) for micro-enterprises. At first, loans were given direct to individuals, but this proved problematic, so Yunus experimented with aggregating borrowers in groups of ten or more (Fuglesang and Chandler, 1986, p. 57). These groups were relatively ineffective, however, as they did not foster financial self-discipline and many members did not bother to take part in group meetings. This finding led to experimentation with smaller groups and Yunus found that results were particularly promising when they had only five members and when several groups (from the same village) were federated into centres. There was also experimentation with procedures and gradually a set of experiences emerged from which a novel operational banking system, appropriate to the requirements of poorer borrowers, could be designed.

By 1979, these structures and procedures had been formalised as by-laws and in 1980 the Grameen Bank began to scale up its activities when the International Fund for Agricultural Development (IFAD) provided a loan of US$3.4 million. In 1983, the Bank was officially gazetted as an independent bank by the Bangladesh government. The following year IFAD loaned the Bank US$23.6 million for a second expansionary phase that seeks to permit it to operate across the entire country (IFAD, 1987, p. 8). By early 1987 the Bank had more than 247,000 active members in 10,800 centres (Hossain, 1988, p. 33) and was well on the way to its target of one million borrowers by the end of the decade. To understand the Bank's achievements it is necessary to examine its structures and procedures and see how these have evolved out of its four basic principles – discipline, unity, courage and hard work.

At the group level, unity is fostered by drawing members from a homogeneous socio-economic group. The Bank has eligibility criteria that exclude people owning more than 0.4 acres of land from becoming members. In this way the local elite is barred from the Bank's activities and the likelihood of capture or co-optation by powerful local interests is made unlikely. The five members who band together to form a group must know and trust each other as, although loans are made to individuals, group members can only take out new loans if the other group members are up-to-date with their loan repayments. The group takes responsibility for analysing the feasibility of each member's loan proposal and ensuring that every loan is repaid, either through social pressure or social support if there is a risk of default. Loans are used for a wide range of purposes including paddy husking, purchasing cows, weaving, cycle repair, goat rearing, cloth manufacture, lime-making and petty trading. Groups contribute to a group fund from which they can make loans as they wish, and from which defaults can be covered. Each group is led by a chairperson selected by members on an annual basis. To ensure that groups are not dominated by an individual, and that all members understand how the Bank operates, leadership must be rotated and no member can chair a group for a second time until all the other members have held the chair. Members of the same family and close relatives are not permitted to join the same group.

Six groups are organised into a centre comprised of thirty members. A centre must construct a shelter for its weekly meetings with bank workers, and must follow a defined procedure at each meeting. Groups arrange themselves in rows with their chairpersons at the end of each row and with the elected centre chief at the front leading the meeting with the Bank field officer. The centre chief can hold her/his position for only one year and then the position must be rotated to reduce opportunities for oligarchy. All members are expected to attend meetings which involve the raising of the Grameen Bank flag, completing a routine of physical exercises, singing Bank songs, discussing any issues that are raised, openly making compulsory savings of one taka (about US$0.03), making any loan repayments that are due and receiving new loans. All transactions are conducted in public view, so as to minimise opportunities for malpractice, and procedures are kept as simple as possible. Whenever difficult decisions have to be made the centre chief attempts to get a consensus agreement by allowing lengthy discussion, as it is believed that voting on such matters can encourage factionalism. The flag, physical exercises and songs help to build solidarity among members and serve to make members closely identify themselves with their centre and the Bank. In deference to Bangladesh's predominantly Muslim culture, centres are strictly segregated in terms of gender and women now comprise about 75 per cent of total membership.

The Bank field workers usually service two centres each day, making them each responsible for overseeing approximately 300 members (Fuglesang and Chandler, 1986). Centres are usually within a five mile radius of a Bank branch, so that workers can reach them by walking or cycling. Generally, a branch has five or six field workers under the supervision of a branch manager. As with groups and centres, bank workers are rotated on an annual basis to work in different villages administered by the branch. This broadens their experience and also reduces the likelihood of the establishment of vested interests and favouritism. The expansion of the Bank has created promotion opportunities at all levels, but it has been at a pace that generally ensures that an individual does not attain a supervisory or training position until they have performed the function to be supervised for a lengthy period. The Bank runs on commercial lines, so that financial discipline is emphasised at all levels and interest rates of 16 per cent, in 1986, are charged (Hossain 1988, p. 178). Each branch is accounted for as a profit centre and, as an inducement to performance, a 10 per cent share of any profit a branch makes is distributed to branch employees.

By adopting an experimental approach to structure and procedure the Grameen Bank has managed to disburse loans to the poor. Its design has been tightly monitored and controlled by Professor Yunus and his staff. Members have limited influence over these design features, but they do control a number of key local-level decisions, most particularly whether or not a loan should be granted. The limits to member participation are rigidly laid down by head office. Despite this centralisation of decision-making, some might call it paternalism, a management process has been established which fosters member and staff commitment to the organisation.

The performance of the Grameen Bank has been praised by many writers. Mosley and Dahal (1987) present a favourable summary of the Bank's results for its early years and more recently Hossain (1988) conducted a survey of 975 borrowers that broadly confirms these findings. The Bank has achieved loan recovery rates of around 98 per cent, a figure which stands in sharp contrast to the recovery rates for rural credit attained by other banks in Bangladesh, which are generally in the 35 per cent to 65 per cent range. Hossain's study concludes that the Bank is reaching its defined target group and that only 4.2 per cent of Bank members in his sample had landholdings above the specified limit. There is considerable evidence that the loans have a beneficial impact on member household incomes as Grameen Bank members have, on average, household incomes 43 per cent higher than those of similar control groups in non-Bank villages (Hossain 1988, pp. 9–11). Only 27 months after receiving his/her first loan from the Grameen Bank, the average borrower has trebled the value of capital at his/her disposal. Hossain also records beneficial employment effects, especially for women. However, he does find that the Bank's plans to move into lending for larger scale collective enterprises have had to be scaled down because such businesses have encountered financial difficulties.

The Bank itself has reported a profit since 1984/85 but this has only been achieved by depositing a significant proportion of IFAD supplied concessional credit on deposit with other banks. Hossain estimates that in 1986 the cost of loan operations was 21.7 per cent of the value of outstanding loans. He doubts that this high level of operating costs subsidy can be counted on as the Bank expands and so the Bank may be forced to change some of its policies in the near future.

Overall, then, there is considerable evidence that the Bank has developed a lending programme that successfully meets the needs of a group of poor borrowers who have not previously had access to formal sector credit. From modest local beginnings the Bank has scaled up its operations to cover several thousand villages. Its performance has stimulated experimentation by other banks and agencies so that its impact is being felt throughout the financial sector. For some commentators the Bank is not merely a credit agency but is a 'socio-economic formation' (Fuglesang and Chandler, 1986) engendering the conscientisation of the poor and the creation of an organisational capacity that may permit previously powerless groups to push for social change. In some localities it is believed that centres have managed to drive up agricultural labour rates and this can be cited as evidence of their growing strength. However, other commentators claim that the Bank only operates in villages where it has the approval of the local elite and that far from empowering the poor it provides a new mechanism for local elites to maintain their position. A lack of empirical research on this topic makes it difficult to draw conclusions on this issue at present.

The management of the Bank's relationship with the state is a key issue that the Bank's leadership has carefully considered. As the Bank's membership expands the political influence that accrues because of this increase becomes more and more significant. At present the Bank's board has twelve members, three of whom are directly appointed by the government. When, and if, Bangladesh returns to democracy, the temptation to align with political parties promoting social change may become a question that diverts the Bank from its financial activities. Takeover by the government is also a possible development. Such an eventuality would most likely destroy the organisational culture that is at the heart of the Grameen Bank.

At the international level the Bank has had a major impact and entertains a constant stream of overseas visitors. Its success has led to a renewed interest in aid policies that target finance towards the poor. There are moves to replicate the Grameen Bank in Malaysia, Sri Lanka, Malawi, Egypt and the Sudan. In some situations the idea of using the Bank as a model has been approached relatively pragmatically as part of a learning process in which Grameen principles are used to design pilot projects as part of an action-research initiative. The Redd Barnna SAVECRED scheme in Sri Lanka falls into this category. Official assistance agencies are more constrained in terms of their ability to mount open-ended experiments. However, the Malawi Mudzi Fund, part of a World Bank–IFAD project, shows a more sensitive approach to donor-assisted 'replication' than occurred in earlier decades with co-operatives and community development.

CONCLUSION

The materials reviewed in this chapter demonstrate the need for continued involvement by sociologists and other social scientists in the analysis of the organisations and organisational changes that are an inevitable aspect of any form of planned development. This involvement entails the elaboration of theoretical frameworks alongside detailed empirical studies. A major objective of such work should be the development of more sophisticated, and useful, methodologies for action. These methodologies should not be of a mechanistic form that presupposes the possibility of identifying a best option organisational form and procedure. Rather, sociologists should aim to develop tools that permit the local level organisations engaged in development to be monitored and redesigned more effectively.

The consequences of glib prescription and weak conceptualisation have already been well illustrated by the co-operative and community development experiences. Theoretical advances through the 1970s and 1980s have proven the falsity of paradigms that assume that standardised organisational prescriptions can cope with the demand for local-level management capacity created by development initiatives. The design of social organisations is contingent upon so many case-specific factors, which are constantly changing, that a process approach must be adopted, linking knowledge to action and permitting those responsible for organisational development constantly to modify the experiments in which they are involved. These findings indicate the need for small-scale experimentation with organisational forms and procedures and gradual evolution, rather than large-scale interventions that assume such issues can be thought through.

Social scientists can play a key role in this process by creating and using tools for monitoring and systematically documenting experience. In particular they can analyse the ways in which new or modified organisations interact with the social and political frameworks in which they are embedded. In this way their contributions may complement the reductionist approaches of the credit specialist, irrigation engineer, financial analyst, agriculturalist or other subject-specific specialist involved in formulating development plans and policies. Much of the demand for such social analysis will be in rural areas, as illustrated by the cases in this chapter, but there will also be applications in urban areas (for an illustration see Turner, 1976).

In addition to action-research projects of the type that led the NIA to reform its approach to community irrigation systems, there is a pressing need for more focused theoretical and empirical study of the relationships between local organisations, their members, local elites and those who exercise state power. This is of direct relevance to development interventions in terms of determining the environments in which local organisations are best structured on exclusive lines, rather than inclusive lines, and are best served by adopting confrontational tactics with agents of the state, rather than co-operative tactics. In what situations should proponents of local organisation favour approaches that permit the 'excluded strata [of society to] confront the supporters and controllers of sets of social arrangements which determine patterns of access to resources, services, status and power, seeking a new deal' (Stiefel and Pearse, 1982, p. 46), and in what circumstances should they favour approaches that make them a delivery mechanism for state-sponsored policies? Do induced activity-specific social organisations, such as those established by the Grameen Bank and NIA, empower marginalised groups in terms of stimulating a process of social change that enables them to exert greater influence in local and national political arenas? The analysis of this issue will demand a renewed interest in the study of field-level bureaucrats, those that deal directly with the general public and local leaders, alongside the study of senior government officials and national politicians.

The sorely needed task of refining the concept of empowerment that underpins an emphasis on the creation of a greater organisational capacity at local level should be facilitated by such work. Talcott Parsons's (1960, pp. 220–2) distinction between the distributive dimension of power (which refers to the ability of a person or a group to force their will on another) and the generative dimension of power (which refers to actions that enable a society or social unit to increase its ability to change its future as an act of choice) presents one possible starting point for such efforts. Those who assume that power has only a distributive dimension, and thus regard it as having a fixed volume, see little possibility for co-operative action and anticipate that existing powerholders will resist or co-opt any organisational initiative (Korten, 1987, pp. 6–7). The generative dimension of power points to the possibility that 'all members of a society or other social unit may benefit from an increase in its power if the increments in power are broadly shared within the group' (Korten, 1987). In effect, this suggests an alternative to the economist's concept of economic man, based on individualism, selfishness and competitiveness. Is it possible to develop a countervailing concept of socio-economic man, in which a highly rational individual choice leads in certain circumstances to the selection of behaviours which are group-based, generous and co-operative? The construction of a model of socio-economic man is thus another possible starting point for more sophisticated theoretical and empirical analysis. In any practical attempt to create an empowerment process a mix of the distributive and generative aspects of power will occur. The analysis of the modes in which these dimensions interact, and of mechanisms for increasing the likelihood of preferred forms of interaction eventuating, is another direction for inquiry.

Case studies illustrate the feasibility of developing local organisational capacities and improving the status of disadvantaged groups by participatory approaches to development. Our understanding of the complex processes that are set off when such interventions are attempted remains partial, however, and much more must be discovered about the nature of empowerment. Notions of empowerment derive from concepts of power, and it is this theme that forms the basis for the concluding chapter.

8

CONCLUSION

Since its inception in the 1950s the sociology of development has undergone a number of transformations. The optimistic assumptions of the modernisation perspective were confounded by poor developmental performance. The neo-Marxist critique spawned innovative theories but their ambitious global aspirations came unstuck in the diverse empirical experience of the Third World. The gloomy admissions of theoretical impasse in the mid-1980s have now been left behind as the sociology of development shows a renewed dynamism and strives for modes of analysis that will take it 'beyond the impasse' (Sklair, 1988; Vandergeest and Buttel, 1988).

Three elements of this renewal should be noted. First, the sociology of development is a hybrid beast. It is not a pure and exclusive sociology. Rather, it draws from other disciplines such as politics, anthropology and economics in order to better analyse the realities of the Third World. This borrowing from other disciplines is not a new phenomenon but is now more openly acknowledged and actively pursued. Development and poverty do not recognise disciplinary boundaries. Likewise, sociologists who study these subjects range widely in order to furnish the best possible analysis. Where human geography or politics end and the sociology of development begins is anybody's guess. A second element is the widespread abandonment of theoretical and conceptual strait-jackets. Orthodoxy is no longer popular and sociologists do not feel compelled to make their analytical offerings conform precisely to a particular theory. This does not mean that some anarchic, atheoretical eclecticism reigns supreme. Rather, sociologists are able to choose the conceptual and theoretical apparatus which best suits the specific unruly experience which they are trying to understand.

While one may favour a particular approach, it is not necessary to adhere to every pronouncement contained in it. Finally, and most importantly, the sociology of development is becoming more practical. As the examples presented in the last few chapters have demonstrated, there have been concerted moves in the direction of an applied stance. Sociologists have shown an increasing interest in making their discipline useful. Accusations of ivory-tower attitudes are no longer justified as a growing number of sociologists employ both the accumulated wisdom and knowledge of previous years and a new-found ingenuity and imagination in their attempts to deal with the practical problems of development. This does not mean that all sociologists are striving to make an impact on policy formulation, planning or programme evaluation. However, the move towards a more practical stance has gathered momentum and seems likely to gain more adherents and greater popularity in the coming years.

Whether the more active involvement of sociologists in applied work will result in improved developmental performance remains to be seen. The standard indicators of development paint a depressing picture. There are more people in poverty than ever before. Social welfare standards have started to slip in many countries. Real incomes are not rising. In many cases the obstacles seem insurmountable. The tragedy is that technology is often not a constraint. The solutions are frequently available but the international environment, political conditions and organisational incapacity combine to thwart potential advances.

The notion of power is central to the development debate, and future success in bringing development to the millions of poor people hinges on the resolution of certain key issues regarding power. First, there is the international dimension. As numerous social scientists have indicated, the political economy of the modern world is not favourable to many Third World countries. Powerful industrial nations strive to maintain their position in the existing scheme of things while a divided Third World consistently fails to act in a concerted manner to alter the status quo. Efforts to improve the trading position of the Third World come to grief at each UNCTAD or GATT meeting; transnational corporations (TNCs) have been accused of exploitation; enormous foreign debt burdens effectively cripple any chances of development in many countries; and the majority of industrial states fail to supply the volume of foreign aid recommended by the United Nations and the Brandt Commission.

While it would be convenient to blame wicked international actors from the industrial countries for the lack of developmental success in many places, this would be a gross oversimplification. Some of the most intractable problems of power and development are to be found on the domestic front. One frequently overlooked fact is war and widespread civil violence. Armed conflicts rage throughout the Third World and disrupt attempts to bring development. People caught in these conflicts generally experience worsening socio-economic conditions and risk injury or even death. The wars vary in form and size: localised tribal fighting in Papua New Guinea, communist insurgency in the Philippines, ethnic strife in Sri Lanka, drug-related violence in Colombia, separatist movements in Ethiopia, foreign-backed intervention in Nicaragua, and wholesale international conflict between Iran and Iraq exemplify the types of armed clashes which proliferate in the Third World. In a recent report (the *Weekend Australian*, 19–20 March 1988) it was noted that all of the twenty-five wars (i.e. conflicts that have cost 1000 or more lives per year) currently raging round the globe were in the Third World. Since the end of the Second World War there have been 17 million killings in wars. Four million of these killings have been in the 1980s. This is not the environment for development. Even when peace is achieved, the legacy of maimed people, a destroyed infrastructure, abandoned toxic and explosive materials, and a deteriorated environment may take decades to set right, as appears to be the situation in Vietnam.

Even where there are no wars, huge military expenditures are often to be found. This spending takes place in the context of scarce financial resources and so has an adverse impact on expenditure on socio-economic development. It often seems the case that 'arms and armies take precedence over needs basic to human development' (Sivard, 1987, p. 23). For example, developing countries spend almost four times as much on arms as on health care. But rising expenditure on the armed forces is to be expected where 59 of 113 governments in one survey of the Third World are of the military variety (Sivard, 1987, p. 26). Even some of the non-military governments of the Third World reserve a prominent place for the military and maintain a high level of military expenditure. The high level of spending is encouraged by the industrial countries who make large profits from the sales of arms to developing nations. In the 1980s, the world's arms trade has been worth about US$36 billion each year with the Third World accounting for approximately 75 per cent of the imports (Sivard, 1987, p. 10) – and this excludes clandestine deals! The USSR is now by far the major source of weapons for the Third World although some developing countries have themselves taken the plunge into weapon production and export.

Even if the trend towards military affluence and militarisation was reversed, those pursuing development would still have to contend with anti-developmental stances of elites and leading classes in many Third World societies. In the 1950s and 1960s it was predicted that modernising elites would emerge to guide backward nations into the promised land of development. But these dynamic species were found to be much rarer than anticipated. While one can point to sweeping land reform, rapid industrialisation and socio-economic equity in Taiwan and a select few countries, such experience is the exception rather than the rule. Elites have generally propagated and presided over versions of development which do not threaten the status quo. They have defended, and perhaps even extended, their interests in a context of societal change. One cannot accuse elites of trying to preserve some fossilised society in which nothing changes. As we have seen, rapid change is characteristic of Third World societies, and elites are at the helm attempting to steer this change in the direction which they desire. The problem is that the elite-dominated version of development frequently fails to address and solve poverty and other urgent issues. It is typically manifest in watered-down land reform, inequitable resource distribution, minimal investment in social welfare, rural neglect, bimodal agricultural strategies, a predilection for prestige projects, regressive taxation, blaming the poor for their predicament, the denial of active mass participation in decision-making and opposition to moves for social justice. Decision-making by many national elites appears to be grounded in notions of distributive power while generative power is denied. The consequence is the creation of a fragile state. Even at the local level, lower level elites make their contribution to promoting change but defending the status quo. For example, landlords may enthusiastically embrace the technological advances of the Green Revolution and in the process boost rice production but widen socio-economic inequalities and increase poverty. Waiting for the 'inevitable' socialist revolution to liberate society has not proved to be a realistic solution. Most often it simply does not occur. When such revolutions have taken place development has frequently been found to be most elusive. Thus, we need to pay close attention to devising policies which are both acceptable to elites and which offer solutions to major developmental problems such as poverty. It is difficult to see how such solutions can be achieved without conflict. The empowerment of the underprivileged classes necessarily challenges the status quo.

Even if elites co-operated in this joint venture there is still the matter of effective developmental policy-making, planning, implementation and evaluation. The bureaucracies are often ill-equipped to perform these tasks effectively and efficiently. A proliferation of state activity undertaken in the name of development has not resulted in the anticipated improvements in socio-economic welfare. Compared to the input of resources the state has generally registered at best a lacklustre performance in providing its citizens with the developmental goods. Output, or the lack of it, from the swollen ranks of the bureaucracy has been the object of increasing criticism and the notion of greater public sector accountability has been gaining popularity. If development is to succeed and the state is to retain its principal role in it then the bureaucracy has to make dramatic improvements in managing development. Unfortunately, the function of state bureaucracies is most often perceived as providing jobs. They are sources of employment rather than facilitators of development. Once viewed in this light, public sector jobs become a form of patronage for national and local elites to preside over. The absence of accountability also means that corruption can flourish, making the likelihood of development even more remote. Building the requisite state institutions with the appropriate organisational capacity is more than a technical matter. It is basically a matter of power: of generating or enforcing a commitment to development, ensuring that adequate technical skills are available and co-ordinating those skills in the most effective and efficient manner. Whether national elites are both willing and able to take the political measures necessary to bring about this desirable state of affairs is a moot point. So, too, is the issue of whether international agencies and foreign governments have the inclination, the right and the ability to attempt to guide national elites in the Third World into adopting policies that are deemed to be appropriate for development.

Sociological analysis reveals that development is highly dependent on the resolution of some or all of the power issues discussed above.

Third World countries need to secure a better deal in the international economy. War, insurgency and the international arms trade work against development. Peace is essential. Elites and dominant classes resist increased political participation by the underprivileged. A reorientation of elite groups to a generative view of power is desirable. But is it feasible? Swollen state bureaucracies absorb huge resources but produce little in the way of effective developmental outcome. Organisational reform is vital. There will be no miraculous transformation in the short or even the medium term for the Third World. Indeed, things are actually getting worse for many of its inhabitants. But, if substantial development progress is to be made then action must be taken on the major issues of power which we raised above. Even then, there will be no easy or rapid path to development for many countries. At least, however, possibilities will be available as constraints on realising developmental potential are removed. Perhaps, then, dreams of development may be transformed into a more substantial reality.

BIBLIOGRAPHY

Abramovitz, M. (1959) *The Allocation of Economic Resources: Essays in Honour of Bernard Frances Haley*, Stanford: Stanford University Press.

Afshar, H. (1985) 'The position of women in an Iranian village', in H. Afshar (ed.) *Women, Work and Ideology in the Third World*, London: Tavistock, pp. 66–82.

Agar, M.H. (1982) 'Toward an ethnographic language', *American Anthropologist*, vol. 84(4), pp. 779–96.

Aguilar, L.E. (ed.) (1968) *Marxism in Latin America*, New York: Knopf.

Ahluwalia, M.S. (1974) 'Income inequality: some dimensions of the problem', *Finance and Development*, vol. 11(3), pp. 3–8.

Ahmad, A. (1985) 'Class, nation, and state: intermediate classes in peripheral societies', in D.L. Johnson (ed.) *Middle Classes in Dependent Countries*, Beverley Hills: Sage, pp. 43–66.

Amin, S. (1976) *Unequal Development*, Hassocks and New York: Harvester Press and Monthly Review Press.

Andreski, S. (1972) *Social Science as Sorcery*, London: Deutsch.

Apthorpe, R. (1970) 'Development studies and social planning', in R. Apthorpe (ed.) *People Planning and Development Studies*, London: Frank Cass, pp. 1–28.

Apthorpe, R. (ed.) (1970) *Rural Cooperatives and Planned Change in Africa*, Geneva: UNRISD.

Apthorpe, R. (1979) 'The burden of land reform in Taiwan: an Asian model land reform reanalysed', *World Development*, vol. 7(4–5), pp. 519–30.

Asian Development Bank (1978) *Rural Asia: Challenge and Opportunity*, New York: Praeger.

Asian Development Bank (1979) *Sector Paper on Agriculture and Rural Development*, Manila: Asian Development Bank.

Atkins, F. (1988) 'Land reform: a failure of neoclassical theorization?' *World Development*, vol. 16(8), pp. 935–46.

Bacdayan, A.S. (1974) 'Mountain irrigators in the Philippines', *Ethnology*, vol. 13, pp. 247–60; reprinted in E.W. Coward (ed.) (1980) *Irrigation and Agricultural Development in Asia*, Ithaca: Cornell University Press.

Bagadion, B.U. and Korten, F.K. (1985 and 1989) 'Developing irrigators' organisations: a learning process approach', in M.M. Cernea (ed.) *Putting People First: Sociological Variables in Rural Development*, Washington DC: Oxford University Press, pp. 52–90 in 1985 edition, second edition 1989.

Bardhan, P.K. (1974) 'India', in H. Chenery, M.S. Ahluwalia, C.L.G. Bell, J.H. Duloy and R. Jolly (eds) *Redistribution with Growth*, Oxford: Oxford University Press, pp. 255–62.

Barnard, R. (1983) 'Housewives and farmers: Malay women in the Muda Irrigation Scheme', in L. Manderson (ed.) *Women's Work and Women's Roles*, Canberra: Australian National University, Development Studies Centre Monograph no. 32, pp. 129–45.

Barnett, A.S. (1977) *The Gezira Scheme: an Illusion of Development*, London: Frank Cass.

Bartelmus, P. (1986) *Environment and Development*, Boston: Allen and Unwin.

Bates, R.H. (1981) *Markets and States in Tropical Africa*, Berkeley: University of California Press.

Bauer, P. (1984) *Reality and Rhetoric: Studies in the Economics of Development*, London: Weidenfeld and Nicolson.

Benor, D. and Harrison, J.Q. (1977) *Agricultural Extension: the Training and Visit System*, Washington D.C.: World Bank.

Berg, A. (1981) *Accelerated Development in Sub-Saharan Africa: An Agenda for Action*, Washington D.C.: World Bank.

Berman, M. (1988) *All that is Solid Melts into Air: the Experience of Modernity*, New York: Penguin

Béteille, A. (1974) *Studies in Agrarian Social Structure*, Delhi: Oxford University Press.

Bhagwati, J.N. (1988) 'Poverty and public policy', *World Development*, vol. 16(5), pp. 539–55.

Binswanger, H. (1989), 'Fiscal and legal incentives with environmental effects on the Brazilian Amazon', *World Bank Discussion Paper*, no. 69, Washington D.C.: World Bank.

Birdsall, N. (1980) 'Population and Poverty in the Developing World', *World Bank Staff Working Paper* no. 404, Washington D.C.: World Bank.

Black, C.E. (1966) 'Change as a condition of modern life', in M. Weiner (ed.) *Modernization: The Dynamics of Growth*, Washington D.C.: Voice of America, US Information Agency, pp. 17–27.

Black, C.E. (1967) *The Dynamics of Modernization: A Study in Comparative History*, New York: Harper and Row.

Blair, H.W. (1978) 'Rural development, class structure and bureaucracy in Bangladesh', *World Development*, vol. 6(1), pp. 65–83.

Blomström, M. and Hettne, B. (1984) *Development Theory in Transition: The Dependency Debate and Beyond: Third World Responses*, London: Zed Books.

Blumberg, R.L. (1981) 'Rural women in development', in N. Black and A.B. Cottrell (eds) *Women and World Change: Equity Issues in Development*, Beverly Hills: Sage, pp. 32–56.

Boeke, J.H. (1953) *Economics and Economic Policy of Dual Societies*, New York: Institute of Pacific Relations.

Booth, D. (1975) 'André Gunder Frank: an introduction and appreciation', in I. Oxaal, T. Barnett and D. Booth (eds) *Beyond the Sociology of Development: Economy and Society in Latin America and Africa*, London: Routledge and Kegan Paul, pp. 50–85.

Booth, D. (1985) 'Marxism and development sociology: interpreting the impasse', *World Development*, vol. 13(7), pp. 761–87.

Boserup, E. (1970) *Woman's Role in Economic Development*, New York: St. Martin's Press.

Boudon, R. (1986) *Theories of Social Change: A Critical Appraisal*, Cambridge: Polity Press.

Box, L. (1988) 'Experimenting cultivators: a method for adaptive agricultural research', *Sociologia Ruralis*, vol. 28(1), pp. 62–75.

Brandt Commission (1980) *North-South: a Program for Survival. Report of the Independent Commission on International Development Issues*, London: Pan.

Brewer, A. (1980) *Marxist Theories of Imperialism: A Critical Survey*, London: Routledge and Kegan Paul.

Bryant, C. and White, L.G. (1984) *Managing Rural Development with Small Farmer Participation*, West Hartford, Conn.: Kumarian Press.

Buvinic, M. and Youssef, N.H. (1987) *Women Headed Households*, Washington D.C.: USAID.

Byres, T.J. (1979) 'Of neo-populist pipe-dreams: Daedalus in the Third World and the myth of urban bias', *Journal of Peasant Studies*, vol. 6(2), pp. 210–44.

Byres, T.J. and Crow, B. (1983) *The Green Revolution in India*, Milton Keynes: Open University Press.

Camp, S.L. and Speidel, M.D. (1987) *Human Suffering Index*, Washington D.C.: Population Crisis Committee.

Cardoso, F.H. and Faletto, E. (1979) *Dependency and Development in Latin America*, Berkeley: University of California Press.

Casley, D.J. and Lury, D.A. (1982) *Monitoring and Evaluation of Agriculture and Rural Development Projects*, Baltimore: Johns Hopkins University Press.

Cernea, M.M. (1983) 'A social methodology for community participation in local investments: the experience of Mexico's PIDER program', *World Bank Staff Working Paper*, no. 598, Washington D.C.: World Bank.

Cernea, M.M. (ed.) (1985) *Putting People First: Sociological Variables in Rural Development*, New York: Oxford University Press.

Cernea, M.M. (1987a) 'The "production" of a social methodology', in E.M. Eddy and W.L. Partridge (eds) *Applied Anthropology in America*, New York: Columbia University Press, pp. 237–62.

Cernea, M.M. (1987b) 'Farmer organizations and institution building for sustainable development', *Regional Development Dialogue*, vol. 8(2), pp. 1–24.

Cernea, M.M. and Guggenheim, S.E. (1985) 'Is anthropology superfluous in farming systems research?' *Farming Systems Research*, vol. 4(9), pp. 504–17.

Chambers, R. (1969) *Settlement Schemes in Tropical Africa*, London: Routledge and Kegan Paul.

Chambers, R. (1981) 'Rural poverty unperceived: problems and remedies', *World Development*, vol. 9(1), pp. 1–19.

Chambers, R. (1983) *Rural Development: Putting the Last First*, London: Longman.

Chambers, R. and Jiggins, J. (1987a) 'Agricultural research for resource-poor farmers, Part I: transfer-of-technology and farming systems research', *Agricultural Administration and Extension*, vol. 27(1), pp. 35–52.

Chambers, R. and Jiggins, J. (1987b) 'Agricultural research for resource-poor farmers, Part II: a parsimonious paradigm', *Agricultural Administration and Extension*, vol. 27(2), pp. 109–28.

Chayanov, A.V. (1966) *The Theory of Peasant Economy*, Homewood, Ill.: Richard C. Irwin.

Clammer, J. (1975) 'Economic anthropology and the sociology of development: "liberal" anthropology and its French critics', in I. Oxaal, T. Barnett and D. Booth (eds) *Beyond the Sociology of Development: Economy and Society in Latin America and Africa*, London: Routledge and Kegan Paul, pp. 208–28.

Clammer, J. (1978a) *The New Economic Anthropology*, London: Macmillan.

Clammer, J. (1978b) 'Concepts and objects in economic anthropology', in J. Clammer (ed.) *The New Economic Anthropology*, London: Macmillan, pp. 1–20.

Cline, W.R. (1982) 'Can the East Asian model of development be generalised?', *World Development*, vol. 10(2), pp. 81–90.

Cohen, J.M. and Isaksson, N-I. (1988) 'Food prodution strategy debates in revolutionary Ethiopia', *World Development*, vol. 16(3), pp. 323–48.

Cohen, J.M. and Uphoff, N.T. (1980) 'Participation's place in rural development: seeking clarity through specificity', *World Development*, vol. 8(3), pp. 213–36.

Cohen, R. (1987) 'A greater south: a reinterpretation of the prelude to the Nigerian civil war', *Manchester Papers on Development*, vol. 3(3), pp. 1–24.

Cole, J. (1987) *Development and Underdevelopment: a Profile of the Third World*, London: Methuen.

Collinson, M. (1985) 'Farming systems research: diagnosing the problems', in M.M. Cernea, J.K. Coulter and J.F.A. Russell (eds) *Research-Extension-Farmer: a Two Way Continuum for Agricultural Development*, Washington D.C.: World Bank.

Colson, E. (1962) *The Plateau Tonga of Northern Rhodesia: Social and Religious Studies*, Manchester: Manchester University Press.

Committee on Australia's Relations with the Third World (CARTW) (1979) *Australia and the Third World*, Canberra: Australian Government Printing Service.

Commoner, B. (1972) *The Closing Circle: Nature, Man and Technology*, London: J. Cope.

Conyers, D. (1982) *An Introduction to Social Planning in the Third World*, Chichester: Wiley.

Cook, P. and Kirkpatrick, C. (1988) *Privatisation in Developing Countries*, Hemel Hempstead: Harvester Wheatsheaf.

Coombs, P.H. and Ahmed, M. (1974) *Attacking Rural Poverty: How Nonformal Education Can Help*, Baltimore: Johns Hopkins University Press.

Corbridge, S. (1982) 'Urban bias, rural bias and industrialisation: an appraisal of the work of Michael Lipton and Terry Byres', in J. Harriss (ed.) *Rural Development Theories of Peasant Economy and Agrarian Change*, London: Hutchinson, pp. 94–116.

Cornia, G.A., Jolly, R. and Stewart, F. (1988) *Adjustment with a Human Face: Protecting the Vulnerable and Promoting Growth*, vols 1 and 2, Oxford: Clarendon Press.

Coward, E.W. (1985) 'Technical and social change in currently irrigated regions: rules, roles and rehabilitation', in M.M. Cernea (ed.) *Putting People First: Sociological Variables in Rural Development*, Washington D.C.: Oxford University Press, pp. 27–51.

Dasmann, R.F. (1972) *Planet in Peril? Man and the Biosphere Today*, Harmondsworth: Penguin-UNESCO.

De'Ath, C. (1980) *The Throwaway People: Social impact of the Gogol Timber Project, Madang Province*, IASER Monograph 13. Boroko: Institute of Applied Social and Economic Research.

de Figueroa, T.O. (1976) 'A critical analysis of Latin American programs to integrate women in development', in I. Tinker and M.B. Bramsen (eds) *Women and World Development*, Washington D.C.: Overseas Development Council, pp. 45–53.

Deyo, F.C. (1987) 'Introduction', in F.C. Deyo (ed.) *The Political Economy of the New Asian Industrialism*, Ithaca: Cornell University Press, pp. 11–22.

Diamond, L. (1987) 'Class formation in the swollen African state', *The Journal of Modern African Studies*, vol. 25(4), pp. 567–96.

Donges, J.B. (1976) 'A comparative survey of industrialisation policies in fifteen semi-industrial countries', *Weltwirtschaftliches Archiv*, vol. 112(4), pp. 626–59.

Doran, C.F., Modelski, G. and Clark, C. (eds) (1983) *North/South Relations: Studies of Dependency Reversal*, New York: Praeger.

Dore, R. (1976) *The Diploma Disease: Education, Qualification and Development*, London: Allen and Unwin.

Dore, R. (1970) 'Modern cooperatives in traditional communities', in P. Worsley (ed.) *Two Blades of Grass: Rural Cooperatives in Agricultural Modernisation*, Manchester: Manchester University Press, pp. 43–60.

Dorner, P. (1972) *Land Reform and Economic Development*, London: Penguin.

Dube, S.C. (1958) *India's Changing Villages: Human Factors in Community Development*, London: Routledge and Kegan Paul.

Dunham, D. (1982) 'Politics and land settlement schemes in Sri Lanka', *Development and Change*, vol. 13(1), pp. 43–61.

Ehrlich, P.R. and A.H. (1970) *Population, Resources, Environment: Issues in Human Ecology*, San Francisco: W.H. Freeman.

Eisenstadt, S.N. (1970) 'Breakdowns of modernization', in S.N. Eisenstadt (ed.) *Readings in Social Evolution and Development*, Oxford: Pergamon, pp. 421–52.

Elson, D. and Pearson, R. (1981) 'Nimble fingers make cheap workers: an analysis of women's employment in Third World manufacturing', *Feminist Review*, vol. 7, pp. 87–107.

Emmanuel, A. (1972) *Unequal Exchange, A Study of the Imperialism of Trade*, London: New Left Books and Monthly Review Press.

Esman, M.J. and Uphoff, N.T. (1984) *Local Organizations: Intermediaries in Rural Development*, Ithaca: Cornell University Press.

Fals Borda, O. (1969) *Cooperatives and Rural Development in Latin America*, Geneva: UNRISD.

Feldman, R. (1975) 'Rural social differentiation and political goals in Tanzania', in I. Oxaal, T. Barnett and D. Booth (eds) *Beyond the Sociology of Development: Economy and Society in Latin America and Africa*, London: Routledge and Kegan Paul, pp. 154–82.

Feuerstein, M.T. (1986) *Partners in Evaluation: Evaluating Development and Community Programmes with Participants*, London: Macmillan.

Fields, G.S. (1981) *Poverty, Inequality and Development*, Cambridge: Cambridge University Press.

Fitzpatrick, P. (1980) *Law and State in Papua New Guinea*, London: Academic Press.

Forrester, J.W. (1971) *World Dynamics*, Cambridge, Mass.: Wright-Allan.

Foster, G.M. (1962) *Traditional Cultures: the Impact of Technological Change*, New York: Harper and Row.

Foster, G.M. (1965) 'Peasant society and the image of the limited good', *American Anthropologist*, vol. 67, pp. 293–315.

Foster-Carter, A. (1978) 'Can we articulate "articulation"?', in J. Clammer (ed.) *The New Economic Anthropology*, London: Macmillan, pp. 210–49; also published in 1978 in *New Left Review*, vol. 107.

Frank, A.G. (1969) *Capitalism and Underdevelopment in Latin America: Historical Studies of Chile and Brazil*, New York: Monthly Review Press.

Frank, A.G. (1971) *Capitalism and Underdevelopment in Latin America*, Harmondsworth: Penguin, first published in 1969 in New York by Monthly Review Press.

Frank A.G. (1972) *Lumpenbourgeoisie-Lumpendevelopment*, New York: Monthly Review Press.

Freire, P. (1972) *Pedagogy of the Oppressed*, Harmondsworth: Penguin.

French, W. and Walter, M. (1984) *What Worth Evaluation? Experiences from the World Bank Funded Integrated Rural Development Project in the Southern Highlands Province, Papua New Guinea*, Boroko: Institute of Applied Social and Economic Research, IASER Monograph 24.

Freyhold, M. von (1979) *Ujamaa Villages in Tanzania: Analysis of a Social Experiment*, London: Heinemann.

Froebel, F., Heinrichs, J. and Kreye, O. (1980) *The New International Division of Labour*, Cambridge: Cambridge University Press.

Fuglesang, A. and Chandler, D. (1986) *Participation as Process: What Can We Learn from Grameen Bank, Bangladesh*, Oslo: Norwegian Ministry of Development Cooperation.

Geertz, C. (1967) 'Organization of the Balinese *subak*', in Koentjaraningrat, (ed.) *Villages in Indonesia*, Ithaca: Cornell University Press, pp. 210–43; reprinted in E.W. Coward (ed.) (1980) *Irrigation and Agricultural Development in Asia*, Ithaca: Cornell University Press.

Gittinger, J.P. (1982) *Economic Appraisal of Agricultural Projects*, second edn, Baltimore: Johns Hopkins University Press.

Glaeser, B. and Vyasulu, V. (1984) 'The obsolescence of ecodevelopment?', in B. Glaeser (ed.) *Ecodevelopment: Concepts, Projects, Strategies*, Oxford: Pergamon, pp. 23–36

Goode, W.J. (1982) *The Family*, Englewood Cliffs, N.J.: Prentice Hall.

Gorman, R.F. (1984) *Private Voluntary Organizations as Agents of Development*, Boulder, Colo.: Westview Press.

Gow, D.D. and Morss, E.R. (1979) *Local Organizations and Rural Development: a Comparative Reappraisal,* 2 vols, Washington D.C.: Development Alternatives.

Greenhalgh, S. (1985) 'Sexual stratification: the other side of "growth with equity" in East Asia', *Population and Development Review,* vol. 11(2), pp. 265–314.

Grillo, R. and Rew, A. (eds) (1985) *Social Anthropology and Development Policy,* London: Tavistock.

Groth, A.J. (1987) 'Third World Marxism–Leninism: the case of education', *Comparative Education,* vol. 23(3), pp. 329–44.

Hall, A. (1988) 'Sociologists and foreign aid: rhetoric and reality', in A. Hall and J. Midgley (eds) *Development Policies: Sociological Perspectives,* Manchester: Manchester University Press, pp. 33–46.

Hall, A. and Midgley, J. (eds) (1988) *Development Policies: Sociological Perspectives,* Manchester: Manchester University Press.

Hardiman, M. and Midgley, J. (1982) *The Social Dimensions of Development: Social Policy and Planning in the Third World,* Chichester: Wiley.

Hardjono, J.M. (1977) *Transmigration in Indonesia,* Kuala Lumpur: Oxford University Press.

Harrison, D. (1988) *The Sociology of Modernization and Development,* London: Unwin Hyman.

Hawes, G. (1987) *The Philippine State and the Marcos Regime: The Politics of Export,* Ithaca: Cornell University Press.

Hecht, S.B. (1985) 'Environment, development and politics: capital accumulation and the livestock sector in Eastern Amazonia', *World Development,* vol. 13(6), pp. 663–84.

Heller, B. (1988) 'Fund-supported adjustment programmes and the poor', *Finance and Development,* vol. 25(4), pp. 2–5.

Hill, H. (1987) 'Gender and inequality in the South: the gender variable in development policies: was Nairobi a turning point?', in C. Jennett and R.G. Stewart (eds) *Three Worlds of Inequality: Race, Class and Gender,* Melbourne: Macmillan, pp. 340–60.

Hill, P. (1986) *Development Economics on Trial: the Anthropological Case for a Prosecution,* Cambridge: Cambridge University Press.

Holdcroft, L.E. (1978) *The Rise and Fall of Community Development in Developing Countries: a Critical Analysis and an Annotated Bibliography,* MSU Rural Development Paper no. 2, East Lansing: Department of Agricultural Economics, Michigan State University.

Horesh, E. (1981) 'Academics and experts or the death of the high level technical assistant', *Development and Change,* vol. 12(4), pp. 611–8.

Hoselitz, B. (1960) *Sociological Aspects of Economic Growth,* Glencoe, Ill.: Free Press.

Hoselitz, B. (1964) 'Social stratification and economic development', *International Social Science Journal*, vol. 16(2), pp. 237–51.

Hossain, M. (1988) *Credit for Alleviation of Rural Poverty: the Grameen Bank in Bangladesh*, IFPRI Research Report 65. Washington D.C.: International Food Policy Research Institute.

Howell, J. (1982) *UK Aid to Co-operatives in Developing Countries 1977–81: an Evaluation*, London: Overseas Development Administration.

Hugo, G.J. et al. (1987) *The Demographic Dimension in Indonesian Development*, Singapore: Oxford University Press.

Hulme, D. (1983) 'Agricultural extension: public service or private business?', *Agricultural Administration*, vol. 14(2), pp. 65–80.

Hulme, D. (1987) 'State-sponsored land settlement policies: theory and practice', *Development and Change*, vol. 18(3), pp. 413–36.

Hulme, D. (1988) 'Land settlement schemes and rural development: a review article', *Sociologia Ruralis*, vol. 28(1), pp. 42–61.

Hulme, D. (1989) 'Learning and not learning from experience in rural project planning', *Public Administration and Development*, vol. 9(1), pp. 1–17.

Humphrey, J. (1985) 'Gender, pay and skill: manual workers in Brazilian industry', in H. Afshar (ed.) *Women, Work and Ideology in the Third World*, London: Tavistock, pp. 214–31.

Hunter, G. (1969) *Modernising Peasant Societies: a Comparative Study in Asia and Africa*, London: Oxford University Press.

Hunter, G. (1976) 'Organisations and institutions', in G. Hunter, A.H. Bunting and A. Bottrall (eds) *Policy and Practice in Rural Development*, London: Croom Helm, pp. 197–207.

Hunter, G. (1978) *Agricultural Development and the Rural Poor*, London: Overseas Development Institute.

Huntingdon, S. (1968) *Political Order in Changing Societies*, New Haven: Yale University Press.

Hyden, G. (1983) *No Shortcuts to Progress: African Development Management in Perspective*, London: Heinemann.

Illich, I.D. (1972) *Deschooling Society*, London: Calder and Boyars.

Inayatullah, E. (1970) *Cooperatives and Planned Change in Asian Rural Communities*, Geneva: UNRISD.

Inayatullah, E. (1972) *Cooperatives and Development in Asia: a Study of Cooperatives in Fourteen Rural Communities of Iran, Pakistan and Ceylon*, Geneva: UNRISD.

Inglis, C. (1983) 'The feminization of the teaching profession in Singapore', in L. Manderson (ed.) *Women's Work and Women's Roles: Economics and everyday life in Indonesia, Malaysia and Singapore*, Canberra: Australian National University, Development Studies Centre.

International Fund for Agricultural Development (IFAD) (1987) *The Poor are Bankable*, Rome: IFAD.

International Labour Office (ILO) (1977) *Employment, Growth and Basic Needs: a One-World Problem*, New York: Praeger.

INCIDI (International Institute of Differing Civilizations) (1959) *Women's Role in the Development of Tropical and Sub-Tropical Countries*, Brussels: INCIDI.

International Rice Research Institute (IRRI) (1982) *Report of an Exploratory Workshop on 'the Role of Anthropologists and Other Social Scientists in Interdisciplinary Teams Developing Improved Food Production Technology'*, Manila: International Rice Research Institute.

Israel, A. (1987) *Institutional Development: Incentives to Performance*, Baltimore: Johns Hopkins University Press.

Janowitz, M. (1970) *Political Conflict: Essays in Political Sociology*, Chicago: Quadrangle Books.

Johnson, J.J. (1958) *Political Change in Latin America: the Emergence of the Middle Sectors*, Stanford: Stanford University Press.

Johnson, J.J. (1964) 'Introduction', in J.J. Johnson (ed.) *Community and Change in Latin America*, Stanford: Stanford University Press.

Johnson, S.P. (1987) *World Population and the United Nations: Challenge and Response*, Cambridge: Cambridge University Press.

Johnston, B.F. and Clarke, W.C. (1982) *Redesigning Rural Development*, Baltimore: Johns Hopkins University Press.

Johnston, B.F. and Kilby, P. (1975) *Agriculture and Structural Transformation: Economic Strategies in Late-Developing Countries*, Oxford: Oxford University Press.

Kaplinsky, R. (1984) 'The international context for industrialisation in the coming decade', *Journal of Development Studies*, vol. 21(1), pp. 75–96.

Kelly, G.P. (1987) 'Setting state policy on women's education in the Third World: perspectives from comparative research', *Comparative Education*, vol. 23(1), pp. 95–102.

Kerr, C., Dunlop, J.T., Harbison, F. and Myers, C.A. (1973) *Industrialism and Industrial Man*, Harmondsworth: Penguin.

Kilson, M. (1987) 'Autonomy of African class consciousness: agrarian populism in Ghana from 1915 to the 1940s and beyond', in I.L. Markovitz (ed.) *Studies in Power and Class in Africa*, New York: Oxford University Press, pp. 50–66.

Kirk, D. (1979) 'World population and birth rates: agreements and disagreements', *Population and Development Review*, vol. 5(3), pp. 387–403.

Kirkpatrick, C.H., Lee, N. and Nixson, F.I. (1984) *Industrial Structure and Policy in Less Developed Countries*, London: Allen and Unwin.

Kitching, G. (1982) *Development and Underdevelopment in Historical Perspective: Populism, Nationalism and Industrialization*, London: Methuen.

Kohli, A. (1989) 'Politics of Economic Liberalization in India', World Development, vol. 17(3), pp. 305–28.

Korten, D.C. (1980) 'Comunity organization and rural development: a learning process approach', *Public Administration Review*, vol. 40(5), pp. 480–511.

Korten, D.C. (ed.) (1987) *Community Management: Asian Experiences and Perspectives*, West Hartford, Conn.: Kumarian Press.

Korten, D.C. (1987) 'Introduction: community-based resource management', in D.C. Korten (ed.) *Community Management: Asian Experiences and Perspectives*, West Hartford, Conn.: Kumarian Press, pp. 1–15.

Korten, D.C. and Klauss, R. (1984) *People-Centered Development*, West Hartford, Conn.: Kumarian Press.

Kuznets, S. (1953) *Economic Change*, New York: Norton.

Lackner, H. (1973) 'Colonial administration and social anthropology: Eastern Nigeria 1920–1940', in T. Asad (ed.) *Anthropology and the Colonial Encounter*, New York: Humanities Press, pp. 123–52.

Laclau, E. (1971) 'Feudalism and capitalism in Latin America', *New Left Review*, vol. 67, pp. 19–38; reprinted with postscript in Laclau (1977).

Laclau, E. (1977) *Politics and Ideology in Marxist Theory: Capitalism, Fascism and Populism*, London: New Left Books.

Lall, S. (1983) 'The rise of multinationals from the Third World', *Third World Quarterly*, vol. 5(3), pp. 618–26.

Lall, S., Khanna, A. and Alikhani, I. (1987) 'Determinants of manufactured export performance in low-income Africa: Kenya and Tanzania', *World Development*, vol. 15(9), pp. 1219–24.

Lambert, J., translated by H. Katel (1967) *Latin America: Social Structure and Political Institutions*, Berkeley: University of California Press.

Lanly, J.P. (1982) *Les Resources Forestières Tropicales*, Rome: FAO.

Leach, E.R. (1961) *Pul Eliya: a Village in Ceylon*, Cambridge: Cambridge University Press.

Lehmann, D. (1974) *Agrarian Reform and Agrarian Reformism*, London: Faber and Faber.

Leonard, D.K. and Marshall, D.L. (eds) (1982) *Institutions of Rural Development for the Poor: Decentralization and Organizational Linkages*, Berkeley: Institute of International Studies, University of California.

Lerner, D. (1958) *The Passing of Traditional Society: Modernizing the Middle East*, New York: Free Press.

Lewis, H.T. (1971) *Ilocano Rice Farmers: a Comparative Study of Two Philippine Barrios*, Honolulu: University of Hawaii Press.

Lewis, W.A. (1954) 'Economic development with unlimited supplies of labour', *The Manchester School*, vol. 22, pp. 139–91.

Lim, L. (1980) *Women Workers in Multinational Enterprises in Developing Countries*, Geneva: International Labour Organisation.

Lin, V. (1987) 'Women workers in the semiconductor industry in Singapore and Malaysia: a political economy of health', in M. Pinches and S. Lakha (eds) *Wage Labour and Social Change: the Proletariat in Asia and the Pacific*, Melbourne: Monash University Papers in Southeast Asia no. 16, pp. 219–61.

Lipton, M. (1977) *Why Poor People Stay Poor: A Study of Urban Bias in World Development*, London: Temple Smith.

Lipton, M. (1984) 'Urban bias revisited', *Journal of Development Studies*, vol. 20(3), pp. 139–66.

Little, I.M., Scitovsky, T. and Scott, M. (1970) *Industry and Trade in Some Developing Countries*, London: Oxford University Press.

Long, N. (1977) *An Introduction to the Sociology of Rural Development*, London: Tavistock.

Long, N. (1988) 'Sociological perspectives on agrarian development and state intervention', in A. Hall and J. Midgley (eds) *Development Policies: Sociological Perspectives*, Manchester: Manchester University Press, pp. 108–33.

Loup, J. (1983) *Can the Third World Survive?*, Baltimore: Johns Hopkins University Press.

Mabogunje, A.L. (1980) *The Development Process: A Spatial Perspective*, London: Hutchinson University Library.

Mamdani, M. (1972) *The Myth of Population Control: Family, Caste and Class in an Indian Village*, New York: Monthly Review Press.

Marx, K. (1967) *Capital*, vol. 1 (preface to the first German edition), New York: International Publishers.

Marx, K. and Engels, F. (1969) *On Colonialism*, Moscow: Progress Publishers.

Maxwell, N. (1984) *From Knowledge to Wisdom*, Oxford: Blackwell.

May, R. (1982) 'Micronationalism in perspective', in R. May (ed.) *Micronationalist Movements in Papua New Guinea*, Canberra: Department of Political and Social Change, Australian National University, pp. 1–28.

Mazur, R.E. (1988) 'Refugees in Africa: the role of sociological analysis and praxis', *Current Sociology*, vol. 36(2), pp. 43–60.

McCall, G.J. and Simmons, J.L. (1969) *Issues in Participant–Observation: a Text and Reader*, Reading, Mass.: Addison-Wesley.

McClelland, D. (1961) *The Achieving Society*, Princeton: Van Nostrand.

Meadows, D.H. and Meadows, D.L. (1972) *The Limits to Growth*, New York: Universe Books.

Midgley, J. (1986) 'Community participation: history, concepts and controversies', in J. Midgley, A. Hall, M. Hardiman and D. Narine (eds) *Community Participation, Social Development and the State*, London: Methuen, pp. 13–44.

Midgley, J. (1988) 'Sociology and development policy', in A. Hall and J. Midgley (eds) *Development Policies: Sociological Perspectives*, Manchester: Manchester University Press, pp. 10–32.

Miro, C.A. and Potter, J.E. (1980) *Population Policy: Research Priorities in the Developing World*, London: Frances Pinter.

Mishan, E.J. (1967) *The Costs of Economic Growth*, London: Staples Press.

Mishan, E.J. (1977) *The Economic Growth Debate: An Assessment*, London: Allen and Unwin.

Moock, P.R. (1981) 'Education and efficiency in small-farm production', *Economic Development and Cultural Change*, vol. 29(4), pp. 723–39.

Moore, W.E. (1963) *Social Change*, Englewood Cliffs, N.J.: Prentice Hall.

Morris, D.M. (1979) *Measuring the Condition of the World's Poor: The Physical Quality of Life Index*, Oxford: Pergamon.

Mosley, P. and Dahal, R.P. (1987) 'Credit for the rural poor: a comparison of policy experiments in Nepal and Bangladesh', *Manchester Papers on Development*, vol. 3(2), pp. 45–59.

Murdock, G.P. (1949) *Social Structure*, New York: Macmillan.

Mwansasu, B.V. and Pratt, C. (eds) (1979) *Towards Socialism in Tanzania*, Toronto: University of Toronto Press.

Myrdal, G. (1968) *Asian Drama: An Inquiry Into the Poverty of Nations*, New York: Pantheon.

Naipaul, S. (1985) 'The myth of the Third World: a thousand million invisible men', *The Spectator* (London), 18 May.

Nash, M. (1984) *Unfinished Agenda: the Dynamics of Modernization in Developing Nations*, Boulder, Colo.: Westview Press.

Nelson, J.M. (1984) 'The political economy of stabilization: commitment, capacity and public response', *World Development*, vol. 12(10), pp. 983–1006.

Nelson, N. (ed.) (1981) *African Women in the Development Process*, special issue of *Journal of Development Studies*, vol. 17(3), (1981), London: Frank Cass.

Nisbet, R.A. (1970) *The Sociological Tradition*, London: Heinemann, first published in 1966 by Basic Books.

Nyerere, J.K. (1973) *Freedom and Development: a Selection from Writings and Speeches 1968–1973*, Dar-es-Salaam: Oxford University Press.

Obikeze, D.S. (1987) 'Education and the extended family ideology: the case of Nigeria', *Journal of Contemporary Family Studies*, vol. 18(1), pp. 25–46.

O'Brien, P.J. (1975) 'A critique of Latin American theories of dependency', in I. Oxaal, T. Barnett and D. Booth (eds) *Beyond the Sociology of Development: Economy and Society in Latin America and Africa*, London: Routledge and Kegan Paul, pp. 7–27.

O'Donnell, G.A. (1975) *Modernization and Bureaucratic Authoritarian-*

ism: Studies in South American Politics, Berkeley: Institute of International Studies, University of California.

Orivel, F. (1983) 'The impact of agricultural extension services: a review of the literature', in H. Perraton, D. Jameson, J. Jenkins, F. Orivel and L. Wolff, *Basic Education and Agricultural Extension: Costs, Effects and Alternatives*, Washington D.C.: World Bank Staff Working Papers no. 564, pp. 3–57.

Palmer, G.B. (1974) 'The ecology of resettlement schemes', *Human Organization*, vol. 23(3), pp. 239–50.

Parsons, T. (1951) *The Social System*, Chicago: Free Press.

Parsons, T. (1960) *Structure and Process in Modern Societies*, Glencoe, Ill.: Free Press.

Parsons, T. (1966) *Societies: Evolutionary and Comparative Perspectives*, Englewood Cliffs, N.J.: Prentice Hall.

Paul, S. (1982) *Managing Development Programs: the Lessons of Success*, Boulder, Colo.: Westview Press.

Paul, S. (1986) *Community Participation in Development Projects: The World Bank Experience*, World Bank Discussion Paper 6. Washington D.C.: World Bank.

Paul, S. (1987) 'Community participation in World Bank projects', *Finance and Development*, vol. 24(4), pp. 20–3.

Pearson, L.B. (1969) *Partners in Development*, London: Pall Mall Press.

Peel, J.D.Y. (1980) 'Inequality and action: the forms of Ijesha social conflict', *Canadian Journal of African Studies*, vol. 14(3), pp. 473–502.

Peterson, W.L. (1979) 'International farm prices and the social cost of cheap food policies', *American Journal of Agricultural Economics*, vol. 61(1), pp. 12–21.

Petras, J.F. (1981) *Class, State and Power in the Third World*, Montclair: Allanheld, Osmun; also published in London by Zed Press.

Pischke, J.D. von (1983) 'The pitfalls of specialised farm credit institutions in low-income countries', in J.D. von Pischke, D.W. Adams and G. Donald (eds) *Rural Financial Markets in Developing Countries*, Baltimore: Johns Hopkins University Press, pp. 175–82.

Prebisch, R. (1950) *The Economic Development of Latin America and its Principal Problems*, New York: United Nations.

Price, S. (1983) 'Rich woman, poor women: occupation differences in a textile producing village in Central Java', in L. Manderson (ed.) *Women's Work and Women's Roles*, Canberra: Australian National University Development Studies Centre Monograph no. 32, pp. 97–110.

Redclift, M. (1984) *Development and the Environmental Crisis: Red or Green Alternatives*, London: Methuen.

Redfield, R. (1941) *The Folk Culture of Yucatan*, Chicago: University of Chicago Press.

Redfield, R. (1947) 'The folk society', *American Journal of Sociology*, vol. 52(4), pp. 292–308.

de los Reyes, R.P. and Jopillo, S. (1986) *An Evaluation of the Philippine Participatory Communal Irrigation Program*, Quezon City: Institute of Philippine Culture.

Rey, P.P. (1971) *Colonialisme, Néo-Colonialisme et Transition au Capitalisme*, Paris: Maspéro.

Rey, P.P. (1973) *Les Alliances des Classes*, Paris: Maspéro.

Rhoades, R.E. (1984) *Breaking New Ground: Anthropology in Agricultural Research*, Lima: International Potato Centre.

Richards, P. (1985) *Indigenous Agricultural Revolution: Ecology and Food Production in West Africa*, London: Hutchinson.

Roberts, B. (1978) *Cities of Peasants: the Political Economy of Urbanization in the Third World*, London: Edward Arnold.

Robertson, A.F. (1984) *People and the State: an Anthropology of Planned Development*, Cambridge: Cambridge University Press.

Rodriguez, J.L. (1987) 'Agricultural policy and development in Cuba', *World Development*, vol. 15(1), pp. 23–9.

Rogers, B. (1980) *The Domestication of Women: Discrimination in Developing Societies*, London: Tavistock.

Röling, N. (1988) *Extension Science: Information Systems in Agricultural Development*, Cambridge: Cambridge University Press.

Rostow, W.W. (1960) *The Stages of Economic Growth: A Non-Communist Manifesto*, Cambridge: Cambridge University Press.

Roxborough, I. (1979) *Theories of Underdevelopment*, Atlantic Highlands, N.J.: Humanities Press.

Sachs, I. (1977) *Environment and Development – A New Rationale for Domestic Policy Formulation and International Cooperation Strategies*, Ottawa: Canadian International Development Agency.

Sahlins, M. and Service, E. (1960) *Evolution and Culture*, Ann Arbor: University of Michigan Press.

Salmen, L. (1987) *Listen to the People: Participant–Observer Evaluation of Development Projects*, New York: Oxford University Press.

Schmitz, H. (1984) 'Industrialisation strategies in less developed counries: some lessons of historical experience', *Journal of Development Studies*, vol. 21(1), pp. 1–21.

Schumacher, E.F. (1973) *Small is Beautiful: Economics as if People Mattered*, New York: Harper and Row.

Scott, J.C. (1985) *Weapons of the Weak: Everyday Forms of Peasant Resistance*, New Haven: Yale University Press.

Scott, J.C. and Kerkvliet, B.J. (1973) 'How traditional rural patrons lose legitimacy: a theory with special reference to southeast Asia', *Cultures et développement*, 5(3), pp. 510–40.

Scudder, T. (1981) 'The development potential of new lands settlements in the tropics and subtropics: a global state of the art evaluation with specific emphasis on policy implication', unpublished report to USAID.

Scudder, T. (1985) 'A sociological framework for the analysis of new land settlements', in M.M. Cernea (ed.) *Putting People First: Sociological Variables in Rural Development*, New York: Oxford University Press, pp. 121–53.

Seers, D. (1977) 'The meaning of development', *International Development Review*, vol. 19(22), pp. 2–7.

Seers, D. (ed.) (1981) *Dependency Theory: a Critical Reassessment*, London: Frances Pinter.

Shahidullah, M. (1985) 'Class formation and class relations in Bangladesh', in D.L. Johnson (ed.) *Middle Classes in Dependent Countries*, Beverly Hills: Sage, pp. 137–64.

Sheehan, G. and Hopkins, M. (1979) *Basic Needs Performance: an Analysis of Some International Data*, Geneva: International Labour Office.

Simmonds, N.W. (1985) 'Farming systems research: a review', *World Bank Technical Paper* 43, Washington D.C.: World Bank.

Singh, K. (1983) 'Structure of interest rates on consumption loans in an Indian village', in J.D. von Pischke, D.W. Adams and G. Donald (eds) *Rural Financial Markets in Developing Countries*, Baltimore: Johns Hopkins University Press, pp. 251–4; first published in 1968.

Sivard, R.L. (1987) *World Military and Social Expenditures 1987–88*, Washington D.C.: World Priorities.

Sklair, L. (1988) 'Transcending the impasse: metatheory, theory, and empirical research in the sociology of development', *World Development*, vol. 16(6), pp. 697–709.

Sklar, R.L. (1979) 'The nature of class domination in Africa', *The Journal of Modern African Studies*, vol. 17(4), pp. 531–52.

Smelser, N.J. (1963) 'Mechanism of change and adjustment to change', in B.F. Hoselitz and W.E. Moore (eds) *Industrialization and Society*, The Hague: Mouton, pp. 32–54.

Smith, A.D. (1973) *The Concept of Social Change: a Critique of the Functionalist Theory of Social Change*, London: Routledge and Kegan Paul.

Snyder, L.L. (1982) *Global Mini-Nationalisms: Autonomy or Independence*, Westport, Wash.: Greenwood Press.

Staley, E. and Morse, R. (1965) *Modern Small Industry for Developing Countries*, New York: McGraw-Hill.

Steward, J. (1955) *The Theory of Culture Change*, Urbana: University of Illinois Press.

Stiefel, M. and Pearse, A. (1982) 'UNRISD's popular participation programme', *Assignment Children*, vol. 59/60, pp. 145–59.

Stivens, M. (1985) 'The fate of women's land rights: gender, matriliny, and capitalism in Rembau, Negeri Sembilan, Malaysia', in H. Afshar (ed.) *Women, Work and Ideology in the Third World*, London: Tavistock, pp. 3–36.

Streeten, P., with Burki, S.J., Haq, M.U., Hicks, N. and Stewart, F. (1981) *First Things First*, London: Oxford University Press.

Sutherland, A. (1987) 'Sociology in farming systems research', *Agricultural Administration Unit Occasional Paper 6*, London: Overseas Development Institute.

Tapay, N.E., Simbahan, G. and Murray-Rust, D.H. (1987) 'Evaluation of communal irrigation system performance in the Philippines: the case of farmer irrigation organization', *Agricultural Administration and Extension*, vol. 25, pp. 127–41.

Tendler, J. (1976) *Inter-Country Evaluation of Small Farmer Organizations in Ecuador and Honduras: Final Report*, Washington D.C.: Latin American Bureau, USAID.

Thorbecke, E. (1979) 'Agricultural development', in W. Galenson (ed.) *Economic Growth and Structural Change in Taiwan: The Postwar Experience of the Republic of China*, Ithaca: Cornell University Press.

Thompson, A.R. (1981) *Education and Development in Africa*, London: Macmillan.

Tinker, I. (1976) 'The adverse impact of development on women', in I. Tinker and M.B. Bramsen (eds) *Women and World Development*, Washington D.C.: Overseas Development Council, pp. 22–34.

Tipps, D. (1973) 'Modernization theory and the comparative study of societies: a critical perspective', *Comparative Studies in Society and History*, vol. 15(2), pp. 199–226.

Toye, J. (1987) *Dilemmas of Development*, Oxford: Basil Blackwell.

Turner, J.F.C. (1976) *Housing by People*, London: Marion Boyars.

Turner, M.M. (1978) 'Interpretations of class and status in the Philippines: a critical evaluation', *Cultures et développement*, vol. 10(2), pp. 265–96.

Turner, M.M. (1988) 'Patron–client relationships in San Fernando, Northern Philippines', in G.H. Krausse (ed.) *Urban Society in Southeast Asia, Volume 2: Political and Cultural Issues*, Hong Kong: Asian Research Service, pp. 103–22.

Turner, M.M. (1989) ' "Trainingism" revisited in Papua New Guinea', *Public Administration and Development*, vol. 9(1), pp. 17–28.

Turner, M. and Hegarty, D. (1987) *The 1987 National Elections in Papua New Guinea*, Canberra: Australian Institute of International Affairs Occasional Paper no. 6.

United Nations Development Programme (UNDP) (1987) *A Better Environment for Development: World Development, UNDP Annual Report 1986*, New York: UNDP.

UNRISD (1975) *Rural Cooperatives as Agents for Change*, Geneva: UNRISD.

Uphoff, N.T. (1986) *Local Institutional Development: an Analytical Sourcebook with Cases*, West Hartford, Conn.: Kumarian Press.

Uphoff, N.T. (1987) 'Activating community capacity for water management in Sri Lanka', in D.C. Korten (ed.) *Community Management: Asian Experiences and Perspectives*, West Hartford, Conn.: Kumarian Press, pp. 201–19.

Uphoff, N.T. and Esman, M.J. (1974) *Local Organization for Rural Development: Analysis of Asian Experiences*, Ithaca: Rural Development Committee, Cornell University.

Vandergeest, P. and Buttel, F.H. (1988) 'Marx, Weber, and development sociology: beyond the impasse', *World Development*, vol. 16(6), pp. 683–95.

Vyasulu, V. (1984) 'Industrial aspects of ecodevelopment', in B. Glaeser (ed.) *Ecodevelopment: Concepts, Projects and Strategies*, Oxford: Pergamon, pp. 59–70.

Wallerstein, I. (1979) *The Capitalist World-Economy*, Cambridge: Cambridge University Press.

Walton, J. (1987) 'Small gains for big theories: recent work on development', *Latin American Research Review*, vol. 22(2), pp. 192–201.

Warren, B. (1980) *Imperialism, Pioneer of Capitalism*, London: Verso Books.

Warriner, D. (1969) *Land Reform in Principle and Practice*, Oxford: Oxford University Press.

Warwick, D.P. (1982) *Bitter Pills: Population Policies and their Implementation in Eight Developing Countries*, Cambridge: Cambridge University Press.

Weitz, R. (1971) *From Peasant to Farmer: a Revolutionary Strategy for Development*, New York: Columbia University Press.

Welch, R.V. (1984) 'The meaning of development: traditional view and more recent ideas', *New Zealand Journal of Geography*, vol. 76, pp. 2–4.

Wells, L.T. (1983) *Third World Multinationals: the Rise of Foreign Investment from Developing Countries*, Cambridge, Mass.: MIT Press.

Werner, D. (1978) *Where there is no Doctor*, Palo Alto: Hesperian Foundation.

Werner, D. and Bower, B. (1982) *Helping Health Workers Learn*, Palo Alto: Hesperian Foundation.

White, G. (1984) 'Developmental states and socialist industrialisation in the Third World', *Journal of Development Studies*, vol. 21(1), pp. 97–120.

Wilmington, M.V. (1983) 'Aspects of moneylending in Northern Sudan', in J.D. von Pischke, D.W. Adams and G. Donald (eds) *Rural Financial*

Markets in Developing Countries, Baltimore: Johns Hopkins University Press, pp. 255–61; first published in 1955.

Wolf, E.R. (1971) *Peasant Wars of the Twentieth Century,* London: Faber and Faber.

Wolf-Phillips, L. (1987) 'Why "Third World"?: origin, definition and usage', *Third World Quarterly,* vol. 9(4), pp. 1311–27.

World Bank (1975) *The Assault on World Poverty: Problems of Rural Development, Education and Health,* Baltimore: Johns Hopkins Press.

World Bank (1978–89) (annual publication) *World Development Report,* New York: Oxford University Press.

World Bank (1984) *Agricultural Credit: Sector Policy Paper,* second edn, Washington D.C.: World Bank.

Worsley, P. (1970) 'Introduction', in P. Worsley (ed.) *Two Blades of Grass: Rural Cooperatives in Agricultural Modernisation,* Manchester: Manchester University Press, pp. 1–40.

Worsley, P. (1984) *The Three Worlds: Culture and World Development,* London: Weidenfeld and Nicholson.

Youngjohns, B.A. (1977) *Co-operative Organisations: an Introduction,* London: Intermediate Technology Publications.

Yang, Q-H. and Hull T.H. (1987) 'High production or low reproduction? Conflicts between China's reforms and population planning'. Paper presented to the Annual Meeting of the Population Association of America, Chicago; forthcoming in T.H. Hull and J. Wang (eds) *Population and Development Planning in China,* Canberra: Australian National University.

Zeitlin, M., Neuman, W.L. and Ratcliff, R.E. (1976) 'Class segments: agrarian property and political leadership in the capitalist class of Chile', *American Sociological Review,* vol. 41 (December), pp. 1006–29.

INDEX